Acing

Professional Responsibility

**A Checklist Approach to
Professional Responsibility Problems**

Leslie W. Abramson

Frost Brown Todd Professor of Law

*University of Louisville
School of Law*

Series Editor
A. Benjamin Spencer

A Thomson Reuters business

Mat #40776872

Thomson Reuters created this publication to provide you with accurate and authoritative information concerning the subject matter covered. However, this publication was not necessarily prepared by persons licensed to practice law in a particular jurisdiction. Thomson Reuters does not render legal or other professional advice, and this publication is not a substitute for the advice of an attorney. If you require legal or other expert advice, you should seek the services of a competent attorney or other professional.

© 2009 Thomson Reuters
   610 Opperman Drive
   St. Paul, MN 55123
   1–800–313–9378

Printed in the United States of America

ISBN: 978–0–314–19965–2

For Lisa, Sam, Shel and Will

*

Table of Contents

Introduction

Most students spend a good deal of time developing an outline for each course—a lengthy (sometimes well over 100 pages) and exhaustive document that purports to compile the universe of information presented in a course into an organized, accessible format that would simplify studying and provide a useful source for information during the exam (provided the exam is open-book).

Unfortunately, personal outlines often do no more than provide anything more than a restatement of various principles of law or doctrine organized by topic. It remains for you to take those doctrines and apply them to the fact patterns presented on exams. That process of applying legal principles to facts is a large part of what exams and lawyering are all about; knowing the relevant law is only half (oftentimes less than half) of the battle. So why are you and your fellow students devoting all of this time and energy into developing these miniature volumes on the course material and not putting more energy into developing a tool that could help guide your legal analysis of problems presented on exams?

In addition to an outline, another document that some students occasionally develop as an examination aid is the checklist. There is not a single definition for a checklist or a consistent approach to drafting one. But a checklist is meant to present in a sparse and simplified way the basics about a topic that you want to be sure to remember to discuss or evaluate in the course of your examination answer. Some checklists are simply elements or rules under larger topical headings. Others are more involved in linking various concepts together in a logical pattern that facilitates the analysis of legal problems. Regardless of the format, most checklists do not make much of a contribution beyond being a condensed form of the lengthier outline prepared for the course.

Properly conceived and crafted, checklists can fulfill the role of providing a tool that truly aids you in your effort to analyze legal problems in your courses. There is a general structure to legal analysis that involves identifying the issue, articulating the applicable legal rules and principles, applying those principles to a given set of facts, and then arriving at and stating a conclusion. A checklist is the document that organizes a collection of rules, identifying all of the relevant questions and issues that you must consider in order to completely analyze a question.

The purpose of this book is to present you with a comprehensive set of checklists pertaining to each of the topics typically covered in a required Professional Responsibility course. The checklists are meant to provide you with a tool that facilitates analysis of ethical problems. Each chapter focuses on a different topic, first presenting a brief review of the subject followed by the checklist for the subject. After the checklist is presented, problems are analyzed to illustrate how the checklists can be used to resolve such problems. Each chapter concludes with a section entitled "Points to Remember" to recapitulate key points that you need to remember when answering exam questions. A concluding chapter provides some final thoughts on preparing for and taking exams generally. At the end of the book there is an Appendix that presents condensed "mini-checklists" for each topic. You may find these useful during the time crunch of an exam when you need quick access to the full range of major concepts that are pertinent to an issue.

You should use this book to assist yourself in developing your own analytical process for resolving the questions you will face on your examinations. The steps outlined in the checklists presented here can provide you with a map for how you should proceed when evaluating any given legal issue. Funneling your analysis through the checklist will also improve the chances that your answer will fully display a reasoned analysis while also arriving at a sound conclusion. But these checklists can only be used effectively if you have a thorough understanding of the substantive material.

This book does not attempt to explain Professional Responsibility doctrines in great detail; rather, it merely seeks to organize doctrine into a dynamic tool that you can use to apply legal principles to fact patterns you will face on exams. You should use these checklists in conjunction with substantive course material to prepare for your exams. Use of these checklists should enhance your ability to write reasoned and sound responses to examination questions. Further, these checklists should be helpful in putting the course material in perspective and providing a clearer picture of how the concepts you are learning should be integrated into a legal analysis. Finally, you should make sure to modify these checklists according to the areas of emphasis and coverage of your professor.

*

CHAPTER 1

Regulation of the Legal Profession

A. POWERS OF COURTS AND OTHERS TO REGULATE LAWYERS

As an exercise of their police powers, the states regulate the legal profession because it affects the public interest. The courts of each state have the inherent power to regulate members of the legal profession for their conduct, both in-court and elsewhere. The highest court of each state has adopted standards of professional ethics based on models created by the American Bar Association [ABA].

Since 1983, states have adopted a version of the ABA's Model Rules of Professional Conduct [MRPC]. Each state is free to adopt all or part of the MRPC. As with their predecessor standards, each state is free to adopt all or part of each standard. Before you begin to practice in a state, it is essential that you consult that state's ethical standards. You can check the status of each state's review of its professional conduct rules by looking at http://www.abanet.org/cpr/jclr/ethics_ 2000_ status_ chart.pdf Throughout this book, the MRPC are referred to by their number, e.g., "Rule 1.6."

Along with the ABA Model Rules, the ABA has published ethics opinions that respond to specific issues posed to the ABA and that aid lawyers' understanding about how the MRPC operate and interrelate. In this book, those opinions are referred to in shortened form. For example, if the ABA published a formal opinion number 396 in 1995, its official citation would be ABA Formal Opinion 95–396 (July 28, 1995). The short-hand citation for that ethics opinion in this book is: "ABA Formal Opinion 95–396."

In addition to adoption of some form of the MRPC, each state has case law that relates to the rights and duties of lawyers to engage in conduct that may not be directly addressed in the state ethics standards. For example, while the MRPC permits contingent fees to be charged in certain types of cases, the case law may clarify a lawyer's duties in determining how to calculate the amount of the fee for the client. States also maintain rules of court for civil and criminal cases, as well as for cases during the appeals process. While ethics standards may require lawyers to accept court appointments, the court rules may prescribe standards of indigency requiring a court-appointed lawyer.

The American Law Institute in 2000 issued the Third Restatement of the Law Governing Lawyers, which while not binding on courts is often cited as a reliable description of the law. Similar to the Restatement in your doctrinal courses, this Restatement states acceptable standards for lawyer behavior. In the absence of an ABA Formal Opinion on a topic, the Restatement can serve as a useful explanation of subjects addressed by the MRPC. The shortened citation for the Restatement in this book is, for example, "Restatement, § 32."

Federal agencies sometimes issue regulations applicable to the lawyers appearing before them. For example, since the Enron scandal a few years ago, the Securities and Exchange Commission has adopted regulations mandating how lawyers for publicly-held companies must respond to possible wrongdoing by the company or within the company. Those statutes are discussed in Chapter 8, along with the MRPC standards for lawyers who represent entities.

You will read about additional professional standards for lawyers located in the following legal sources: Code of Federal Regulations [CFR], United States Code [U.S.C.], Federal Rules of

Civil Procedure [FRCP], and ABA Standards on the Defense Function. In addition, when the United States Supreme Court has decided an issue relevant to the discussion, that holding and those of other courts are discussed in the text.

Judicial conduct is also governed by an ABA document called the Code of Judicial Conduct [CJC]. Since the first set of Canons of Judicial Ethics were published in 1924, the ABA has issued a new Code of Judicial Conduct in 1972, 1990 and 2007. As with the Rules, the highest court of each state chooses the appropriate norms for appellate and trial judges to follow. Judges can be disciplined for their failure to follow those standards. In this book, an example of the shortened citation for a provision of the CJC is "CJC Rule 2.11." Federal judges are not subject to the ABA Code, although they are subject to a Code of Conduct for Federal Judges which borrows heavily from the ABA Code and became effective July 1, 2009.

B. ADMISSION TO THE PROFESSION

The highest court in each state regulates all aspects of the legal profession, from admission standards to disciplinary enforcement. That court may delegate responsibility to the state bar association for regulating bar admissions and disciplinary enforcement. Mandatory dues from lawyers in good standing fund the state bar associations. Most states require that every lawyer licensed to practice in that state must be a member of that state's bar association. When a lawyer wants to represent a party in a *federal* court, she must be admitted according to the federal court's rules which usually defer to state standards. In other words, a lawyer admitted to practice in a state must be admitted separately to practice in the federal courts of that state.

Applicants for admission to the bar usually must satisfy several requirements. They must: (1) graduate from an accredited law school, (2) pass the Multistate Professional Responsibility Examination (MPRE), (3) pass the bar examination for that state, and (4) have the necessary character and fitness to practice law.

The states differ in how receptive they are to applicants who did not graduate from an ABA-accredited law school. Courts are more demanding that bar applicants be able to read and write

English proficiently. Issues also have been litigated about state bar residency requirements. The United States Supreme Court has held that a state cannot require that its lawyers be United States citizens or residents of that state as a condition of bar admission. *In re Griffiths*, 413 U.S. 717 (1973) (U.S. citizenship); *Supreme Court of New Hampshire v. Piper*, 470 U.S. 274 (1985) (state residency).

Client protection is the most cited rationale for the character and fitness requirement. Restatement, § 2, Comment d. *Douglas v. Noble*, 261 U.S. 165 (1923) permits a state to require good moral character and proficiency in the law before admission. However, an applicant cannot be denied admission based on her beliefs, race, or affiliations. *Schware v. Board of Bar Examiners*, 353 U.S. 232 (1957) (Communist Party members). On the other hand, a state can deny bar admission to an applicant who belongs to an organization which she knows advocates the violent overthrow of the government.

In asking for information from bar applicants, relevant MRPC standards focus on conduct that functionally relates to practicing law. For example, bar applicants who have engaged in cheating, lying, plagiarism, dishonesty in handling money, or criminal conduct probably have violated Rule 8.4(c), which prohibits lawyers from engaging in "dishonesty, fraud, deceit, or misrepresentation." By contrast, issues of "personal morality, such as adultery" lack a specific connection to a person's fitness to practice law. Rule 8.4, Comment 2.

If a bar application seeks information relating to past misconduct, the applicant must respond fully. She then may argue that the conduct, because of its nature or its age, is not predictive of her future conduct. She also may argue for her admission based upon her current candor, as well as her mental state, community service, age at the time of the misconduct, and the opinions of others about her current character. *Schware*.

Rule 8.1 is one of the few Rules that governs nonlawyers and lawyers. It "extends to persons seeking admission to the bar as well as to lawyers." It can apply to (1) a lawyer in one jurisdiction applying for bar admission in another jurisdiction, (2) a new applicant who becomes subject to discipline after admission, (3) a lawyer who is the subject of a disciplinary hearing, and (4) a lawyer who represents either bar applicants or lawyers who face disciplinary hearings. A bar applicant must be candid in the application process, in part because practicing law in a specific state is a privilege not an entitlement.

Under Rule 8.1(a), an applicant for the bar who submits information for bar admission cannot "knowingly make a false statement of material fact." It must be shown that the applicant knew that she was making a misstatement about something important to the determination about her fitness to practice law, such as cheating during a college test. In addition, an applicant must disclose an earlier false statement even if she did not know that it was false when she made it. She also has a duty to clarify any "misunderstanding" by admissions or disciplinary authorities of which she becomes aware. Rule 8.1(b).

Rule 8.1 also applies to you as a practicing lawyer when a bar applicant asks you for advice about her bar application. Suppose a family friend applying for bar admission comes to you and tells you about several examples of clear misconduct in her past, and then asks you to write an affidavit attesting to her good character. Filing the affidavit may subject you to discipline under Rule 8.1(a) for making a knowingly false or misleading statement about your friend, even though the bar application is not yours. If your knowledge about the applicant's prior misconduct is privileged, your duty of confidentiality to your friend under Rule 1.6 is more important than the duty you owe to the bar admission officials.

C. REGULATION AFTER ADMISSION— LAWYER DISCIPLINE

1. Misconduct

While you are subject to discipline for wrongful conduct committed while you are acting in your capacity as a lawyer, you also may be disciplined for your misconduct outside your capacity as a lawyer. Discipline in the latter category is limited to misconduct that functionally relates to your capacity to practice law, as with illegal conduct or conduct involving dishonesty, fraud, deceit, or misrepresentation. Rule 8.4(c).

You are subject to discipline for (1) violating the MRPC, (2) attempting to violate the MRPC, and (3) assisting or inducing another person to violate a Rule. The latter category makes you subject to discipline if you order another lawyer to engage in misconduct or knowingly ratify her misconduct. Rule 8.4(a). As the supervisory lawyer, you also are responsible for the other lawyer's misconduct if you fail to take reasonable remedial action to avoid or mitigate the misconduct. Rule 5.1(c)(2).

Discipline may be imposed for crimes that reflect "adversely on the lawyer's honesty, trustworthiness or fitness as a lawyer." Rule 8.4(b). Discipline is inappropriate for personal morality crimes such as adultery which do not involve a characteristic relevant to the practice of law. While the MRPC refer to the commission of a crime, a *conviction* for that crime is not necessary for discipline. A pattern of minor offenses could be the reason for discipline by showing the lawyer's "indifference to legal obligation." Rule 8.4, Comment 2.

You also are subject to discipline for "conduct that is prejudicial to the administration of justice." Rule 8.4(d). Although the phrase is vague, one example of such misconduct would occur if you made remarks that were racist or sexist. Rule 8.4, Comment 3. The Rule does not punish legitimate advocacy. Thus, "a finding that peremptory challenges were exercised on a discriminatory basis does not alone establish a violation of this rule." Rule 8.4, Comment 3.

You cannot state or even imply an ability to influence improperly a government agency or official, or to achieve results by any means that violate the Rules, even if you actually lack the ability to exercise influence. Rule 8.4(e). You also cannot knowingly assist a judge to violate the Code of Judicial Conduct, e.g., accepting a bribe. Rule 8.4(f). For example, if you represent a judge on a personal matter and also represents a client whose unrelated case is before the judge, if the judge fails to disqualify herself you would be in violation of Rule 8.4(f) if you or anyone else in your firm continues to represent the client before the judge. ABA Formal Opinion 07–449.

2. Disciplinary Authority

If you are admitted in State A, you are subject to discipline there, even if your misconduct occurs outside State A. If you are not admitted to practice in State A, you are nevertheless subject to discipline in State A if you provide or offer to provide legal services there. Because the purpose of lawyer discipline is to determine fitness for legal practice, any misconduct (no matter where it occurs) reflects on your ability to practice in State A. Rule 8.5(a).

3. Choice of Law

If your conduct occurs before a court in State A, you are subject to discipline by that state's disciplinary authority unless their Rules specify differently. If you are admitted to practice in State A but you are temporarily admitted in a court in State B and your alleged misconduct occurred there, discipline by State A would be governed by the Rules of State B. Rule 8.5(b). If your alleged misconduct occurs outside a court, the applicable Rules are those of the state where the misconduct occurred unless the predominant effect of the particular conduct is elsewhere. Rule 8.5(b).

D. REPORTING PROFESSIONAL MISCONDUCT

You have a general obligation to report information about another lawyer's serious disciplinary violation, and your failure to report such misconduct may subject you to discipline. The duty is to report another lawyer, but there is no duty to report yourself. In the well-known case of *In re Himmel*, 533 N.E.2d 790 (Ill. 1988), the lawyer was suspended from practicing law for one year for failing to report another lawyer's misconduct and the charged lawyer was instructed by his client not to make the report.

The scope of your duty to report misconduct does not include a duty to report any and all misconduct. Your obligation to report requires that you know that another lawyer has violated the MRPC. A reasonable belief about the violation does not trigger your obligation. The Rule focuses on conduct that raises a "substantial question" about the other lawyer's "honesty, trustworthiness or fitness as a lawyer." Rule 8.3(a). "Substantial" refers to the "seriousness of the possible offense." Rule 8.3, Comment 3. Just as you have a duty to report another lawyer who has engaged in substantial misconduct, you must report a judge to the "appropriate authority" any nonconfidential information showing that she has committed a violation of judicial conduct raising a substantial question about her fitness for office. Rule 8.3(b).

Your duty includes reporting another lawyer who is suspected of alcoholism, drug addiction, or other mental impairment. ABA Formal Opinion 03–431. If you recognize the symptoms of mental impairment that significantly harm her ability to represent clients, you have the discretion to consult with the affected lawyer, members of her law firm, mental health professionals, or members of an established lawyer assistance program. Your disclosure cannot relate to the representation of the reported lawyer's client. Rule 8.3(c).

There are two contexts when the duty to report is extinguished. It is superseded by the duty of confidentiality under Rule 1.6, as when your client tells you that another lawyer has engaged in serious misconduct, or when you represent a lawyer who has herself committed serious misconduct. In each instance, you learned the information during the lawyer-client relationship. The reporting requirement also does not apply to lawyers who participate in lawyer assistance programs. Rule 8.3, Comment 5.

E.   UNAUTHORIZED PRACTICE OF LAW

As you know, only licensed professionals can practice law in the United States. While the definition of unauthorized practice of law is defined by the statutes, rules and case law of each state, the MRPC incorporate that law by reference. Rule 5.5, Comment 2. As a lawyer, you may have disciplinary problems with the unauthorized practice rules, either by practicing in a state where you are not admitted or by helping a lay person (or even a lawyer unadmitted in that jurisdiction). Rule 5.5(a). If that lay person is your employee, you also may face discipline under Rule 5.3 for not supervising your employees. Unauthorized practice is remedied by criminal penalties, injunctive relief, or holding the offender in contempt. A common example of concern about unauthorized practice is whether the sale of legal forms or kits constitutes unauthorized practice by those who write and sell them. As long as no personalized advice is included by the authors or anyone distributing them, courts have found that there is no unauthorized practice associated with their sale or use.

Unauthorized practice rules also do not apply to persons who represent themselves, either as a result of court rules or as a matter of constitutional law. Defendants in criminal cases have a Sixth Amendment right to represent themselves. *Faretta v. California*, 422 U.S. 806 (1975). Unauthorized practice laws *do* apply when one lay person represents another lay person. As a lawyer you can assist a person who is authorized to represent herself. Rule 5.5, Comment 2. You also can use support staff to assist you, as long as you supervise them adequately.

F. MULTIJURISDICTIONAL PRACTICE

Being admitted to practice in one state does not automatically entitle you to practice in another state where you have not been admitted. Each state has its own rules for admission to practice, and failure to comply with them constitutes unauthorized practice in the state. Rule 5.5(a). You cannot hold yourself out to the public that you are licensed to practice there when you are not. Likewise, you cannot open a law office in a state where you are not admitted, but you may open an office with a lawyer admitted there. Rule 5.5(b).

Under certain circumstances, you can offer temporary legal services in another jurisdiction from where you are admitted. First, you may associate yourself with local counsel who actively partici-pates in any representation of your clients. Rule 5.5(c)(1). Second, you also may be admitted by a court to practice one case *pro hac vice*, and you work in the other state in anticipation of such an admission. Rules 5.5(b); 5.5(c)(2). Your subordinates may work on the case even if they will not enter their appearances before the court. Rule 5.5, Comment 11. Third, you may participate in an alternative dispute resolution proceeding in the other state if it is reasonably related to or arises out of a representation in the place where you are admitted to practice. Rule 5.5(c)(3). Finally, as a catch-all, you also may represent a client in a matter in that other state when that matter is closely related to your representation of a client in the state where you are admitted. Rule 5.5(c)(4).

If you are an employee-lawyer for an entity like a corporation, you may represent only your employer anywhere in the United States where you are not admitted to practice. Rule 5.5, Comment

16. A 2008 amendment to Rule 5.5(d)1) requires lawyers practicing as in-house counsel to register in a state within 180 days of employment. If the representation results in litigation, you must seek *pro hac vice* admission to the court where the lawsuit is pending. Rule 5.5(d)(1). If you are in good standing and there is authorization by federal or other law, you may also provide legal services beyond the state where you are admitted. Rule 5.5(d)(2).

After a finding by a court that a major disaster exists, lawyers from other states can provide *pro bono* representation temporarily in another state affected by that disaster. Rule 5.5, Comment 14. The scope of that Rule includes allowing lawyers from the disaster state to practice in a state outside where they ate admitted to practice.

G.   FEE DIVISION WITH A NONLAWYER

Generally, you or your firm cannot share legal fees with a nonlawyer, in order to control nonlawyer involvement in the delivery of legal services. Rule 5.4(a). For example, if you hire a nonlawyer to assist you in litigation, you must pay her an hourly or fixed fee, but not a contingent fee which would amount to fee sharing with a nonlawyer. The MRPC recognize several exceptions to the general Rule.

First, a temp lawyer agency may charge you a percentage of the temp's compensation, because the payment does not affect the temp lawyer's professional independence. ABA Formal Opinion 88–356. Second, your firm may pay money to the estate of a deceased lawyer for a reasonable period of time after her death. Rule 5.4(a)(1). Third, if you buy the law practice of a deceased lawyer, you may pay the purchase price to the nonlawyer executor of the estate. Rule 5.4(a)(2). Fourth, you can include nonlawyer employees in a compensation plan even though the plan is based on a profit-sharing arrangement. Rule 5.4(a)(3). Finally, you can agree in advance to give your court-awarded fees to a non-profit organization. Rule 5.4(a)(4). On the other hand, it violates Rule 5.4(c) for in-house counsel to share with her corporate employer a lawyer's fee that exceeds the cost of the corporation employing the lawyer. ABA Formal Opinion 95–392.

While you may include nonlawyers in your profit-sharing plan, they cannot assume any of its managerial control including being the officers or directors of a professional legal corporation. Similarly, you cannot be in a partnership with a nonlawyer if practicing law is any part of the partnership's business. Rule 5.4(b). A contrary principle allows law partnerships of many lawyers even though not all of them are admitted in every jurisdiction where the partnership has an office. Rule 7.5(b).

H. LAW FIRM AND OTHER FORMS OF PRACTICE

Law-related Services. In your law practice, you also may offer law-*related* services, such as "title insurance, financial planning, accounting, trust services, real estate counseling, legislative lobbying, economic analysis, social work, psychological counseling, tax return preparation, and patent, medical or environmental consulting." Rule 5.7, Comment 9. Providing these services subjects you to the requirements of Rule 1.8(a) for business transactions with a client.

Before you contract for law-related services in a manner that is distinct from your law practice, you must disclose to your client that those law-related services do not constitute law practice. Under those circumstances, you are not subject to the MRPC that apply to lawyers who are acting as lawyers, such as conflicts of interest, advertising, or confidentiality. Regardless of whether you provide those services separately or as part of your law practice, you are subject to the MRPC that apply to lawyers without regard to whether you are acting in your capacity as a lawyer. When your legal services and the law-related services are intertwined, you must follow Rule 5.3's requirement that you supervise the non-lawyers in the delivery of those services.

Short-term Legal Services. Rule 6.5 applies to your participation in a short-term legal services program sponsored by a nonprofit organization or a court, when you have no expectation of a continuing lawyer-client relationship. Under that circumstance, the current client or former client conflict Rules (1.7 and 1.9) do not apply unless you are aware of a conflict of interest at the time. Rule 6.5(a)(1). If there is a conflict, you cannot represent the client even in this short-term context. If you are unaware of a conflict, you may form a lawyer-client relation with her and give short-term legal advice. Imputed disqualification under Rule 1.10 applies only if you know that a current or former client conflict exists for other lawyers in your law firm. Rule 6.5(a)(2).

Sale of a Law Practice. Rule 1.17 permits a lawyer to sell either his entire practice or an entire area of practice to one or more lawyers or law firms. In other words, you cannot sell some cases of one type but keep other cases of the same type. Several collateral restrictions on the sale of a law practice accompany the sale. The seller must cease practicing law or an entire area of practice unless there are unanticipated circumstances. Rule 1.17, Comment 2. Becoming in-house counsel, working for the government, or working for a legal services entity does not constitute a return to private law practice. Rule 1.17, Comment 3.

As the seller of your law practice you cannot disclose to a potential buyer confidential information about your clients, their cases, or their files. Once there is an agreement about a sale, your clients must have a reasonable chance to consent or withhold consent before confidences are revealed to the buyer. Each client must receive written notice of the proposed sale, the right to retain other counsel, and the right to take possession of her file. Rule 1.17(c)(1)–(3). Consent to disclosure is presumed if a client does not object or respond within ninety days. Rule 1.17(c)(3). If a client cannot be given notice, the buyer must obtain a court order authorizing the transfer, and the court then decides whether reasonable efforts to locate and notify the client have occurred.

The buyer of the practice cannot increase the fee charged to the clients. Rule 1.17(d). The fee-splitting provisions of Rule 1.5(e)(1) do not apply to the sale of a practice. Rule 1.17, Comment 15. You may purchase the law practice from the representative of a deceased lawyer under the conditions described in Rule 1.17. Rule 5.4(a)(2).

Disposition of Client Files and Property When Lawyer Dies. When a sole practitioner dies, she should have a plan to protect her clients' interests and to assure that their cases are not neglected.

ABA Formal Opinion 92–369. The plan should designate a lawyer who would notify the clients, review the files only to identify the clients, and decide which cases needed immediate attention. Rule 1.3, Comment 5.

I. RESPONSIBILITIES OF PARTNERS, SUPERVISORY AND SUBORDINATE LAWYERS

1. Supervisory Responsibilities of Lawyers

The partners or others in a law firm with "managerial authority" must make reasonable efforts to assure that all lawyers in their firm comply with the MRPC. Rule 5.1(a). The same duty also applies to the general counsel of a corporation or the head of a government agency's legal department. Rule 5.1, Comment 1. Even if you outsource legal or nonlegal support services, you still must comply with Rules 5.1. ABA Formal Opinion 08–451. All firms must have procedures to detect and resolve ethics issues, such as conflicts of interest and a system for the intake of prospective clients.

Even if you are not a partner in a firm, you may have supervisory authority over another lawyer, e.g., a senior associate supervising a junior associate. Your responsibilities are the same as a partner in order to assure compliance with ethics standards by the lawyers working under your authority, but your responsibilities relate only to them. Those responsibilities extend to the performance and quality of those lawyers' work, and includes being available to answer their questions. Rule 5.1(b).

When you know that you are supervising an impaired lawyer, you must take care to reasonably assure that their (physical or mental) impairment will not cause a Rule violation. If that lawyer leaves your supervision, you may have obligations to her clients who are considering whether to continue to use her services. ABA Formal Opinion 03–429. If you try to take steps to assure that she does not represent clients while materially impaired but she is not responsive to your concerns, you do not have to speak with her before reporting her to the appropriate professional authority. Rule 8.3; ABA Formal Opinion 03–431.

You cannot knowingly assist another lawyer to violate the MRPC or knowingly violate them through that person's acts. Rule 8.4(a). You are responsible for another lawyer's ethical violation if either you order her to engage in misconduct or you knowingly ratify her misconduct. Rule 5.1(c)(1). The second situation may occur if she tells you about her proposed misconduct and you either tell her to "go ahead" or otherwise do nothing to stop her misconduct. As a partner or supervisory lawyer, you also have an ethical responsibility to act when you can avoid or mitigate the consequences of the supervised lawyer's ethical violation. Rule 5.1(c)(2). In a law firm, as each partner learns about the Rule violation, each becomes responsible for taking action or each violates the Rule for failing to act.

2. Subordinate Lawyers' Responsibilities

You cannot escape your responsibility for ethical misconduct by claiming that you were just following orders. Rule 5.2(a). On the other hand, if the existence of an ethical violation is not clear, you can defer to the judgment of your supervising lawyer when you followed the "reasonable resolution of an arguable question of professional duty." Rule 5.2(b). Courts often decide instead that, as the supervised lawyer, your reasonable course was to look up the law rather than relying on your supervising lawyer's opinion about the proper course of action. Lawyers have brought wrongful discharge claims against their law firms or their clients when they have been fired for their refusal to engage in unethical activity. The typical case relates to being fired for not following the supervising lawyer's unethical directive. Rule 5.2(a). The supervised lawyer claims that her termination was wrongful, even though she was an at-will employee of the firm.

3. Lawyers' Responsibilities for Nonlawyer Assistants

You have a duty to instruct your nonlawyer employees about the ethical aspects of their employment, because you must exercise "reasonable care" to prevent them from violating confidentiality norms. Rule 5.3, Comment 1. You may have periodic discussions with them about the duties of lawyers, such as the duty of confidentiality. The essence of the disciplinary violation is the failure to supervise the employee, even if she discloses no confidential information. If she does improperly disclose, you have no ethical responsibility if you adequately supervised her. The Rule applies to any law partner, lawyers with managerial authority, and lawyers who supervise nonlawyer employees or independent contractors such as law clerks. Rule 5.3(a). When you hire outside contractors for nonlawyer tasks, you must exercise care in selecting those people because they may have access to client files. Rule 5.3, Comment 1. If a breach of confidential information were to occur, you may have to inform your affected clients. ABA Formal Opinion 95–398.

J. RESTRICTIONS ON RIGHT TO PRACTICE

Except for agreements for retirement benefits, the Rules prohibit agreements that restrict your right to practice after you leave your law firm. You cannot offer or make a contract restricting another lawyer's right to practice law after the termination of the relationship created by a partnership, operating, shareholder, or employment agreement. Rule 5.6(a). Such restrictive covenants can subject you to discipline even if they are reasonable in length and geographic area. ABA Formal Opinion 300 (1961). Courts likewise will not enforce such restrictive covenants.

An exception to Rule 5.6(a) permits a restriction on your right to practice that is part of an agreement on retirement benefits. ABA Formal Opinion 06–444. If you are retiring, you would not be available to represent clients anyway. A court will examine the benefits and restrictions as a whole to decide whether a law firm has properly used the retirement label to implement a covenant not to compete with the remaining lawyers.

No one, including you, can restrict your right to practice law as part of the settlement of a client's case. Rule 5.6(b). This Rule qualifies the language of Rule 1.2(d), which requires you to go along with your client's decisions about settlements. The rationale for the Rule relates to both your freedom and your client's freedom.

REGULATION OF THE LEGAL PROFESSION CHECKLIST

A. Powers of Courts and Others to Regulate Lawyers

1. The courts of each state have the inherent power to regulate members of the legal profession for their conduct, both in-court and elsewhere.

2. The legal profession is governed by state ethics standards, case law, and court rules.

B. Admission to the Profession

1. A bar applicant cannot "knowingly make a false statement of material fact."

2. You cannot make a knowingly false or misleading statement in a statement of support for the bar application of another applicant.

C. Regulation after Admission—Lawyer Discipline

1. Misconduct

   a. You are subject to discipline for wrongful conduct committed while you are acting in your capacity as a lawyer.

   b. You may be disciplined for your misconduct outside your capacity as a lawyer, i.e., illegal conduct or conduct "involving dishonesty, fraud, deceit, or misrepresentation."

   c. You are subject to discipline for violating the MRPC, and assisting or inducing another person to violate a Rule.

   d. Discipline may be imposed for crimes that reflect "adversely on the lawyer's honesty, trustworthiness or fitness as a lawyer."

   e. You are subject to discipline for "conduct that is prejudicial to the administration of justice," as when you make remarks that are racist, sexist, or politically incorrect.

2. Disciplinary Authority

    a. If you are admitted in State A, you are subject to discipline there, even if your misconduct occurs outside State A.

    b. If you are not admitted to practice in State A, you are nevertheless subject to discipline in State A if you provide or offer to provide legal services there.

3. Choice of Law

    a. If you are admitted to practice in State A but you are temporarily admitted in a court in State B and your alleged misconduct occurred there, discipline by State A would be governed by the Rules of State B.

    b. If your alleged misconduct occurs outside a court, the applicable Rules are those of the state where the conduct occurred unless the predominant effect of the particular conduct is elsewhere.

D. **Mandatory and Permissive Reporting of Professional Misconduct**

1. You have a general obligation to report information about another lawyer's serious disciplinary violations.

2. Your duty to report misconduct focuses on conduct that raises a "substantial question" about the other lawyer's "honesty, trustworthiness or fitness as a lawyer."

3. Your duty extends to reporting to regulatory authorities another lawyer who is suspected of alcoholism, drug addiction, or other mental impairment.

4. There are two contexts when the duty to report is extinguished.

    a. The duty to report is superseded by the duty of confidentiality under Rule 1.6, as when your client tells you that another lawyer has engaged in serious misconduct, or you represent a lawyer who has herself committed serious misconduct.

b. The reporting requirement also does not apply to lawyers who participate in lawyer assistance programs.

E. Unauthorized Practice of Law

1. The definition of unauthorized practice of law is defined by the statutes, rules and case law of each state, and the MRPC incorporate that law by reference.

2. You violate the unauthorized practice Rules, either by practicing in a state where you are not admitted or by helping a lay person in her unauthorized practice of law.

F. Multijurisdictional Practice

1. You cannot open a law office in a state where you are not admitted, but you may open an office with a lawyer admitted there.

2. You can offer *temporary* legal services in a jurisdiction where you are not admitted.

   a. You may associate yourself with local counsel who actively participates in representation of your clients.

   b. You may be admitted by a court to practice one case *pro hac vice*.

   c. You can participate in an ADR proceeding in another state if it is reasonably related to or arises out of a representation in the place where you are admitted to practice.

   d. You may represent a client in a matter in another state when that matter is closely related to your representation of a client in the state where you are admitted.

3. If you are an employee-lawyer for an entity like a corporation, you may represent it anywhere you are not

admitted to practice. If that representation results in litigation, you must seek *pro hac vice* admission to the court where the lawsuit is pending.

G. Fee Division with a Nonlawyer

1. Generally, you or your firm cannot share legal fees with a nonlawyer. Rule 5.4(a).

2. Exceptions.

   a. Your firm may pay money to the estate of a deceased lawyer for a reasonable period of time after her death.

   b. If you buy the law practice of a deceased lawyer, you may pay the purchase price to the nonlawyer executor of the estate.

   c. You can include nonlawyer employees in a compensation plan even though the plan is based on a profit-sharing arrangement.

   d. You can agree in advance to give your court-awarded fees to a non-profit organization.

3. You cannot be in a partnership with a nonlawyer if practicing law is any part of the partnership's business. Rule 5.4(b).

H. Law Firm and Other Forms of Practice

1. Law-related Services. Before you contract for such law-related services such as title insurance, you must disclose to your client that those law-related services do not constitute law practice.

2. Short-term Legal Services. You may participate in a short-term legal services program sponsored by a non-profit organization or a court, as when you have no expectation of a continuing lawyer-client relationship. Under that circumstance, the current or former client conflict Rules (1.7 and 1.9) do not apply.

3. Sale of Law practice. You may sell either your entire practice or an entire area of practice to one or more lawyers or law firms.

4. Collateral restrictions on the sale of a law practice

    a. You must cease practicing law or an entire area of practice unless there are unanticipated circumstances.

    b. Becoming in-house counsel, working for the government, or working for a legal services entity does not constitute a return to private law practice.

    c. Each of the seller's clients must receive written notice of the proposed sale, the right to retain other counsel, and the right to take possession of her file.

I. **Responsibilities of Partners, Supervisory, and Subordinate Lawyers**

1. Supervisory Responsibilities of Lawyers

    a. The partners in a law firm must make reasonable efforts to assure that all the lawyers in their firm comply with the MRPC.

    b. If you have supervisory authority over another lawyer, your responsibilities are the same as a partner.

    c. When you are supervising a physically or mentally impaired lawyer, you must take care to reasonably assure that their impairment will not cause a MRPC violation.

    d. You are responsible for another lawyer's ethical violation if either you order her to engage in misconduct or you knowingly ratify her misconduct.

2. Subordinate Lawyers' Responsibilities

    a. You cannot escape your responsibility for ethical misconduct by claiming that you were just following orders.

    b. If the existence of an ethical violation is not clear, you can defer to the judgment of your supervising lawyer.

3. Lawyers' Responsibilities for Nonlawyer Assistants

    a. You have a duty to instruct your nonlawyer employees about the ethical aspects of their employment.

    b. When you hire outside contractors, you must exercise care in selecting those people because they may have access to client files.

J. Restrictions on Right to Practice

1. Except for agreements for retirement benefits, the MRPC prohibit agreements that restrict your right to practice after you leave your law firm.

2. Rule 5.6(a) prohibits the corporation from restricting your later representation of a client against the corporation even in unrelated matters.

3. No one, including you, can restrict your right to practice law as part of the settlement of a client's case.

ILLUSTRATIVE PROBLEM

During her college years, Miriam Maney probably enjoyed herself too much. She was on academic probation during her freshman year and was briefly suspended from her college a semester later. In her sophomore year, she was arrested twice and had one conviction for forgery. When she applied to law school, she denied that she had been suspended from an institution of higher education and she failed to mention the forgery conviction when asked about prior arrests and convictions. Having both lied and hidden her past in her law school application, should Miriam attempt to correct her law school application while she is in law school, or should she rely on her law school application when she applies to take the bar examination?

Analysis

In an application to take the bar examination, Miriam must be completely truthful in her written responses as well as when an admissions or character and fitness committee assesses her character. Rule 8.1(a) requires that she must not knowingly make a false statement of material fact in connection with her bar application. Having failed to answer the law school application questions truthfully, she cannot continue to rely on those false answers and hidden information when she applies for admission to the bar. Making false statements about her academic record and failing to disclose information about her burglary conviction may result in her being denied admission to the bar, per Rule 8.1(a).

Further, she cannot fail to disclose a fact that is necessary to correct a misapprehension known by her to have arisen. Rule 8.1(b). In certifying her to take the state's bar examination, her law school in part will be relying on her law school application's false answers. Ideally, she should correct her law school application as soon as possible. Thereafter, she should must respond truthfully in her bar application to all questions no matter how embarrassing her answers may be.

POINTS TO REMEMBER

- The courts of each state have the inherent power to regulate members of the legal profession for their conduct, both in-court and elsewhere.

- A bar applicant cannot "knowingly make a false statement of material fact."

- You are subject to discipline for wrongful conduct committed while you are acting in your capacity as a lawyer.

- You also may be disciplined for your misconduct outside your capacity as a lawyer, i.e., illegal conduct or conduct "involving dishonesty, fraud, deceit, or misrepresentation."

- You are subject to discipline for violating the MRPC, and assisting or inducing another person to violate a Rule.

- Discipline may be imposed for

  - Crimes that reflect "adversely on the lawyer's honesty, trustworthiness or fitness as a lawyer." Rule 8.4(b).

- Conduct involving dishonesty, fraud, deceit, or misrepresentation. Rule 8.4(c).

- "Conduct that is prejudicial to the administration of justice," e.g., if you made remarks that were racist, sexist, or politically incorrect. Rule 8.4(d).

- Stating or implying an ability to influence improperly a government agency or official, or to achieve results by any means that violate the Rules. Rule 8.4(e).

- Knowingly assisting a judge to violate the Code of Judicial Conduct. Rule 8.4(f).

- If you admitted in State A, you are subject to discipline there, even if your misconduct occurs outside State A. Rule 8.5(a).

- The partners in a law firm must make reasonable efforts to assure that all the lawyers in their firm comply with the MRPC. Rule 5.1(a).

- If you have supervisory authority over another lawyer as a senior associate supervising a junior associate, your responsibilities are the same as a partner. Rule 5.1(b).

- You are responsible for another lawyer's ethical violation if you order her to engage in misconduct or you knowingly ratify her misconduct. Rule 5.1(c)(1).

- You cannot escape your responsibility for ethical misconduct by claiming that you were just following orders. Rule 5.2(a).

- You have a general obligation to report information about another lawyer's serious disciplinary violations, unless that information is confidential under Rule 1.6.

- Your duty to report misconduct focuses on conduct that raises a "substantial question" about the other lawyer's "honesty, trustworthiness or fitness as a lawyer." Rule 8.3(a).

- The duty to report is superseded by the duty of confidentiality under Rule 1.6, as when your client tells you that another lawyer has engaged in serious misconduct, or you represent a lawyer who has herself committed serious misconduct.

- Generally, you or your firm cannot share legal fees with a nonlawyer, to control nonlawyer involvement in the delivery of legal services. Rule 5.4(a).

- You cannot be in a partnership with a nonlawyer if practicing law is any part of the partnership's business. Rule 5.4(b).

- You may violate the unauthorized practice rules, either by practicing in a state where you are not admitted or by helping a lay person in her unauthorized practice of law. Rule 5.5(a).

- You cannot open a law office in a state where you are not admitted, but you may open an office with a lawyer admitted there. Rule 5.5(b).

- Except for agreements for retirement benefits, the MRPC prohibit agreements that restrict your right to practice after you leave your law firm. Rule 5.6(a).

- No one, including you, can restrict your right to practice law as part of the settlement of a client's case. Rule 5.6(b).

- You may sell either your entire practice or an entire area of practice to one or more lawyers or law firms.

- Collateral restrictions on the sale of a law practice are: you must cease practicing law or an entire area of practice unless there are unanticipated circumstances, and each of the seller's clients must receive written notice of the proposed sale, the right to retain other counsel, and the right to take possession of her file.

CHAPTER 2

The Lawyer–Client Relationship

A. FORMATION OF LAWYER–CLIENT RELATIONSHIP

There are several ways for the creation of a lawyer-client relationship with a client to occur. First, you may form such a relationship with a client who intentionally wants you to provide legal services to her and you agree. Second, a relationship may be created when she intends for you to provide her with legal services, but you fail to be clear that you do not agree to represent her, and you know or should know that she is reasonably relying on you to provide those services. The third way in which a relationship is created occurs when a judge appoints you to represent a client. Restatement, § 14. As discussed in Chapter 11, Rule 6.2 may or must require you to decline the court's appointment.

You *must* refuse to create a lawyer-client relationship if (1) your client's motive is to harass another person, Rule 4.4(a), (2) you are being asked to take a position that is either factually or legally frivolous, Rule 3.1, (3) you are too busy or inexperienced to be competent in the matter, Rule 1.1, or (4) your own mental or physical condition materially impairs your ability to represent her, Rule 1.16(a)(2). For example, you may have strong personal feelings about the client's case.

The lawyer-client relationship with your client is governed by both general contract principles and the specific agreement with her. Regardless of the terms of the contract with a client, lawyers owe their clients duties of confidentiality and loyalty as well as a duty to protect their property.

B. SCOPE, OBJECTIVE, AND MEANS OF THE REPRESENTATION

1. Limits on the Scope of the Representation

The scope and objectives of your representation of a client may be defined by your agreement to represent her. Without such a descriptive or limiting agreement, you have a duty to use available legal methods to pursue her objectives. As long as you do not assist a client in criminal or fraudulent conduct, you can explain to her the consequences of possible actions. Rule 1.2(d). You also may help her to determine whether specific conduct is criminal or fraudulent under applicable law. If you find yourself tempted to violate the MRPC, you must withdraw from representing your client. Rule 1.16.

You may limit the scope of your representation if the limitation is reasonable and your client gives you her informed consent. Rule 1.2(c). Before she can give informed consent, you must explain the risks of limited representation and any available alternatives to such limitations. Rule 1.0(e). Even though it often is the client and not the lawyer who places limitations on the scope of the representation, you must still explain the risks and document her informed consent in writing.

When you and your client disagree about what you should do to accomplish her objectives, the MRPC encourage clients to defer to your expertise, especially on "technical, legal, and tactical matters." On the other hand, you should defer to her decisions which involve added expense or harm to others. Rule 1.2, Comment 2. Although the MRPC do not prescribe how to resolve such disagreements, a fundamental disagreement may permit or require you to withdraw. Rule 1.16(b)(4); 1.16(a)(3).

2. Client With Diminished Capacity

In the typical lawyer-client relationship, your client sets the goals of the representation and participates in many of the decisions, e.g., whether to settle a civil case, whether to have a jury trial, plead guilty, or testify in a criminal case. Rule 1.2(a). Sometimes, your client has a diminished capacity, as a result of their mental abilities or because of their age (juveniles).

Determining that a client has a diminished capacity. "As far as reasonably possible," you should maintain a "normal client-lawyer relationship" with a person of diminished capacity. You have to explain things to her in words that she can understand and then allow her to make decisions. Rules 1.4(b); 1.14(a).

An adult or juvenile client who may not appreciate the significance of what is going on may be under a mental disability. If your client has a diminished capacity, you may take action when she "is at risk of substantial physical, financial, or other harm unless action is taken." Rule 1.14(b). The Comments provide guidance about how to make this determination and includes the option of seeking help from a diagnostician. You must assess your client's mental capacity, considering several factors: her "ability to articulate reasoning leading to a decision, variability of state of mind and ability to appreciate consequences of a decision; the substantive fairness of a decision; and the consistency of a decision with the known, long-term commitments and values of the client." Rule 1.14, Comment 6.

If you seek assistance in reaching a conclusion about your client's capacity, you are implicitly authorized to reveal otherwise confidential information about your client, but only to the extent necessary to protect her interests. Rule 1.14(c). That implied authorization may even override your client's directive to the contrary. Rule 1.14, Comment 8.

When she suffers from a diminished capacity, maintaining a normal lawyer-client relationship which includes keeping her informed and consulting with her about her situation is not realistic. In that situation, you may override her choices because of your concern that to follow her chosen course of action will cause her to suffer substantial injury. Rule 1.14(b). The Rule permits you to override the client's allocation of decision-making authority normally provided by Rule 1.2. The action you take must be the "least restrictive action under the circumstances." For example, appointment of a guardian should not be an option if other, less drastic, solutions are available. ABA Formal Opinion 96–404. Such choices must be due to the necessity of the situation, rather than because of a family member's request.

Emergency situations. In emergencies, a person may seek your services even if she cannot establish a lawyer-client relationship or make decisions about her situation. Before acting on her behalf, you must "reasonably believe that the person has no other lawyer, agent, or other representative available." And you may act only to the extent that is "reasonably necessary to maintain the *status quo* or otherwise avoid imminent irreparable harm." Rule 1.14, Comment 9. If you appear before a tribunal, you must inform the tribunal of the nature of the relationship with the person and confidential information necessary to accomplish the intended protective action. Rule 1.14, Comment 10. You are supposed to take steps to establish a lawyer-client relationship as soon as possible. Normally, you would not charge a legal fee under these circumstances.

C. DECISION–MAKING AUTHORITY— ACTUAL AND APPARENT

Generally, you have the authority to make decisions on issues that do not either affect the merits of your client's case or substantially prejudice her rights. For example, you may agree unilaterally to an extension of time for the opposing party to file a pleading. Otherwise, your client has the exclusive authority to make decisions. As the agent for your client, you must follow her "decisions concerning the objectives of representation," but you also can act on your client's behalf in a manner which is "impliedly authorized to carry out the representation." Rule 1.2(a). For example, she can delegate her settlement authority to you by saying, "you do not have to contact me if the other side offers less than $1,000,000."

Because of the difficulty in drawing clear lines, the MRPC offer examples about decision-making authority between client and lawyer. Your client has the authority to decide whether to accept a settlement offer, to plead guilty, to waive a jury trial, to testify in her own defense in a criminal case, or to appeal. Rule 1.2(a). As to the decision to testify, you have a duty to explain the benefits and burdens of testifying so that she can make an informed decision. Rule 1.4(b).

Your authority extends to strategic decisions about issues like which witnesses to call, methods of cross-examination, jury selection, motions and objections to make, and other strategic or tactical decisions. ABA Standards Relating to the Administration of Criminal Justice, The Defense Function, Standard 4–5.2(b). Although decisions about which objections to make are within your tactical choices, the effect of your failure to object can result in forfeiting a client's constitutional right. *Wainwright v. Sykes*, 433 U.S. 72 (1977).

You and your client may agree about which nonfrivolous issues to present to a tribunal. Constitutionally, while your indigent client can compel you as her appointed counsel to pursue a nonfrivolous appeal, *Anders v. California*, 386 U.S. 738 (1967), she cannot force you to assert a specific nonfrivolous issue on appeal. *Jones v. Barnes*, 463 U.S. 745 (1983).

D. TERMINATION OF THE LAWYER–CLIENT RELATIONSHIP

Throughout these chapters, there are references to varying circumstances by which you must or you may withdraw from representing your client. This section focuses exclusively on the Rule for withdrawal. In proceedings before a tribunal, you must follow its rules about withdrawing from representing a litigant. If a court refuses to grant its permission to withdraw, you have to continue representing your client even though the MRPC may provide a duty or right to withdraw. Rule 1.16(c). If the court asks the reason you seek to withdraw, your duty to preserve confidential information can prevent you from responding. Rule 1.16, Comment 3.

If your client fires you, but the court refuses to approve your withdrawal, you must comply with the court's order. Rule 1.16(a)(3). She is still liable to you for any fees you earned in representing you, and you must return any money you had not yet earned. Rule 1.16(d).

When your representation does not involve litigation, your client "has a right to discharge [you] at any time, with or without cause, subject to liability for payment for the lawyer's services." Rule 1.16, Comment 4. Regardless of whether you resign or are fired, you must make reasonable efforts to protect your client's interests, e.g., turning over her papers and property. Rule 1.16(d).

Mandatory withdrawal. Under Rule 1.16(a), you *must* withdraw from representation under three circumstances: 1) your continued employment would result in violating the MRPC or other law, 2) your physical or mental condition has a materially adverse effect on your client, or 3) she fires you.

Permissive withdrawal. You *may* withdraw for any reason if it does not have a materially adverse effect on your client's interests. Rule 1.16(b)(1). The Restatement takes the opposite view, given your fiduciary obligation to your client, that the harm to your client should not be disproportionate to your justification for withdrawal. Restatement, § 32(4), Comment h.

You *may* withdraw for seven other reasons, per Rule 1.16(b)(2)–(7): (1) your client persists in a course of action that you reasonably believe is criminal or fraudulent, (2) she has used your services to perpetuate a crime or fraud, (3) she insists on taking action which you consider repugnant or with which you have a fundamental disagreement, (4) she fails substantially to fulfill an obligation to you relating to your services and has been reasonably warned that you will withdraw unless the obligation is met, (5) she has made the representation unreasonably difficult, (6) the representation will result in an unreasonable financial burden, or (7) for other good cause.

Wrongful discharge. Even if you can be fired for no reason and you usually have no expectation of continued employment, your discharge cannot be for an improper reason. For example, when employers discharge associates in private law firms or in-house counsel for their refusal to engage in unethical activity, the employee may be able to sue the employer for wrongful discharge.

E. COMMUNICATIONS WITH THE CLIENT

The only way for clients to participate effectively in being represented by a lawyer is for her to keep them informed about what is going on. When clients complain about lawyers neglecting their case, their complaint is usually about the failure to keep them reasonably informed about the progress of their case. You may be justified in delaying the sharing of information about your client's case if you believe that she may react negatively or unwisely. Rule 1.4, Comment 6.

Many Rules require that you communicate with your client in order to obtain her "informed consent" as a prerequisite to your next act. The essence of informed consent from your client is that you have first given her adequate information and explanation about the risks attendant to a course of action by you. Rule 1.0(e). Your effective communication with her enables her to make an informed consent.

It is a basic obligation for you to keep your client reasonably informed about the representation and to promptly answer her reasonable requests. Rule 1.4(a); Restatement, § 20(1). Notice the use of the term "reasonable." Clients who contact you constantly with requests and demands may be viewed as unreasonable. If your client makes a specific request to you for information, your duty is to respond promptly to a reasonable request. Part of your duty to her also is to voluntarily inform her. Rule 1.4 specifies five contexts in which you should provide information to your client.

First, whenever the MRPC prescribe that you obtain your client's informed consent, you must promptly consult with her and obtain her consent. Rule 1.4(a)(1). That consultation is unnecessary if you already had discussed the issue and she had instructed you about what to do, and nothing important about your client's situation has changed since your client initially instructed you. The prior consent also is inapplicable when the current, informed consent must be written, per the MRPC.

Second, you must "reasonably consult with the client about the means by which the client's objectives are to be accomplished." Rule 1.4(a)(2). After your client sets the goals for your representation, you are responsible for deciding the necessary means to accomplish those objectives. Rule 1.2(a). While you are not expected to describe "negotiation strategy" in detail for your client, she needs sufficient information to participate intelligently in discussions about how to accomplish her objectives. Rule 1.2, Comment 5. Her sophistication and the nature of the representation determines the types of information you need to communicate. There is a need for discussions at important times about what you have done and what lies ahead. Rule 1.4, Comment 2.

Your third obligation is to "keep the client reasonably informed about the status of the matter." Rule 1.4(a)(3). Unless she has told you not to communicate such information, you should inform her about what you and the opposition have done in her case, judicial rulings and, consistent with Rule 1.2, settlement offers from the opposing party.

Fourth, you must "promptly comply with reasonable requests for information." Rule 1.4(a)(4). This part of the Rule is about returning phone calls and other communications like email, and responding to your client's reasonable requests for information. If your client calls you daily to ask when a court may decide her case on appeal, your best response is to tell her that you will call her when the court of appeals informs you of its decision.

Finally, you must "consult with the client about any relevant limitation on the lawyer's conduct when the lawyer knows that the client expects assistance not permitted by the Rules of Professional

Conduct or other law." Rule 1.4(a)(5). If you conclude that your client's "proposed course of conduct of action will constitute a violation," Rule 1.4(a)(5) requires consultation "with the client about the legal limits" of your assistance. ABA Formal Opinion 08–453. You cannot, for example, engage in illegal and unethical conduct, such as being a member of a criminal conspiracy, or violating the rules of procedure.

At the beginning of the representation, you should prepare an "engagement letter" for your client to read and sign. It should specify the identity of the client, which may be especially important in the case of a corporation with subsidiaries, or when you are drafting a document for one member of a couple but not the other. The letter also should include information about: (1) what you intend to do for your client (and maybe what you will not be doing as part of the representation), (2) your fee, as well as how you will bill your client, how promptly you expect to be paid, and the consequences for the relationship of your client not meeting her fee obligations, and (3) any conflicts of interest and sufficient information for your client to give informed consent to waive any conflicts. If you decide not to represent a person, you should send her a "disengagement letter" to record that fact so that she will not later claim that she reasonably believed that you still represented her.

Rule 1.4(b) requires you to explain to your client the possible consequences of any proposed action you intend to take. If you are prohibited from complying with Rule 1.4(b) due to your duty of loyalty to another client, you must withdraw from representing both of them under Rule 1.16(a)(1). ABA Formal Opinion 08–450.

F. FEES

1. Types of Fees

When you charge your client a fee in return for your professional services, issues about your fee usually arise only when your client becomes unhappy about the size of the fee or the manner in which you are earning that fee by representing her. Your fee must be reasonable. Rule 1.5(a). Whether a fee is reasonable may come before a court in several ways: (1) judicial approval of a fee in connection with a settlement, (2) you may sue your client to recover a fee, (3) your client may sue to recover a fee already paid, (4) in disciplinary proceedings, (5) when one party is assessed the other party's lawyer's fee under a fee-shifting statute, e.g., 42 U.S.C. § 1988, or a court rule authorizing sanctions, e.g., FRCP 11, or (6) probate or bankruptcy proceedings requiring court approval of a lawyer's fee out of an estate or trust.

You may encounter several types of fee arrangements: (1) a flat fee for a legal service, e.g., an uncontested divorce, (2) an hourly rate on a particular matter, e.g., $200 per hour, (3) a proportional fee, e.g., handling a real estate matter for a percentage of the purchase price, (4) a contingent fee, e.g., one-third of whatever amount is recovered, (5) a retainer, or down payment on future services to be drawn against when legal services are provided, (6) budgeted fee arrangements, e.g., a budget is prepared to control legal costs on a particular issue (a memorandum of law on an issue) or a particular task (a dollar amount for each deposition), (7) blended hourly rates, e.g., a partner's rate and an associate's rates blended to yield one rate, or (8) project pricing, a fixed fee for a given project before the work begins.

If your fee is alleged by a court or by a client to be unreasonable, Rule 1.5(a) lists eight factors as examples of relevant concerns in determining the fair market value of your services.

2.   Factors Relating to the Reasonableness of a Fee

Time and labor required, novelty and difficulty of the questions involved, and skill requisite to perform the legal service properly. Rule 1.5(a)(1). The time reasonably necessary for the services required is more important than the time actually spent on the matter. Your time must be fairly and properly used. An experienced lawyer may accomplish more in a short time than a new lawyer.

Likelihood that accepting employment will preclude other employment by the lawyer. Rule 1.5(a)(2). In setting your fee, you may consider the loss of other employment due to the time taken by this case. In any case you take, there may be certain aspects which might cause you to lose future business because of your association with this case. Representing your client in this case also may lead to conflicts of interest that may prevent you from accepting future work.

When someone pays you in advance, you charge your fee against the advance payment as you earn it. You should deposit the advance fee in your client trust account until you earn it. Rule 1.15(a). If you do not earn the entire amount of the advance fee, you must return the unearned portion to your client. Rule 1.16(d). After the advance is used, you and your client may negotiate how she will pay any additional fee.

Fee customarily charged in the locality for similar legal services. Rule 1.5(a)(3). In setting a fee, you may consider the amount set for similar legal services in that locality. To prove this factor, you may obtain affidavits from other lawyers who practice this type of case. By setting your fee at the customary local rate, you are not necessarily part of a conspiracy to fix prices that violates antitrust laws. *Goldfarb v. Virginia State Bar*, 421 U.S. 773 (1975).

Amount involved and results obtained. Rule 1.5(a)(4). When you set a fee, you may consider how much money is involved and how successful you are in the particular case. The resistance by the other side is likely to be greater when a large amount is involved. In a contingent fee case, the only factor is the result obtained as a precise measure of the value of the services. Other things besides material gain may be important, e.g., establishing a precedent, overturning a landmark decision, or obtaining a result that benefits others as well as your client.

Time limitations imposed by the client or by the circumstances. Rule 1.5(a)(5). Your fee may reflect any special time limitations, e.g., you must perform the work by the following day. Time constraints imposed by your client's circumstances may lead to a higher than normal fee.

Nature and length of the professional relationship with the client. Rule 1.5(a)(6). The reasonableness of your fee may depend on the nature and length of your relationship with your client. For an existing client, you may reduce your bill.

Experience, reputation, and ability of the lawyer or lawyers performing the services. Rule 1.5(a)(7). Your fee may also reflect your experience, reputation and ability in that type of case. You may decide that your services are worth a lot more than other lawyers. Your client may agree and hire you, or she may go elsewhere for legal services. Your general income is not relevant to this factor, and your success in earning large fees is not a true indication of your reputation or ability generally. Your unique skill or experience is relevant when the particular case calls for your specialized ability.

Whether the fee is fixed or contingent. Rule 1.5(a)(8). The reasonableness of a fee may depend on whether it is fixed or contingent on the outcome of the representation. Contingent fees may appear large in retrospect, but not if your client considers that you risked earning nothing in the matter.

3.   Contingent Fees

A contingent fee arrangement provides that you will receive a fee if you are successful in obtaining a recovery for your client. Contingent fees are customarily used by plaintiff's counsel, but there is no *per se* ethical prohibition against their use by defense counsel. ABA Formal Opinion 93–373. Because of the controversy that sometimes surrounds their use, ethics standards often treat contingent fee arrangements with provisions not used in other fee contexts. If "applicable law" requires, you must offer your client an alternative to a contingent fee arrangement. Rule 1.5, Comment 3.

Written details. All contingent fee arrangements must be in writing and signed by your client, in order to avoid later claims that she never saw or signed a written agreement. The contents must include (1) the percentage of the recovery you will earn, (2) whether the percentage to be charged depends on how far the case proceeds, (3) whether expenses are to be deducted before or after the fee is calculated, and (4) which expenses she must pay if she gets no recovery. When the representation is concluded, you must also provide a detailed statement in writing to your client. Rule 1.5(c)

Conflicts of interest. Contingent fees raise potential conflicts of interest between you and your client. For example, you might believe that settling her case is inappropriate before trial, but you cannot require her to give up her right to settle. Rule 1.2, Comment 5.

Criminal and divorce cases. You cannot ethically use a contingent fee in a criminal case or a domestic relations matter. Rule 1.5(d)(1)–(2). For criminal cases, the rationale is that there is no *res* from which a fee can be paid. In divorce cases, contingent fees are forbidden because you might be tempted to prevent reconciliation of the married couple in order to recover your fee. After a divorce is granted, in cases to collect an alimony or child support arrearage, there is a *res* that enables you to use a contingent fee. Rule 1.5, Comment 6.

Early termination. If you terminate the representation of a contingent fee client without good cause or your client's consent, your ability to recover a fee depends on the reason for the termination. If you withdraw due to an unforeseen circumstance on your part, you probably will be unable to collect any fee. But if the cause for the termination is the result of your client's conduct, you may be able to enforce the contract with your client and recover a fee based on a *quantum meruit* standard.

4. Fee Sharing and Other Fee Issues

The MRPC do not address how lawyers in the same firm divide legal fees. Lawyers in *different* firms may divide fees only under specified conditions. First, the division must either be divided in proportion to the services performed by each lawyer or have each of them assume joint financial and ethical responsibility for the case. Each lawyer has a duty of supervision under Rule 5.1, which makes you responsible for ethical compliance by those you supervise. Second, the client agrees in writing to the division, including the share for each of you. Rule 1.5, Comment 7. Finally, as with all fees, the total fee must be reasonable. Rule 1.5(e)(1)–(3).

When you hire a temporary lawyer, the ethical standards treat her the same as if she is an associate working under your supervision. Therefore, when you pay her, you are not sharing a legal fee with someone in a different law firm. ABA Formal Opinion 88–356.

Ability to pay. Within the context of reasonableness, your fee may be a function of how much your client can afford to pay. Rule 1.5, Comment 3. When you charge poorer clients a "substantially reduced fee for services," you are effectively charging affluent people a higher fee. Rule 6.1, Comment 6. You cannot charge *any* client more than a "reasonable" fee.

Time manipulations in fee-setting. If you charge your clients by the hour, you cannot charge them for wasteful or repetitious tasks, charge them for more hours than they actually worked, or bill several clients for the same hour. "A lawyer who spends four hours of time on behalf of three clients has not earned twelve billable hours." ABA Formal Opinion 93–379. It is reasonable for your client to think that you have passed on any efficiency that results in fewer hours being charged. An efficient lawyer may charge a higher hourly rate.

Modifying the fee agreement. A reviewing court examining a fee agreement considers its reasonableness as of the time that the agreement was made, rather than with the benefit of hindsight. When you modify a fee agreement with your client, you are engaging in a business transaction with your client under Rule 1.8(a), which requires disclosure of factual information and the opportunity for your client to consult with independent counsel.

Written fee agreements The MRPC express the preference that fee agreements should be reduced to writing, Rule 1.5(b), but only a contingent fee agreement *must* be written. Rule 1.5(c).

Fee disputes. Disputes about fee agreements are construed from the perspective of the reasonable person in the circumstances of the client. Restatement, § 18(2). If a dispute develops midway through the representation about a modification to the fee, a fee alteration must be fair and reasonable to the client who has less bargaining power at that point. Restatement, § 18. Because non-refundable fee agreements have a chilling effect on your client's ability to end her lawyer-client relation with you, many courts regard such agreements as unenforceable because they are inconsistent with public policy.

If there is an established procedure for resolving fee disputes, such as mediation or arbitration, the MRPC *require* that you "should conscientiously consider submitting to it." Rule 1.5, Comment 9. The Restatement *permits* you to use any fee collection method not prohibited by law. Restatement, § 41.

Withdrawal after your client fails to pay your fee. If your client intentionally fails to pay your fee, you may withdraw from representing her, but only after you take reasonable steps to protect her interests. Rule 1.16(b)(4) & (d). In a case pending before a court, you must obtain the court's permission to withdraw. Until the court consents, you cannot neglect your client's case. Rule 1.16(c).

Use of credit cards. You may charge interest and accept credit cards as long as any accompanying advertising is not false, fraudulent, or misleading. ABA Formal Opinion 00–420.

THE LAWYER–CLIENT RELATIONSHIP CHECKLIST

A. **Formation of Lawyer–Client Relationship**

    1. There are several ways for the creation of a lawyer-client relationship with a client to occur.

        a. A client intentionally wants you to provide legal services to her and you agree.

        b. A client intends for you to provide her with legal services, but you fail to be clear that you do not agree to represent her, and you know or should know that she is reasonably relying on you to provide those services.

        c. A judge appoints you to represent a client, though Rule 6.2 may require you to decline the court's appointment.

2. The lawyer-client relationship with your client is governed by both general contract principles and the specific agreement with her.

B. Scope, Objective, and Means of Representation

1. Limits on the Scope of the Representation

    a. You may limit the scope of your representation if the limitation is reasonable and your client gives you her informed consent.

    b. You cannot assist a client in criminal or fraudulent conduct. However, you may help her to determine whether specific conduct is criminal or fraudulent under applicable law.

2. Client with Diminished Capacity

    a. If a client lacks the capacity to make considered decisions, "as far as reasonably possible," you should maintain a "normal client-lawyer relationship," explaining things to her in words that she can understand and that allow her to make decisions.

    b. If your client has a diminished capacity, you may take action when she "is at risk of substantial physical, financial, or other harm unless action is taken."

    c. You are implicitly authorized to reveal information about your client, but only to the extent necessary to protect her interests. That implied authorization may even override your client's directive to the contrary, because of your concern that her chosen course will cause substantial injury. You must take the "least restrictive action under the circumstances," e.g., appointment of a guardian should not be an option if there are less drastic solutions available.

C. Decision–Making Authority

1. Generally, you have the authority to make decisions on issues that do not either affect the merits of your client's case or substantially prejudice her rights.

2. As the agent for your client, you must follow her "decisions concerning the objectives of representation," but you also can act on your client's behalf in a manner which is "impliedly authorized to carry out the representation." Rule 1.2(a).

   a. She can delegate her settlement authority to you.

   b. She decides whether to accept a settlement offer, to plead guilty, to waive a jury trial, to testify in her own defense in a criminal case, or to appeal.

   c. You have a duty to explain the benefits and burdens of testifying so that she can make an informed decision.

3. Your authority extends to decisions about which witnesses to call, methods of cross-examination, jury selection, motions and objections to make, and other strategic or tactical decisions.

4. When you and your client disagree, the MRPC encourage clients to defer to your expertise, especially on "technical, legal, and tactical matters."

   a. You should defer to her decisions on matters which involve added expense or harm to others.

   b. A fundamental disagreement may permit or require you to withdraw.

D. **Termination of the Lawyer–Client Relationship**

1. You must follow the Rules about withdrawing from representing a litigant.

   a. If a court refuses to grant its permission to withdraw, you have to continue representing your client even though the Rules may provide a duty or right to withdraw.

   b. If the court asks the reason you seek to withdraw, your duty to preserve confidential information can prevent you from responding.

c.   If your client fires you, but the court refuses to approve your withdrawal, you must comply with the court's order.

2.   Outside litigation, your client "has a right to discharge [you] at any time, with or without cause, subject to liability for payment for the lawyer's services."

3.   Regardless of the reason for the withdrawal, you must make reasonable efforts to protect your client's interests, e.g., turning over her papers and property.

4.   Under Rule 1.16(a), you **must** withdraw under three circumstances:

    a.   Your continued employment would result in violating the ethical rules or other law,

    b.   You physical or mental condition has a materially adverse effect on your client, or

    c.   She fires you.

5.   You **may** withdraw for any reason if:

    a.   It does not have a materially adverse effect on your client's interests.

    b.   Your client persists in a course of action that you reasonably believe is criminal or fraudulent,

    c.   She has used your services to perpetuate a crime or fraud,

    d.   She insists on taking action which you consider repugnant or with which you have a fundamental disagreement,

    e.   She fails substantially to fulfill an obligation to you relating to your services and has been reasonably warned that you will withdraw unless the obligation is met,

    f.   She has made the representation unreasonably difficult,

    g.   The representation will result in an unreasonable financial burden, or

    h.   There is other good cause.

E. **Communication**

1. You must keep your clients informed about what is going throughout the representation and to promptly answer their reasonable requests.

2. Rule 1.4 specifies five contexts in which you should provide information to your client.

   a. When the MRPC prescribe that you obtain your client's informed consent, you must promptly consult with her and obtain her consent.

   b. You must "reasonably consult with the client about the means by which the client's objectives are to be accomplished."

   c. Keep her reasonably informed about the status of the matter.

   d. You must "promptly comply with reasonable requests for information."

   e. Inform her about the limits on what you can do on her behalf.

3. You must explain to your client the possible consequences of any proposed action you intend to take. Rule 1.4(b).

F. **Fees**

1. You may not negotiate for, charge, or collect an unreasonable fee or an unreasonable amount for expenses. Rule 1.5(a) lists eight factors as examples of relevant concerns in determining the fair market value of your services.

   a. Time and labor required, novelty and difficulty of the questions involved, and skill requisite to perform the legal service properly.

   b. Likelihood that accepting employment will preclude other employment by the lawyer.

    c.   Fee customarily charged in the locality for similar legal services.

    d.   Amount involved and results obtained from the representation.

    e.   Time limitations imposed by the client or by the circumstances.

    f.   Nature and length of the professional relationship with the client.

    g.   Experience, reputation, and ability of the lawyer or lawyers performing the services.

    h.   Whether the fee is fixed or contingent.

2.   Contingent Fees.

    a.   A contingent fee arrangement provides that you will receive a fee if you are successful in obtaining recovery for your client.

        1.   If "applicable law" requires, you must offer your client an alternative to a contingent fee arrangement.

        2.   All contingent fee arrangements must be in writing and signed by your client, specifying the percentage of the recovery you will earn, whether the percentage to be charged depends on how far the case proceeds, whether expenses are to be deducted before or after the fee is calculated, and which expenses she must pay if she gets no recovery.

        3.   When the representation is concluded, you must also provide a detailed statement to your client.

    b.   Contingent fees raise potential conflicts of interest between you and your client. You might believe that settling her case is inappropriate before trial, but you cannot require her to give up her right to settle.

      c. You cannot ethically use a contingent fee in a criminal case or a domestic relations matter.

3. Fee Sharing and Other Fee Issues

      a. Lawyers in different firms may divide fees only under specified conditions.

            1. The division must either be divided in proportion to the services performed by each lawyer or have each of them assume joint responsibility for the case.

            2. The client agrees in writing to the division, including the share for each lawyer.

      b. Lawyers who charge their clients by the hour are prohibited from charging clients for using wasteful tasks, charging them for more hours than they actually worked, or billing several clients for the same hour.

      c. The reasonableness of a fee agreement is considered as of the time that it was made, rather than with the benefit of hindsight.

      d. The Rules express the preference that fee agreements should be reduced to writing, but only a contingent fee agreement *must* be written.

      e. Disputes about fee agreements are construed from the perspective of the reasonable person in the circumstances of the client.

ILLUSTRATIVE PROBLEM

Pam Prosecutor was attempting to negotiate a plea bargain with Damien Defendant, who was charged with burglary. Prosecutor offered Defendant's defense lawyer Mason the following deal: Defendant could plead to a reduced charge and serve sixty days. Mason thought about the offer for five seconds and said, "No deal. We're going to trial." Defendant indeed did have a trial and was sentenced to the maximum statutory penalty of ten years. Three months later, a conscience-stricken Prosecutor wrote Defendant in prison, informing him that Mason had "sold him down the river." Defendant immediately filed a petition for post-conviction relief, claiming that Mason had been ineffective as his counsel. At the hearing on whether to grant post-conviction relief, Mason will testify for the state to uphold the conviction and Prosecutor will be a witness for Defendant to support Defendant's allegations. An assistant district attorney from Prosecutor's office will represent the state at the hearing. Did Mason act improperly?

Analysis

Mason probably had an obligation under Rules 1.4 and 1.2 to communicate with his client about important matters such as plea bargaining in criminal cases. Rule 1.4(a)(1) prescribes that "a lawyer who receives from opposing counsel . . . a proffered plea bargain in a criminal case must promptly inform the client of its substance unless the client has previously indicated that the proposal will be acceptable or unacceptable or has authorized the lawyer to accept or to reject the offer." Unless Mason and Defendant had a prior understanding about what period of time Defendant was willing to accept as part of a plea bargain, Mason had a duty under Rule 1.2(a) to communicate with Defendant about whether to accept the plea offer and change his plea from not guilty to guilty. "In a criminal case, the lawyer shall abide by the client's decision, after consultation with the lawyer, as to a plea to be entered. . . . " Rule 1.2(a).

POINTS TO REMEMBER

- Methods by which a lawyer-client relationship is formed:
  - A client intentionally wants you to provide legal services to her and you agree.
  - She intends for you to provide her with legal services, but you fail to be clear that you do not agree to represent her, and you know or should know that she is reasonably relying on you to provide those services.

- A judge appoints you to represent a client. Rule 6.2 may or must require you to decline the court's appointment.

- If a client lacks the capacity to make considered decisions, "as far as reasonably possible," maintain a "normal client-lawyer relationship," explaining things to her in words that she can understand and that allow her to make decisions. Rules 1.4(b); 1.14(a).

- If your client has a diminished capacity, you may take action when she "is at risk of substantial physical, financial, or other harm unless action is taken." Rule 1.14(b).

- If you seek assistance in reaching a conclusion about your client's capacity, you are implicitly authorized to reveal information about your client, but only to the extent necessary to protect her interests.

- When she suffers from a diminished capacity, you may override her decision-making authority because of your concern that her chosen course will cause substantial injury.

- As the agent for your client, you must follow her "decisions concerning the objectives of representation," but you also can act on your client's behalf in a manner which is "impliedly authorized to carry out the representation."

- When you and your client disagree, the MRPC encourage clients to defer to your expertise, especially on "technical, legal, and tactical matters."

- You may limit the scope of your representation if the limitation is reasonable and your client gives you her informed consent.

- Rule 1.4 specifies several contexts in which you should provide information to your client.

    - When the MRPC prescribe that you obtain your client's informed consent, you must promptly consult with her and obtain her consent.

    - You must "reasonably consult with the client about the means by which the client's objectives are to be accomplished."

- Keep her reasonably informed about the status of the matter.

- "Promptly comply with reasonable requests for information."

- You must "consult with the client about any relevant limitation on the lawyer's conduct when the lawyer knows that the client expects assistance not permitted by the Rules of Professional Conduct or other law."

- You must explain to your client the possible consequences of any proposed action you intend to take.

- You may not negotiate for, "charge, or collect an unreasonable fee or an unreasonable amount for expenses." Examples of relevant concerns are the:

  - Time and labor required, novelty and difficulty of the questions involved, and skill requisite to perform the legal service properly.

  - Likelihood that accepting employment will preclude other employment by the lawyer.

  - Fee customarily charged in the locality for similar legal services.

  - Amount involved and results obtained.

  - Time limitations imposed by the client or by the circumstances.

  - Nature and length of the professional relationship with the client.

  - Experience, reputation, and ability of the lawyer or lawyers performing the services.

  - Whether the fee is fixed or contingent.

- All contingent fee arrangements must be in writing and signed by your client.

- You cannot ethically use a contingent fee in a criminal case or a domestic relations matter.

- Lawyers in different firms may divide fees only under specified conditions.

- The MRPC express the preference that fee agreements should be reduced to writing, but only a contingent fee agreement *must* be written.

- If your client intentionally fails to pay your fee, you may withdraw from representing her, but only after you take reasonable steps to protect her interests.

*

CHAPTER 3

Client Confidentiality

The duty of confidentiality is probably *the* most important duty of a lawyer. It enables the lawyer to protect his client, and it lasts beyond the termination of the lawyer-client-relationship. Confidentiality is controversial because it enables lawyers to protect their clients in situations where many believe they deserve no such protection. The duty of confidentiality has two facets—the ethical duty of confidentiality and the evidentiary principle known as the lawyer-client privilege. Historically, there is a substantial difference between the scope of the lawyer's duty of confidentiality and the evidentiary lawyer-client privilege.

A. LAWYER–CLIENT PRIVILEGE

1.   Lawyer–Client Privilege

The lawyer-client privilege arose at common law and has been defined and refined through evidentiary rules and judicial precedent. Under the lawyer-client privilege, case law determines if the information sought is privileged, but a lawyer may reveal privileged materials or communications if compelled by legal process. The rationale for the lawyer-client privilege "is to encourage full and frank communication between attorneys and their clients and thereby promote broader public interests in the observance of law and administration of justice." *Upjohn Company v. United States*, 449 U.S. 383, 389 (1981).

Before a lawyer or a client can raise the lawyer-client privilege, there must be a lawyer-client relationship. The person seeking to invoke the privilege has the burden of proof on the relationship issue. In order to establish the relationship, the lawyer need not have entered an appearance in the court record on the client's behalf. The lawyer-client privilege contains several elements. It protects communications made in confidence to a lawyer by a client for the purpose of seeking or obtaining legal advice.

Communications. In order for the lawyer-client privilege to be invoked, the client must communicate with the lawyer. The client's communication may be oral, written, electronic, or any other method of transmitting information. Excluded from the privilege are physical characteristics of the client, such as her complexion, demeanor, and her dress, which are observable by anyone who talked with the client. The privilege applies not only to communications from the client to her lawyer, but also to communications from the lawyer to her client.

It is the communication of facts themselves that are privileged. The facts that are communicated are not privileged. Thus, a client cannot insulate herself from disclosing facts simply by disclosing them to her lawyer. If someone asks your client during a deposition a question about factual information she already told you, she cannot claim the lawyer-client privilege unless the question asked is, "What did you tell your lawyer . . . ?"

Made in confidence. Whether a communication is confidential depends on the client's intent in disclosing the information to her lawyer. For the lawyer-client privilege to apply, the client must intend for the information to be treated as confidential. If a client writes or speaks to her lawyer, while seeking legal advice, and gives her permission for the lawyer to disclose that information to a third party, the client's communication is not made in confidence. If the client makes statements to unknown persons in her lawyer's reception area, the privilege does not apply even if the persons work for the lawyer.

If the lawyer suggests that the defendant contact an expert to assist in the preparation of his case, the client's communications with the expert are not privileged. For the privilege to apply, the expert must be under the control of the lawyer as a consultant. Only then can the client's communications with the expert be deemed a confidential communication to the lawyer.

If a third party happens to overhear a communication made in confidence, most courts look at the totality of the circumstances to determine whether the eavesdropping was foreseeable. When the client transmits information to the lawyer via a third person or in the presence of a third person, courts find that the communication was not made in confidence. By contrast, when the third parties are employees or associates of the lawyer, the privilege remains because they are necessary adjuncts to the lawyer.

To a lawyer. A person's status as a lawyer does not necessarily supply the lawyer component of the lawyer-client privilege. The lawyer must be acting as a legal advisor with respect to the particular client. Thus, the lawyer-client privilege does not apply to situations in which the lawyer acts merely as a scrivener or as a conduit for the client. Written and oral communications to and from the lawyer's staff may be included within the lawyer-client privilege.

By a client. If a prospective client consults a lawyer, their preliminary communications are privileged even if the lawyer is not ultimately retained. When a lawyer is appointed to represent an indigent defendant, the communications between them are privileged even though the defendant pays no fee. A client enjoys the same evidentiary privilege even if she has not paid her lawyer's fees. The payment of legal fees by a third person by itself does not create a lawyer-client relationship between the lawyer and the client's benefactor sufficient to sustain a claim of privilege. The client may use an agent to facilitate the client's communications with her lawyer. For example, an incompetent client or a client who does not speak English needs an agent to communicate on her behalf.

For the purpose of seeking or obtaining legal advice. A communication must be made primarily for obtaining the lawyer's legal advice or services. A client is not using a lawyer for securing legal advice when the lawyer is acting merely as a scrivener or as a courier to pay bail and legal fees, because these activities could be performed by persons with other occupations.

2.   Specific Examples of Lawyer–Client Privilege

Lawyer-client privilege for government lawyers. If you are a lawyer for an entity such as the government, an unincorporated association, a union, a partnership, or a corporation, you owe it the same duty of confidentiality that you owe a human client. Rule 1.6, Comments 6, 16. Confidentiality "aids government entities and employees in obtaining legal advice founded on a complete and accurate factual picture." Restatement, § 74, Comment b. You have a lawyer-client relationship with your governmental client, not with a specific government official. Case law supports the position that the government rather than an official controls the lawyer-client privilege.

Lawyer-client privilege for corporate lawyers. The lawyer-client privilege protects communications when your client is an organization such as a corporation. Organizations have rights to the protection of their confidential information. People throughout a corporation may have information which a corporation can use to comply with its legal obligations. The problem is defining which corporate agents' communications are confidential.

Several tests have been used to measure when the corporations's lawyer-client privilege applies. Under the popular control group test, the lawyer-client privilege only extended "who play a substantial role in deciding and directing the corporation's response to the legal advice given." *United States v. Upjohn Co.,* 600 F.2d 1223, 1226 (6th Cir. 1979), *rev'd,* 449 U.S. 383 (1981).

The Supreme Court in *Upjohn Co. v. United States,* 449 U.S. 383 (1981), rejected the control group test, but declined to formulate an alternative test for federal law. In *Upjohn,* the corporation learned from auditors that one or more of its corporate divisions had made illegal payments to foreign governments. The general counsel for the corporation prepared a confidential questionnaire for lower level employees to learn about the payments. The

Internal Revenue Service tried to compel production of the questionnaire answers from the internal investigation.

The Court had the clear opportunity to adopt another popular standard, the so-called "subject matter test," a broader formulation that applies "to communications with lower-echelon employee or agent as long as the communication relates to the subject matter of the representation." Restatement, § 73, Comment d. This test encourages employees who have engaged in wrongdoing to be forthright with their employers' lawyer.

The Court in *Upjohn* did not accept the "subject matter" test *per se* but listed several significant factors which may be relevant in applying the privilege to a corporate communication between a corporate agent and the entity's lawyer. A court must consider whether (1) the communications were made by employees at the direction of corporate superiors, so that the corporation could receive legal advice from counsel, (2) the communications concerned matters within the scope or the employee's duties which information was not available from upper-level directors, (3) the employees were told the purpose of the communications, and (4) the communications were considered confidential when made and were not disseminated outside the corporation. At this point, there is no uniform dispositive test. The states have split in adopting the *Upjohn* standard.

When the client is an organization, the person in charge at that time controls the waiver of confidential information. Neither the privilege nor the duty of confidentiality prevents new managers from learning what the former managers told corporate counsel.

B. WORK PRODUCT DOCTRINE

1. Work Product Defined

Like the lawyer-client privilege, the work product doctrine protects a lawyer from disclosing certain types of information. Work product consists of tangible material or its intangible equivalent in oral and unwritten form, other than underlying facts, prepared by or for a lawyer either for current litigation or in anticipation of future litigation. There are two types of work product materials. *Opinion* work product consists of opinions and mental impressions of a lawyer, such as what you remember from a conversation or from reading a document. Opinion work product is protected from disclosure.

Ordinary work product is the other type of work product, and protects disclosure of information such as a person's pretrial statement. While you may use discovery to find out who has given statements to the litigation adversary and who has possession of those statements, work product prevents you from obtaining the statement itself. However, you may be able to obtain the statement by showing that you have a "substantial need" for the document and that a substantial equivalent for the document cannot be obtained without "undue hardship" to your client.

Work product provides an independent ground upon which litigants may rely for protection of materials prepared by lawyers for trial. *Hickman v. Taylor*, 329 U.S. 495 (1947). "Not even the most liberal of discovery theories can justify unwarranted inquiries into the files and the mental impressions of an attorney." When your litigation opponent has information essential to the preparation of your case, that information could be discovered when witnesses are no longer available or can be contacted only with difficulty.

2. Comparing the Lawyer–Client Privilege With the Work Product Doctrine

The bases for work product differ from those underlying the lawyer-client privilege. What your client reveals to you may be covered by the privilege, but they may not constitute disclosures that are "prepared in anticipation of litigation." On the other hand, many facts developed during trial preparation do not come from your client and therefore are not privileged.

The lawyer-client privilege protects communications between clients and their lawyers, thus encouraging an open dialogue. The work product doctrine is broader and precludes lawyers from capitalizing on an adversary's work efforts. The work product doctrine is codified as to tangible items, such as letters, in FRCP

26(b)(3). It is well-settled that work product is aimed at protecting your legal theories and strategies that you develop in preparation for litigation.

Like the lawyer-client privilege generally, work product is protected even after the termination of the litigation for which it was prepared. *F.T.C. v. Grolier, Inc.*, 462 U.S. 19 (1983). Work product extends to subsequent litigation. The rationale is that FRCP 26, which governs discovery, does not explicitly confine the work product privilege to the litigation in which it is sought.

C. PROFESSIONAL OBLIGATION OF CONFIDENTIALITY—GENERAL RULE

1. The General Rule of Confidentiality

The ethical duty of confidentiality is based upon the MRPC. Under the ethical duty of confidentiality, you cannot talk about a client's case to anyone in the course of the representation, except as the client authorizes. The rationale for the ethical duty encourages your client to tell you all the information she knows about her case and also encourages you to learn additional information about her case from other sources. If you violate your duty of confidentiality, you may be subject to discipline, held liable for damages, disqualified from representing a client, or enjoined from further disclosures.

Your ethical duty to protect information about your client's case "applies not only to matters communicated in confidence by the client but also to all information relating to the representation, whatever its source." Rule 1.6, Comment 3. You must maintain confidentiality whether you learn the information from the client, a third party, the media, or elsewhere.

You must safeguard your client's information from "inadvertent or unauthorized disclosure." Rule 1.6, Comment 15. Your need to safeguard client confidences requires training your support staff to understand and follow the ethical duty. Confidentiality exists as to *any* information that relates to the representation, regardless of whether it was acquired before or after the inception of the lawyer-client relationship.

Disclosure to others of information otherwise confidential under Rule 1.6 may occur if such disclosures

- are "implicitly authorized" to facilitate a satisfactory conclusion to a matter (e.g., a disclosure during plea bargaining may be intended to lead to a mutually satisfactory result),

- are made with the client's informed consent (through communications with your client about the risks of and alternatives to disclosure, followed by her agreement that you disclose, per Rule 1.0(e)), or

- are authorized under the Rule's six enumerated exceptions.

2. Prohibited Uses of Confidential Information

Using confidential information to client's disadvantage. Just as you cannot disclose information relating to your client's representation, you also cannot use your current client's confidential information to her disadvantage. Rule 1.8(b). As to a former client, you cannot use such information unless that information has become generally known. Rule 1.9(c)(1). The classic example involves the lawyer learning in confidence that his client is planning to renew the lease on the building where his business is located. The lawyer cannot use that confidential information to visit his client's lessor and obtain a lease in order to raise his client's rent on the building. Without disclosing confidential information, the lawyer has used it to his client's disadvantage and is subject to discipline.

Using confidential information to lawyer's advantage. You cannot use your client's confidential information for personal enrichment, even if your client is not harmed. Restatement, § 60(2). A classic example has the client telling the lawyer about her plan to purchase and develop several parcels of land, after which the lawyer uses that information either to purchase one of the parcels in competition with the client or to recommend to another client that he purchase the land. If you do engage in self-dealing, your (presumably former) client can force you to disgorge any profits you made under the law of agency.

Interception of lawyer-client communications by government. Courts have expressed concern about governmental intrusion into the lawyer-client relationship. For example, in *O'Brien v. United States*, 386 U.S. 345 (1967), the Supreme Court vacated criminal convictions and remanded the cases for a new trial after the government admitted intercepting lawyer-client communications. Indictments have been dismissed where the prosecution has deliberately used informants to obtain confidential information about defense strategy.

3. Comparing the Duty of Confidentiality With the Lawyer–Client Privilege

The ethical duty of confidentiality is broader than the evidentiary privilege. The lawyer-client privilege differs from the ethical duty of confidentiality on three key issues—scope, source of information, and disclosure.

- Scope: For the privilege to apply, the client must intend that the communication to be in confidence. The ethical duty applies to you whether or not your client has told others the same information that she had told to you.

- Source: Only information obtained from the client or his agent is privileged. Any information relating to the representation of your client is protected by the ethical duty.

- Disclosure: No privileged information can be disclosed, even involuntarily, unless your client consents or if the information is within your discretion to disclose. For the ethical duty, you cannot voluntarily disclose; only by court order, consent, or by a discretionary exception can you disclose information relating to the representation.

Waiving the evidentiary privilege does not waive the ethical duty of confidentiality. Suppose your client in the course of seeking professional advice from you discloses that she committed the crime with which she is charged. Later that same day she tells her bank teller, grocery clerk and furnace repairman of her criminal acts. As for the lawyer-client privilege, you cannot claim it and refuse to reveal your client's admission. The privilege belongs to the client, who has lost it by revealing the information about the representation to others. Even if you attempt to resist disclosure by asserting the privilege, the court can order you to disclose matters not falling within the evidentiary privilege.

Even if your client loses the evidentiary privilege, you still have an ethical obligation to maintain your client's confidential information. If you are called to testify about your client's admission, you must assert her ethical duty of confidentiality but the court may order you to disclose the information.

Duration of lawyer-client relationship. Your obligation to preserve your client's confidential information generally survives the end of your lawyer-client relationship with her. Rules 1.6, Comment 18; 1.9(c)(2). Your duty also survives the death of your client. When the Office of Independent Counsel sought notes of conversations between a White House aide and his lawyer shortly before the aide's death, the Supreme Court upheld that principle.

> Knowing that communications will remain confidential even after death encourages the client to communicate fully and frankly with counsel. While the fear of disclosure, and the consequent withholding of information from counsel, may be reduced if disclosure is limited to posthumous disclosure in a criminal context, it seems unreasonable to assume that it vanishes altogether. Clients may be concerned about reputation, civil liability, or possible harm to friends or family. Posthumous disclosure of such communications may be as feared as disclosure during the client's lifetime.

Swidler & Berlin v. United States, 524 U.S. 399, 410 (1998).

Lawyers sometimes have to testify about privileged conversations to explain the terms of a will or otherwise to carry out the wishes of a deceased client. "It would be desirable that a tribunal be empowered to withhold the privilege of a person then deceased as to a communication that bears on a litigated issue of pivotal significance. Permitting such disclosure would do little to inhibit clients from confiding in their lawyers." Restatement, § 77, Comment d.

4.   Waiving Confidentiality

Although the elements of the lawyer-client privilege exist, the privilege may be waived. Because the lawyer-client privilege and the ethical duty of confidentiality belong to your client (and not to you), she is the only one who can waive her right to the protection provided both by the privilege and by your duty of confidentiality towards her. She may waive explicitly or implicitly. An express waiver requires that her consent be informed, which means that you must give her sufficient information to permit her to understand the significance of the waiver. Rules 1.0(e), 1.6(a), 1.8(b).

Implicit waiver. She also may implicitly waive confidentiality in order for you "to carry out the representation." Rule 1.6(a). By her conduct, she may authorize you to disclose information otherwise covered by the privilege or the ethical duty of confidentiality in order to represent her effectively. For example, in order to settle a case for her, you may disclose information to conclude that negotiation, or you may admit a fact that "cannot properly be disputed." Rule 1.6, Comment 5. She also may effect a waiver by omission if she discloses privileged information to another lawyer before you object to her statements.

When the client discloses information to a third person after giving the same information to her lawyer in confidence, the privilege exists but her subsequent conduct waives the privilege. Subsequently, the lawyer can be required to disclose the information.

Selective waiver. Once waived, the privilege cannot be reasserted. A client cannot selectively choose to assert the privilege in some instances and waive it in others. A client cannot disclose some privileged communications supporting his case, and yet claim the privilege for other information.

Waiver by inaction. The privilege may also be waived without any action being taken by you or your client. If a third party witness testifies that he relied on an otherwise privileged document to reach his conclusion, the document is no longer privileged and the author of the document can be questioned about its contents.

Potentially harmful waivers of the privilege can be avoided by not allowing third parties to view privileged materials.

5. Treating Confidential Information With Reasonable Care

Inadvertent disclosure of confidential information. As noted, your client may inadvertently waive the protection of the lawyer-client privilege, if she reveals some or all of a privileged communication to someone other than you, her lawyer. She must treat confidential papers with reasonable care, or a court will rule that she has relinquished the privilege. If your client tells her friends about the information she disclosed to you confidentially, she has lost the protection of the privilege.

Lawyer's use of email and wireless technology. As in other contexts, you must take reasonable care in using telephones, emails, and wireless technology. For example, you have an obligation to your client "to prevent [confidential] information from coming into the hands of unintended recipients." Rule 1.6, Comment 17.

New Federal Rule of Evidence 502 is aimed at guarding against the inadvertent disclosure of privileged information. It generally provides that inadvertent disclosures do not waive the privilege if the holder of the privilege took reasonable steps to prevent disclosure and also promptly took reasonable steps to rectify any inadvertent disclosure.

The use of unencrypted email for communicating with clients does not waive the lawyer-client privilege. The client may decide against some forms of communication due to unusual circumstances, which "might include the avoidance of email, just as they would warrant the avoidance of the telephone, fax, and mail." ABA Formal Opinion 99–413. But that Opinion concluded that a failure to use encryption does not violate your duty of confidentiality or waive the privilege, unless your client insists or unusual circumstances require heightened security.

Mistaken fax. Your duty to maintain confidentiality extends not only to intentional disclosures of information but also to inadvertent disclosure of confidential information, as when opposing counsel receives a misdirected fax. The MRPC and the Restatement require only that you take "reasonable efforts" to protect your client's information. Rule 1.6, Comment 17; Restatement, § 60(1)(b); § 79, Comment h.

"A lawyer who receives a document from opposing parties or their lawyers and knows or reasonably should know that the document was inadvertently sent should promptly notify the sender in order to permit the sender to take protective measures," such as obtaining a protective order so that his client has not lost the protection of the lawyer-client privilege. ABA Formal Opinion 05–437. It goes on to state that "Rule 4.4(b) . . . does not require the receiving lawyer either to refrain from examining the materials or to abide by the instructions of the sending lawyer." If a court decides that the fax did not waive the privilege, the recipient cannot take advantage of the sender's mistake. But if the court concludes that the fax's disclosure effectively waived the privilege, the recipient can take advantage of the sender's mistake without concern that the recipient is violating the MRPC.

In the case of an inadvertent fax, ABA Formal Opinion 06–440 recognizes that Rule 4.4(b) requires only that the receiving lawyer notify the sender if she knows or reasonably should know that the fax was sent inadvertently. Comment 3 to Rule 4.4(b) leaves it to the recipient's professional judgment to determine whether to return the document unread.

Duty to client about disclosed information. Suppose that you learn that someone in your firm has disclosed a client's confidential information to a third party, as in the case of a misdirected fax. You owe a duty to your client to inform her that confidential information has been disclosed. Your duty to communicate also includes an obligation to disclose to her information about your own negligence.

Rule 5.1(b)(2) requires you to take reasonable remedial measures to protect your client's interests. Those measures may include asserting your client's lawyer-client privilege and seeking a court's protection for the disclosed information. If another lawyer was involved in the disclosure, you may need to comply with Rule 8.3 and disclose the misconduct to the appropriate authority.

Metadata. Metadata is confidential information that is hidden in the coding of electronic files, and may include deleted text, information about when changes were made, and information about the person making the changes which could provide confidential information to the opposition. The MRPC do not prohibit lawyers from learning about and using metadata in documents received from other lawyers even if the sending lawyer is unaware of the existence of the metadata. ABA Formal Opinion 06–442.

D. DISCLOSURES EXPRESSLY OR IMPLIEDLY AUTHORIZED BY CLIENT

1. Disclosure Within Articulated Exceptions

In enumerated situations, the MRPC permit or require you to disclose confidential information. For the discretionary disclosure provisions, your decision to reveal confidential information is within your discretion without securing a waiver from your client. Rule 1.6, Comment 15. Most of the articulated exceptions for discretionary disclosure are limited by a rule of reasonable necessity. You must have a good reason to believe that disclosure of the confidential information is necessary, but you cannot disclose all the negative facts that you know about your client.

Discretionary disclosure to prevent death or substantial bodily harm. You "*may* reveal information relating to the representation of a client to the extent the lawyer reasonably believes necessary" to "prevent reasonably certain death or substantial bodily harm." Rule 1.6(b)(1) (emphasis added). The provision is discretionary, not mandatory. The language enables you to disclose client information to prevent a threatened suicide, even if suicide is not a crime under the applicable state law. The disclosure is intended to address *future* death or bodily harm. Recall that you cannot disclose client information that she *already* has killed or has caused serious harm to someone. That information is protected by your duty of confidentiality.

The reference to "certain" death or substantial bodily harm includes imminent, lingering, and delayed death or bodily harm. You may reveal that your client's environmental law violation will likely cause death to people. Rule 1.6. Comment 6. "Substantial" refers to life-threatening injuries or illnesses and the consequences of events such as imprisonment for a substantial period, and child sexual abuse. Restatement, § 66, at Comment b.

As noted, your duty of confidentiality to your client generally appears to survive the death of your client. Under Rule 1.6(b)(1), you may be able to disclose the confession of your dead client if you believe that disclosure is reasonably necessary to prevent a wrongfully accused person from reasonably certain death or substantial bodily harm. Despite the United States Supreme Court's disagreement with disclosure of a dead client's confidential statements, you may be permitted or required to make disclosures "against" your former client if other Rules permit. Rule 1.9.

Discretionary disclosure to secure legal advice. In order to obtain advice about your compliance with the MRPC, you *may* reveal information relating to the representation of your client. Rule 1.6(b)(4). Bar associations offer services to lawyers for the purpose of obtaining advice from other members of the bar about their ethical conduct. ABA Formal Opinion 98–411 cautions you to (1) consult in hypothetical terms, (2) to obtain permission from your client if the consultation might put her at risk, (3) not to consult a lawyer who might represent the adverse party, and (4) to obtain assurances of confidentiality for the information.

Discretionary disclosure to establish a claim or defense. You *may* disclose confidential information if you reasonably believe that disclosure is necessary to sue your client for an unpaid fee, or to defend a malpractice, disciplinary, or criminal charge. Rule 1.6(b)(5). The purpose of this exception is to prevent your client, who benefits from the fiduciary relationship, from taking advantage of the relationship to your detriment. Rule 1.6, Comment 11. As with all of the discretionary disclosure provisions, you may reveal client confidences only when it is "reasonably necessary." Threatening to disclose confidential information to your client's detriment in order to receive your fee is not a reasonably necessary disclosure. Rule 1.6, Comment 10.

You have the discretion to disclose confidential information to establish that your client owes you a fee, as well as the amount of the fee. If your client fails to pay you after you have rendered services for her, you may sue her for the fee she still owes and disclose confidential information if she defends the fee action by attacking your representation. Or, you may reveal confidential information to establish that she has the assets to pay you.

An adverse party can effectively strip your client of the protection of confidentiality by naming both you and your client as co-parties, to encourage you to disclose what you know about your client or what you advised her to do. After disclosure, you are dropped from the suit as a co-defendant. Judges supervise this trick to prevent an adverse party from seeking to manipulate your discretionary disclosure.

If your client were to sue you for legal malpractice, you may disclose confidential client information in order to defend yourself against her claim for compensatory damages. She has effectively waived confidentiality by putting the quality of your representation in issue.

Your discretion to disclose is subject to two qualifications. First, you do not have to wait for a formal proceeding to be brought against you challenging your conduct before you may reveal client information. Rule 1.6, Comment 10. Second, if it is practical, before disclosing you should give your client a chance to avoid the need for your disclosure. If that attempt fails, you should limit the scope of disclosure or dissemination. Rule 1.6, Comments 14 and 17.

Discretionary disclosure to comply with other law or court order. You *may* disclose confidential information in order "to comply with other law or a court order," such as revealing client perjury, per Rule 3.3(b). Rule 1.6(b)(6). When a disclosure is permitted or required under federal law, such as disclosing information to the SEC under the Sarbanes Oxley Act, federal law preempts the application of a contrary state ethics rule. Or, if a state law, such as a child abuse reporting requirement, requires that you disclose confidential client information, Rule 1.6(b)(6) overrides the general confidentiality requirement.

If a court orders you to disclose information that you believe is protected by the lawyer-client privilege, you may either reveal it or challenge the court's order. You do not have to be held in contempt before obeying the court's order to disclose. You may comply with the court's order and disclose, without first violating the order and risk being held in contempt.

The MRPC allow you to make a good faith effort to determine the validity of a court's application of the law, but you cannot "knowingly disobey an obligation under the rules of a tribunal except for an open refusal based on an assertion that no valid obligation exists." Rule 3.4(d). In other words, you can challenge the court's order or obey it, but you cannot ignore it. When ordered to disclose, you should be cautious to disclose only what the court has ordered you to reveal and avoid disclosing more information than required. Rule 1.6, Comment 14.

Discretionary disclosure of future and past crime or fraud. The MRPC permit you to disclose confidential information about past, present, or future client fraud or client crime that has caused or reasonably certain to cause financial harm to another person. You *may* reveal information reasonably necessary to prevent your client from carrying out a plan to commit a crime or fraud that is reasonably certain to cause substantial injury to another person's financial interests or property *and* which involved your client's use of your services. Rule 1.6(b)(2). This discretionary disclosure provision was adopted by the ABA in 2003, in response to the Enron scandals. Your right to disclose this category of confidential client communication is based on your client's breach of her duty to you not to use your services in this manner.

You also *may* reveal information to prevent, mitigate or rectify substantial injury to another person's financial interests or property that is reasonably certain to result or already *has resulted* from your client's commission of a crime or fraud *and* which involved your client's use of your services. Rule 1.6(b)(3). Under this provision, you can reveal client confidences *after* the criminal or fraudulent behavior but before its effects are complete. Your disclosure is intended to prevent further conduct, or mitigate or rectify the conduct which has already occurred. The discretionary disclosure "does not apply when a person who has committed a crime or fraud thereafter employs a lawyer for representation concerning that offense." Rule 1.6, Comment 8.

Without your client's past or current use of your services to commit a fraud or crime, you have no discretion to disclose under either Rule 1.6(b)(2) or (b)(3). If your client uses your services to further her "criminal or fraudulent conduct," you *must* withdraw. Rule 1.6, Comment 7; Rule 1.16(a)(1). That withdrawal may effectively constitute a disclosure of your client's communications.

Rule 1.2, Comment 10 and Rule 4.1, Comment 3 both authorize you to file a notice of withdrawal and to disaffirm any opinion, document, or affirmation. Although your notice to the other side does not describe the precise reasons for the withdrawal, it effectively warns others that your client is up to no good. This "noisy withdrawal" represents a middle ground between blowing the whistle on your client and doing nothing.

Discretionary disclosure to prevent a fraud on an entity. If an entity such as a corporation is your client, you may disclose client confidential information when corporate action or inaction would involve a clear violation of the law that is reasonably likely to result in substantial injury to the entity. As lawyer for the organization, you "may reveal information relating to the representation whether or not Rule 1.6 permits such disclosure, but only if and to the extent [you] reasonably believe[ ] necessary to prevent substantial injury to the organization." Rule 1.13(c).

Required disclosure to prevent client fraud on a tribunal. You must not permit your client to commit a fraud on a tribunal. Rule 3.3. When you discover that your client is committing or has committed a fraud on a tribunal, you *must* take action to correct it. First, you are supposed to attempt to persuade your client to correct the fraud. Second, if that attempt fails, you must disclose the fraud to the court regardless of whether Rule 1.6 permits you to disclose. Rule 3.3.

In addition, if you have offered material evidence and later learn that it was false when you submitted it, you "must take reasonable remedial measures." Rule 3.3(a)(3). Your duty applies "even if compliance requires disclosure of information otherwise protected" by Rule 1.6. Your duty continues "to the conclusion of the proceeding" even if "compliance requires disclosure of information otherwise protected under Rule 1.6." Rule 3.3(c). "Direct disclosure under Rule 3.3 to the opposing party or, if need be to the court, may prove to be the only reasonable remedial measure" before trial. ABA Formal Opinion 93–376. That Opinion made clear that a lie in response to a deposition question or to a discovery request is "perjury", which requires you to correct the record in spite of the dictates of Rule 1.6.

2. Disclosures Implicitly Authorized to Carry Out the Representation

Disclosure of confidential communications to others. One example of implied authorization of a lawyer to disclose confidential communications about a client's case occurs when lawyers in the same firm frequently discuss their clients' cases, even if the client hired only one of the lawyers. ABA Formal Opinion 08–453. Your client may choose to instruct you not to discuss all or some of that information, even with your professional colleagues.

If you want to discuss your client's confidential information with a lawyer in *another* firm, perhaps due to the other lawyer's expertise, it is preferable to obtain your client's express consent. The MRPC do suggest that you may share confidential information with that other lawyer to obtain his advice about your compliance with an ethical standard. Rule 1.6, Comment 9. In either event, you must take care to avoid compromising your duty of confidentiality to your client, because there is no lawyer-client relationship between your client and the consulted lawyer. ABA Formal Opinion 98–411.

Co-parties. Lawyers for co-parties have recognized the benefits in pooling their information to the extent that it does not compromise their clients' positions. The pooling may involve exchange of witnesses' statements, joint efforts in interviewing witnesses and hiring experts, and coordination of positions to be asserted in conferences with prosecutors. Whether these communications are protected depends on the existence of the joint defense privilege, an extension of the lawyer-client privilege.

In order to safeguard the joint defense privilege, it is prudent to have a written agreement. At a minimum the agreement should state that: (1) the information transmitted contains confidential lawyer-client communications that are privileged, (2) the information is being transmitted only to counsel for other subjects of the pending investigation, (3) the exchange is made to facilitate presentation of common defenses, (4) the documents must not be furnished to any other person by way of production of copies or disclosure of their contents, and (5) each of the parties agrees to voluntarily waive any civil actions that she (or it) may currently or in the future be able to prosecute against any or all of the signatories to the agreement. *Continental Oil Co. v. United States*, 330 F. 2d 347 (9th Cir. 1964).

When separately represented clients decide to cooperate because their interests are identical or similar, you as one of the lawyers owe a duty to the other co-parties. As the agent of your client, you have a duty to maintain the confidentiality of information that your client must keep confidential as the result of the co-parties' cooperation. Restatement, § 132, Comment g(ii) at 85. That information relates to the representation and also is protected by Rule 1.6.

Multiple clients in the same matter. When you represent more than one client in the same matter, you must tell them about the joint client exception to the lawyer-client privilege. Under the exception, the privilege does not apply between joint clients. Rule 1.7, Comment 30. In litigation, a risk exists that someone who sues your joint clients may include in settlement negotiations a request that one of your joint clients waive the privilege.

You should "advise each client that information will be shared and that the lawyer will have to withdraw if one client decides that some matter material to the representation shall be kept from the other." Rule 1.7, Comment 31. You must inform your joint clients about any confidentiality issues that may arise in the representation so that they can decide if they want one lawyer to represent them in the same matter. In effect, tell them that, if any of them has anything to hide or keep confidential from the others, she should obtain separate counsel. Without an agreement about shared confidential information, if one client asks you not to share her confidential information with the co-parties, issues of competence, communication, and conflicts of interest may arise and require you to withdraw from representing *any* of the co-parties. Rule 1.16.

CONFIDENTIALITY CHECKLIST

A. **Lawyer–Client Privilege**. Before a lawyer or client can raise the lawyer-client privilege, he must establish the existence of a lawyer-client relationship. Its elements are:

    1. **Communication**. The client must communicate with the lawyer, orally, in writing, electronically, or using any other method of transmitting information.

        a. Excluded from the privilege are physical characteristics of the client, such as her complexion, which is observable by anyone who talked with the client.

        b. The privilege applies to communications from the client to her lawyer, and to communications from the lawyer to his client.

        c. It is the communication of facts themselves that are privileged. The facts that are communicated are not privileged. Thus, a client cannot insulate herself from disclosing facts simply by disclosing them to her lawyer.

    2. **Made in confidence**. The client must intend for the information to be treated as confidential.

        a. If a client gives her permission for the lawyer to disclose that information to a third party, the client's communication is not made in confidence.

        b. For the privilege to apply, an expert must be under the control of the lawyer (not the client) as a consultant.

        c. If a third party overhears a communication made in confidence, the totality of the circumstances determine whether the eavesdropping was foreseeable.

      d.   When the client transmits information to the lawyer in the presence of a third person, the communication was not made in confidence.

3. **To a lawyer**. The lawyer must be acting as a legal advisor with respect to the particular client.

      a.   The privilege does not apply when a lawyer acts as a scrivener or as a conduit for the client.

      b.   Written and oral communications with the lawyer's staff may be privileged.

4. **By a client**.

      a.   If a prospective client consults a lawyer, their preliminary communications are privileged even if the lawyer is not ultimately retained.

      b.   When a lawyer is appointed to represent an indigent defendant, the communications between them are privileged even though the defendant pays no fee.

5. **For the purpose of seeking or obtaining legal advice**. Communications while using a lawyer as a scrivener are not covered by the privilege, because these activities could be performed by persons with other occupations.

6. **Specific Examples of Lawyer–Client Privilege**.

      a.   Lawyers for an entity like the government, an unincorporated association, a union, a partnership, or a corporation owe the same duty of confidentiality as they would owe to a human client.

      b.   In *Upjohn Co. v. United States*, 449 U.S. 383 (1981), the Court listed relevant factors in applying the privilege to a communication between a corporate agent and the entity's lawyer, whether:

            1.   The communications were made by employees at the direction of corporate superiors, so that the corporation could receive legal advice from counsel,

2. The communications concerned matters within the scope or the employee's duties which information was not available from upper-level directors,

3. The employees were told the purpose of the communications, and

4. The communications were considered confidential when made and were not disseminated outside the corporation.

B. Work Product Doctrine

1. Work product consists of tangible material or its intangible equivalent in oral or unwritten form, other than underlying facts, prepared by a lawyer either for current litigation or in anticipation of future litigation.

   a. Opinion work product is the opinion and mental impression of a lawyer.

   b. Other work product is known as ordinary work product. Subject to exceptions, ordinary work product is not discoverable.

2. Work product provides an independent ground upon which litigants rely for protection of materials prepared by lawyers for trial. *Hickman v. Taylor*, 329 U.S. 495 (1947).

3. The bases for work product differ from those underlying the lawyer-client privilege.

   a. What your client reveals to you may be covered by the privilege, but they may not be disclosures that are "prepared in anticipation of litigation."

   b. Many facts developed during trial preparation are work product although they do not come from your client and therefore are not privileged.

C. **Professional Obligation of Confidentiality—General Rule**

1. The ethical duty of confidentiality is based upon the MRPC. Generally you are not to talk about a client's case to anyone in the course of the representation, except as the client permits.

    a. The confidentiality principle applies regardless of whether the information came from the client or from another source.

    b. Even if the information is widely known, you cannot disclose it.

    c. The duty encourages your client to tell you all the information she knows about her case and it also encourages you to learn additional information about her case from other sources.

    d. Disclosure of information otherwise confidential under Rule 1.6 may occur if such disclosures are implicitly authorized, with the client's informed consent, or are authorized under Rule 1.6's enumerated exceptions.

2. Prohibited Uses of Confidential Information.

    a. You cannot use your current client's confidential information to her disadvantage.

    b. You cannot use your client's confidential information for personal enrichment, even if your client is not harmed. Restatement, § 60(2).

3. Comparing the Duty of Confidentiality with the Lawyer–Client Privilege

    a. The ethical duty of confidentiality is broader than the lawyer-client privilege. The privilege differs from the duty of confidentiality on three key issues—scope, source of information, and disclosure.

        1. Scope: For the privilege to apply, the client must intend that the communication to be in confidence. The ethical duty applies to you whether

or not your client has told others the same information that she had told to you.

2. Source: Only information obtained from the client or her agent is privileged. By contrast, any information relating to the representation of your client is protected by the ethical duty.

3. Disclosure: No privileged information can be disclosed, even involuntarily, unless your client consents or if the information is within your discretion to disclose. For the ethical duty, you cannot *voluntarily* disclose. Only by court order, consent, or by a discretionary exception can you disclose information about the representation.

b. Waiving the evidentiary privilege does not waive the ethical duty of confidentiality.

1. Even if your client loses the evidentiary privilege, you still have an ethical obligation to maintain your client's confidential information.

2. If you are called to testify about your client's admission, you must assert her ethical duty of confidentiality but the court may order you to disclose the information.

3. The privilege belongs to the client, who loses it by revealing information about the representation to others. A court can order you to disclose matter not falling within the evidentiary privilege.

        c.   Duration of Lawyer–Client Relationship

            1.   Your obligation to preserve your client's confidential information generally survives the end of your lawyer-client relationship with her and continues after her death.

            2.   Lawyers sometimes have to testify about privileged conversations to explain the terms of a will or otherwise to carry out the wishes of a deceased client.

4.   Waiving Confidentiality

        a.   Although the elements of the lawyer-client privilege exist, the privilege may be waived.

        b.   Your client may waive explicitly or implicitly.

            1.   An express waiver requires that her consent be informed. You give your client sufficient information to permit understanding of the significance of the waiver.

            2.   She may implicitly waive confidentiality in order for you "to carry out the representation," e.g., disclosing information to settle a case for her.

        c.   A client cannot selectively choose to assert the privilege in some instances and waive it in others.

        d.   If a third party witness testifies that he relied on an otherwise privileged document to reach his conclusion, the document is no longer privileged and the author of the document can be questioned about its contents.

5.   Treating Confidential Information with Reasonable Care

        a.   Your client may inadvertently lose protection of the lawyer-client privilege, if she reveals a privileged communication to someone other than her lawyer.

b. You must take reasonable care in using telephones, emails, and wireless technology "to prevent [confidential] information from coming into the hands of unintended recipients."

c. A lawyer-recipient must promptly notify the sender of a misdirected fax so that he can "take protective measures," such as obtaining a protective order so that his client has not lost the protection of the lawyer-client privilege.

e. Duty to client about disclosed information

1. If you learn about a misdirected fax, you must inform your client that confidential information has been disclosed.

2. If another lawyer was involved in the disclosure, you may need to comply with Rule 8.3 and disclose the misconduct to the appropriate authority.

D. Disclosures Expressly Authorized by Client

1. In enumerated situations, the MRPC permit or require you to disclose confidential information. For the discretionary disclosure provisions, your decision to reveal confidential information is within your discretion without securing a waiver from your client.

2. Most of the articulated exceptions for discretionary disclosure are limited by a rule of reasonable necessity.

3. You "may reveal information relating to the representation of a client to the extent the lawyer reasonably believes necessary" to "prevent reasonably certain death or substantial bodily harm."

a. The disclosure is intended to address *future* death or bodily harm.

b. "Substantial" refers to life-threatening injuries or illnesses and the consequences of events such as imprisonment for a substantial period, and child sexual abuse.

4. In order to obtain legal advice about your compliance with the MRPC, you may reveal information relating to the representation of your client.

5. You may disclose confidential information if you reasonably believe that disclosure is necessary to sue your client for an unpaid fee, or to defend a malpractice, disciplinary, or criminal charge.

6. You may disclose confidential information in order "to comply with other law or a court order" such as revealing client perjury.

   a. When a disclosure is permitted or required under federal law, such as disclosing information under the Sarbanes Oxley Act, federal law preempts the application of a contrary state ethical rule.

   b. A state law, such as a child abuse reporting requirement, may require that you disclose confidential client information.

   c. If a court orders disclosure of confidential information, inform your client to get her informed consent or obtain her permission in order to challenge the court's order. You are not required to be held in contempt before obeying the court's order to disclose.

   d. You can challenge the court's order or obey it, but you cannot ignore it. When ordered to disclose, disclose only what the court has ordered you to reveal.

7. The MRPC permit you to disclose confidential information about past, present, or future client fraud or client crime that has caused or is reasonably certain to cause financial harm to another person.

   a. Your right to disclose this category of confidential client communication is based on your client's breach of her duty not to use your services in this manner.

b. You can reveal client confidences *after* the criminal or fraudulent behavior but before its effects are complete. Your disclosure is intended to prevent further conduct, or mitigate or rectify the conduct which has already occurred.

c. Without your client's past or current use of your services to commit a fraud or crime, you have no discretion to disclose under either Rule 1.6(b)(2) or (b)(3).

d. If your client uses your services to further her "criminal or fraudulent conduct," you must withdraw which may effectively constitute a disclosure of your client's communications.

8. If an entity such as a corporation is your client, you may disclose confidential information when corporate action or inaction would involve a clear violation of the law that is reasonably likely to result in substantial injury to the entity.

9. When you discover that your client is committing or has committed a fraud on a tribunal, you *must* take action to correct it.

a. Try to persuade your client to correct the fraud.

b. If that attempt fails, you must disclose the fraud to the court.

c. If you have offered material evidence and later learn that it was false when you submitted it, you "must take reasonable remedial measures."

1. Your duty apples even if "compliance requires disclosure of information otherwise protected under Rule 1.6."

2. Disclosure to the opposing party or to the court may be the only reasonable remedial measure before trial.

E. **Disclosures Implicitly Authorized to Carry Out the Representation**

     1. Disclosure of Confidential Communications to Others.

         a. Lawyers in the same firm frequently discuss their clients' cases, even if the client hired only one of the lawyers.

         b. If you want to discuss your client's confidential information with a lawyer in another firm, it is preferable to obtain your client's express consent.

     2. Lawyers for co-parties have recognized the benefits in pooling their information. To safeguard the joint defense privilege, a written agreement should describe the nature of the information exchanged and the purpose for the pooling.

     3. When you represent more than one client in the same matter, advise each client that information will be shared and that you will have to withdraw if one client decides to keep some matter from the other client.

ILLUSTRATIVE PROBLEMS

■ PROBLEM 3.1 CONFIDENTIAL INFORMATION ABOUT PAST CONDUCT ■

Continental Towing Company is the nation's largest operator of towboats. It also has a small manufacturing plant. A large Spanish corporation has been trying to acquire Continental. Very few people at Continental know about the acquisition possibility and the corporate CEO has instructed those few (including Maris, the General Counsel) not to tell anyone about it. The takeover almost certainly would result in the Spanish company selling off most of Continental's operations business with nothing remaining of the current Continental business but the small manufacturing entity.

Jordan is the Associate General Counsel for Continental and seeks your advice. Two years ago, she learned from a recently-fired executive (who was her mentor) that Maris had secretly tried to take over Continental without the corporate CEO's knowledge. Last week, Continental's outside counsel told her that Maris and he were promoting the takeover by the Spanish corporation so that they could begin their own towing operation. Did Maris violate his ethical duty of confidentiality to the organization?

Analysis

When a client discloses information to a lawyer, generally that information cannot be disclosed by the lawyer without the client's consent. Model Rule of Professional Conduct 1.6(a). Rule 1.6(a) requires a lawyer to maintain inviolate information relating to the representation of a client. Here, the CEO did not give permission to Maris to disclose information about the acquisition possibility. He clearly told the Maris *not* to disclose the information to anyone. Thus, Maris violated the duty of confidentiality owed by an attorney to the client.

■ PROBLEM 3.2 PERMISSIVE DISCLOSURE OF CONFIDENTIAL INFORMATION ■

Arthur Kirkland practices law in Hartford, primarily representing plaintiffs in civil litigation. Recent events have made him concerned about the ethics of his behavior. After successfully obtaining a hefty settlement for Sam Jones in a personal injury case, Arthur was troubled by the fact that, in preparing for trial, Jones had told him that he is a cocaine trafficker and plans to continue engaging in that work. Arthur contacted the local police to about Sam's admissions to him. Did Arthur violate the rules on confidentiality by reporting his client's admissions?

Analysis

Rule 1.6 generally prohibits an attorney from revealing "information relating to representation of a client" without the client's consent. Arthur would have a duty not to disclose Jones's past criminal activities, but Rule 1.6(b)(1) does permit disclosure of information relating to a client's future criminal conduct to the extent the lawyer reasonably believes necessary to "prevent reasonably certain death or substantial bodily harm." The provision is discretionary, not mandatory. The disclosure is intended to address *future* death or bodily harm. Arthur would have to assess whether Jones intends to continue committing the crime and whether the crime of cocaine trafficking would cause reasonably certain death or substantially bodily harm. For example, if Arthur knows that people die or become seriously ill from ingesting cocaine, reporting Jones's activities can prevent others from experiencing death or substantial bodily harm.

POINTS TO REMEMBER

- The lawyer-client privilege is a rule of evidence that applies to communications made in confidence to a lawyer by a client for the purpose of seeking or obtaining legal advice.

- The lawyer-client privilege protects communications between clients and their lawyers to encouraging open dialogue, while the work product doctrine is broader and precludes lawyers from capitalizing on an adversary's work efforts.

- The ethical duty of confidentiality applies to any information you learn about your client's case, from your client and from anyone else.

- You cannot use confidential information to your client's disadvantage or to your advantage.

- Government and corporate lawyers owe a duty of confidentiality to the entity, which is the client, rather than an individual.

- The obligation to preserve your client's confidential information generally survives the end of your lawyer-client relationship with her.

- Because the lawyer-client privilege and the ethical duty of confidentiality belong to your client, she is the only one who can waive her right to their protection.

- A client may waive explicitly or implicitly. An express waiver requires that you obtain her informed consent.

- As in other contexts, you must take reasonable care with your client's confidential information when using telephones, emails, and wireless technology.

- You have the discretion to "reveal information relating to the representation of a client to the extent the lawyer reasonably believes necessary" to

  - prevent reasonably certain death or substantial bodily harm.

  - secure legal advice.

  - establish a claim or defense.

  - comply with other law or a court order.

  - prevent your client from carrying out a crime or fraud reasonably certain to cause substantial injury to another person's financial interests or property and which involved your client's use of your services.

  - prevent, mitigate or rectify substantial injury to another person's financial interests or property that is reasonably certain to result or has resulted from his commission of a crime or fraud and which involved her use of your services.

  - prevent fraud on an entity.

- You *must* disclose confidential information to prevent client fraud on a tribunal.

- Implicitly authorized disclosure occurs when lawyers in the same firm discuss their cases, even if the client hired only one of the lawyers.

- When lawyers for co-parties pool their information, whether these communications are protected depends on the existence of the joint defense privilege, an extension of the lawyer-client privilege. When you represent more than one client in the same matter, you must tell each of them about the joint client exception to the lawyer-client privilege.

*

CHAPTER 4

Conflicts of Interest

The MRPC describe standards for identifying conflicts of interest that arise between your (1) current clients, (2) current and future clients, (3) current and former clients, (4) current client and interested third parties, and (5) current client and your own interest. The consequences of a conflict of interest may include: (1) professional discipline by a state's highest court, (2) disqualification from representing a particular client pursuant to a court's inherent power to regulate who practices before it, (3) breaching a duty of loyalty to a client, and (4) forfeiture of your fee.

A. CURRENT CLIENT CONFLICTS— MULTIPLE CLIENTS AND JOINT REPRE- SENTATION

1. Current Client Conflicts

When you look at a set of circumstances to determine whether you have a conflict of interest with a current client, you should consider several issues. First, do you have a conflict of interest under the MRPC? If not, you can continue your representation. If you have a conflict of interest you move to the inquiry about whether you can still represent your client with her "informed consent." If so, you can continue the representation. If not, you cannot represent her even if she is willing to consent.

Your duties to protect your client's confidential information and to be loyal to her are the primary rationales for the ethics rules for conflicts of interest. Suppose that you are representing Client A at trial and your current Client B appears as a witness for the adversary. If you cross-examine Client B by revealing the confidential information from Client B, you are violating your duty of confidentiality to Client B. If you do not use that information in your representation of Client A in order to protect the confidences of Client B, you are violating your duty of loyalty to Client A because you are not representing Client A properly.

Most lawyers have computerized data bases with information about their current and former clients. When a new client seeks representation, you should do a conflict of interest check to inquire about whether a conflict exists or may arise later.

"Directly adverse" conflict. One example of a concurrent client conflict exists under Rule 1.7(a)(1), which prohibits you from representing a client if that representation "will be directly adverse to another client." The nature of the conflict is between two current clients. The Rule is based on your obligation of loyalty to your current clients, who expect that you will not represent someone whose interests are "directly adverse" to theirs. The most egregious example would occur if you represent both the plaintiff and the defendant in the same lawsuit. Suing a current client even on an unrelated matter is a directly adverse conflict. A directly adverse conflict also arises in a non-litigation setting when you negotiate the sale of property for the buyer where the seller is also your client, regardless of who represents the seller in the negotiation.

"Materially limited" conflict. A second example of a concurrent client conflict occurs under Rule 1.7(a)(2), which prohibits representation if there is a significant risk that the representation will be "materially limited" by your responsibilities to another, whether that client is a current client, a former client, a third person, or even yourself. "Materially limited" conflicts focus on client harm, implicating significant risks that your ability to represent your client is limited by your other obligations. In other words, is there a "significant risk" that your representation of one client will affect your obligations to other clients or to yourself? A significant risk is less than one that actually exists but it is more than merely a possibility of subsequent harm. Rule 1.7, Comment 8.

This type of conflict may relate to current clients whom you represent in the same lawsuit or negotiation. In a class action where you represent the plaintiff class, you have a "materially limited" conflict if one of the potential defendants is also a current client. But for your representation of the potential defendant, your advice to the plaintiff class about whether to name that person as a defendant might differ. Or, if you represent several people who are forming a business, you cannot permit any responsibility to one of those clients to materially limit your responsibilities in representing the others.

All current conflicts are not subject to client consent. To resolve the "directly adverse" or "materially limited" conflict of interest, Rule 1.7(b) has four requirements. You must (1) independently decide whether you can competently and diligently represent all the affected clients, (2) decide whether some other law precludes you from accepting the representation, and (3) not represent one client against another client "in the same litigation." Finally, each of your affected clients must give you "informed consent, confirmed in writing." Rule 1.7(b)(1)–(4).

There are situations when a conflict cannot be saved by client consent. First, you cannot continue a conflicted representation unless you "reasonably believe" that you can provide competent, diligent representation to those clients whose circumstances present your conflict. Rule 1.7(b)(1). When you have the opportunity to represent multiple parties on the same side of a lawsuit or criminal case, you must carefully evaluate your abilities to render competence and diligence to each of your clients.

Second, if the contemplated representation is prohibited by law, your client's consent is irrelevant. Rule 1.7(b)(2). Some states, for example, prohibit individual lawyers from representing more than one capital defendant in the same criminal case. Third, under Rule 1.7(b)(3), in any case before a tribunal, you cannot represent two or more clients who are asserting claims against each other.

This provision obviously prevents you from representing both plaintiff and defendant in a civil case. It also prevents you from representing multiple defendants when one files a cross-claim against the other.

2. Consent to the Current Client Conflict

If none of the above circumstances precludes consent for your continued but conflicted representation, Rule 1.7(b)(4) provides that your client can give informed consent, confirmed in writing, for you to continue the representation. For a consent to be "informed," you must explain to your client the "material risks" and "reasonably available alternatives" of going forward with or without you as her counsel. Rule 1.0(e).

You make a full disclosure to your clients, in part by explaining to them the relevant circumstances that created the conflict. For concurrent representation, you would explain the risks and benefits of one lawyer representing all of the people as opposed to each of them having separate lawyers. Rule 1.7, Comment 19. It is insufficient for each of your clients simply to be aware of your other representation.

The content of the conversation leading to informed consent should highlight several topics. Tell each client that if she has information to protect from your other clients she needs to have her own lawyer. In the multiple representation context, all information is shared with all of your clients. Rule 1.7, Comment 31. If you cannot share information relating to the representation with each co-client, you must withdraw from one or more of the representations. ABA Formal Opinion 08–450.

In order for a consent to be informed, it is also possible that you would have to disclose to your client confidential information from another client. If your other client refuses to permit that disclosure, no consent can occur and your representation cannot go forward. You should listen for indications that concurrent representation is inappropriate. Any client needing special assistance needs separate counsel. If any of them is unequal in bargaining power, you should not represent all the clients.

Your client's consent must be confirmed in writing, which has a broad meaning. It confirms your client's oral consent by giving her "a tangible or electronic record of a communication or representation, including handwriting, typewriting, printing, photostating, photography, audio or videorecording and e-mail." The requirement of a written consent should impress the client about the seriousness of the situation. A conversation with each client to explain and respond to their questions confirms that each understands the importance of consenting after each has exercised her opportunities to seek information about the situation.

Outside the litigation context, you may be able to represent adverse parties such as the buyer and seller of the same parcel of real estate. To represent them both, you would need to follow the aforementioned Rule 1.7 steps for a valid informed consent in writing.

Clients have the authority to waive a conflict of interest in advance. Rule 1.7, Comment 22. A prospective waiver means the same as the phrase "informed consent" in the MRPC. Such a waiver is more likely to be effective if it relates to a future conflict that is unrelated to the subject matter of the current representation. ABA Formal Opinion 05–436 stated that a waiver of a future conflict may be valid even though it is very general. An effective disclosure depends on your ability to explain all important risks connected to the future conflict.

After obtaining an informed consent, the circumstances of the representation may change and affect the consent's validity. When the consent becomes invalid, your representation violates Rule 1.7. You then must withdraw from representing all of your clients who are involved in your representation of conflicting interests. Rule 1.16(a).

3. Current Conflicts in Unrelated Matters

Just as you cannot represent both sides of the same case, the general rule is that you cannot sue Client B on behalf of Client A, while you represent Client B on an unrelated matter. Even though the cases are unrelated and create no danger of using the confidential information from one case to assist the representation in the other case, you would breach your duty of loyalty to Client B by accepting Client A's case. Rule 1.7, Comment 6.

> We think it would be questionable conduct for an attorney to participate in any lawsuit against his own client without the knowledge and consent of all concerned. . . . [T]he mainte- nance of public confidence in the bar requires an attorney to decline employment adverse to his client, even though the nature of such employment is wholly unrelated to that of his existing representation.

Cinema 5, Ltd. v. Cinerama, Inc., 528 F.2d 1384, 1386–87 (2d Cir. 1976). The rule exists to prevent either an actual or apparent conflict in loyalties or a reduction in the zeal of the representation.

If you are representing two clients in unrelated cases and they compete daily for market share in their businesses, they are generally adverse but not "directly adverse." There is no conflict of interest under the MRPC. You are not suing either of them, you are not giving legal advice to one that could be used against the other, and you are not using confidential information from one to the disadvantage of the other. Rule 1.7, Comment 6.

If you represent two directly adverse clients in different lawsuits, you cannot avoid the conflicts issue by dropping one of the clients. If the parties do not consent to the conflict, you usually must withdraw from representing *both* parties in the two cases. The exception to the general rule occurs when the conflict arose through no fault of the lawyer, as when an unforeseen event such as a corporate merger of two or more companies was the source for the conflict of interest.

4. Other Examples of Current Client Conflicts

Questioning a current client as an adverse witness. In order for you to represent Client A at trial and cross-examine an adverse material witness (Client B) who is also your client, there must be consent from both clients even if Client B's case is unrelated. The cross-examination ordinarily would constitute a conflict under Rule 1.7(a)(1). If the conflict arises only after the representation of Client A begins, you may have to withdraw from representing both of your clients.

Multiple representation in criminal cases. A criminal convic- tion must be reversed if the trial judge required that the defendants be tried together, over the defendant's timely trial objection, because the joint representation was presumed to be prejudicial. *Holloway v. Arkansas*, 435 U.S. 475 (1978). In the absence of a trial objection, the defendant must prove that an actual conflict of interest adversely affected his lawyer's performance but he does not have to prove prejudice. *Cuyler v. Sullivan*, 446 U.S. 335 (1980).

Job negotiations between lawyer for one party and adversary. If you negotiate for a new job with an opposing party or that party's lawyer, there is a "materially limited" conflict. Rule 1.7, Comment 10. Both you as the job-seeking lawyer and the firm trying to hire you must take steps to protect your clients' interests.

Related or married lawyers representing adverse parties. The Rule 1.7 analysis applies to lawyers who are related or married to each other and who are on opposite sides of the same case. Inadvertent disclosure of confidential information is the primary concern, such as voice mail messages on the answering machine used by both lawyers. The related counsel must disclose the existence and the implications of the relationship between them before each lawyer agrees to the representation. Rule 1.7, Comment 11. Both clients should consent before you and your relative or spouse represent them. Because of the personal nature of the conflict, it is not imputed to others in your firm.

Lawyer's client is another lawyer. When a lawyer from another firm retains you, you may have a conflict of interest if the two of you concurrently represent clients who are adverse to each other in a separate case. You are "directly adverse" to your lawyer-client if you attack your client's credibility in the case where you both have clients. A risk also exists that you may temper your advocacy on behalf of your client in the other case so as not to alienate your lawyer-client whose representation you want to maintain. The importance of the case to your lawyer-client, the relative size of your fee for representing your lawyer-client, and the relative importance of the two cases are factors which may "materially" limit your relationship with your lawyer-client. ABA Formal Opinion 97–406. Informed consent by both clients may be impossible if you do not permit your lawyer-client to make a full disclosure to her client. Rule 1.7, Comment 14.

Lawyer as director of corporate client. If you represent a corporation, you may be asked to serve on the its board of directors. Your corporate client may not understand whether you are giving business advice in your role as director or legal advice as counsel for the corporation. If your obligations in the dual role are "materially adverse" to each other, you must withdraw from representation unless your corporate client consents. Rule 1.7, Comment 35; Restatement, § 125, Comment d.

Insured and insurer. Conflicts of interest may arise when the insured is sued for more than the policy limits and the insured wants to settle for an amount less than the policy limits. Another conflict arises when the insured and insurer disagree about whether the claim is covered under the policy. Most of the case law treats the insured as the client and the insurer as the third-party payer of the fee. Restatement, § 134, Comment f. See Section H of this Chapter on third party compensation.

Positional conflict. A positional conflict exists when you represent a client in one matter seeking a particular result, and at the same time you represent another client in a different case in which you are taking a contrary *legal* position. You may advocate antagonistic legal positions in different cases, as long as the positional conflict does not materially limit your representation of one of your clients. Rule 1.7(b). Relevant factors include "where the cases are pending, whether the issue is substantive or procedural, the temporal relationship between the matters, the significance of the issue to the immediate and long term interests of the clients involved, and the clients' reasonable expectations in retaining the lawyer." Rule 1.7, Comment 24.

B. CURRENT CLIENT CONFLICTS— LAWYER'S PERSONAL INTEREST OR DU- TIES

1. Sexual Relations With Your Client

You cannot have a sexual relationship with a client, unless that consensual relationship already existed prior to the beginning of the lawyer-client relationship. Rule 1.8(j); Restatement, § 16, Comment e. (Pre-relationship relations are governed by Rule 1.7.) Your fiduciary obligation requires that you not take unfair advantage of your client. Sexual relations with a client create an ethical problem for you because of your potential undue influence and her emotional vulnerability, both of which affect your independent personal judgment and rebut your client's meaningful consent. ABA Formal Opinion 92–364.

2. Accepting Gifts From Clients

Suppose you want your client to recognize and reward you for your outstanding legal work. Any gift transaction from her to you must meet general standards of fairness. Agency and fiduciary duty law treat client gifts to you as presumptively fraudulent. Rule 1.8, Comment 6; Restatement § 127(2). Ethically, the idea for a "substantial gift" needs to come from your client and not from you. You cannot ask a client to give you a substantial gift, even in her will. Rule 1.8(c).

If your client does make a substantial gift to you which requires the preparation of a legal instrument, you cannot draft it. Rule 1.8(c) prevents you from drafting a will for your client when the will gives you a disproportionate percentage of her assets. Because of Rule 1.8(k)'s imputed disqualification, a lawyer in another firm should draft the instrument. That lawyer's obligation to your client is to explain to her that she is not obligated to give you any gift. Even when another lawyer advises your client about making the gift, it "remains subject to invalidation if the circumstances warrant under the law of fraud, duress, undue influence, or mistake." Restatement, § 127, Comment g.

There are two stated exceptions to Rule1.8(c)'s operation. First, if you cannot accept a gift, no one related to you can accept unless you or the other gift recipient is related to the client. Rule 1.8(c). ("Related persons include a spouse, child, grandchild, parent, grandparent or other relative or individual with whom" you or your client "maintains a close, familial relationship." Rule 1.8(c).) Second, the Rule does not prohibit you from seeking an appointment as executor of your client's estate. Rule 1.8, Comment

8. Your law firm may represent you in the administration of the estate but the combined fee for acting as fiduciary and as lawyer must be reasonable under Rule 1.5(a). ABA Formal Opinion 02–426.

C.   FORMER CLIENT CONFLICTS

If you *used* to represent a client in a matter, you cannot represent a new client in the same or substantially related matter if your new client has interests that are "materially adverse" to your former client. Rule 1.9(a). The Rule recognizes loyalty and client confidences as the two interests of the client that must be protected.

1.   Definition of a "Matter"

You cannot in effect switch sides in the same or a substantially related matter. *T.C. Theatre Corp. v. Warner Bros. Pictures, Inc.*, 113 F.Supp. 265 (S.D.N.Y. 1953). A "matter" is not limited to lawsuits. For example, a lawyer cannot seek on behalf of Client A to rescind a contract he had drafted for Client B. A "specific transaction" is a matter. Rule 1.9, Comments 1 & 2. Whether matters are so related that they are regarded as the same or even substantially related is a question of degree and is defined in terms of the reason for Rule 1.9. "Substantially related" includes the "same transaction or legal dispute or if there otherwise is a substantial risk that confidential factual information as would normally have been obtained in the prior representation would materially advance the client's position in the subsequent matter." Rule 1.9, Comment 3.

2.   Examples of Successive Representation

Suppose you represent the seller in the sale of a business. Later you represent the buyer of that business and tell her to stop making payments to the seller who has not complied with the terms of the deal. Your advice to the buyer breached your continuing duty of loyalty to the prior client, the seller, even in the absence of any showing that the seller's confidential information was disclosed to the buyer.

Suppose you previously represented a material witness for the litigation opponent. You should disqualify yourself if confidential information you gained when you represented the prior client in the prior case would enable you to examine and impeach your prior client more effectively.

Suppose you switch law firms. Your old firm represented Client A in a lawsuit against a defendant, though you were not involved in representing Client A and received no confidential information about her case. If you leave your firm and join the firm that represents the defendant in that same lawsuit, you may still represent that defendant even though the Client A's and defendant's interests are materially adverse, because you have no actual knowledge of Client A's confidential information. Rule 1.9(b). In Section E of this Chapter, there is a discussion about whether your new firm would be disqualified if you are not.

If you had acquired confidential information about Client A with your old firm, you are personally disqualified from representing the defendant unless Client A waives the conflict. Rule 1.9(b). You cannot use confidential information about a prior client to her disadvantage, unless that information has become generally known and therefore does not require protection. Rule 1.9(c)(1). (The MRPC do not prohibit your use of confidential information unless it disadvantages the prior client. Rule 1.8, Comment 5.)

3. Waiver of Successive Conflict

Rules 1.9(a) and 1.9(b) permit the prior client to waive the successive conflict of interest. With a waiver, the otherwise disqualified lawyer may represent a new client against the prior client who gives informed consent in writing. As in other contexts, an informed consent requires you to explain to your prior client the relevant risks, as well as their significance. Rule 1.0(e).

Future waivers of a prior client conflict are unlikely to be valid, because they include permission to disclose future confidential information. Clients normally do not know at the time of a future waiver what their future confidences might be, much less their relevance or significance. A consent to her lawyer's future representation of another client with adverse interests "does not amount to consent to breach of confidential disclosure or the use of that information against the consenting party." *Westinghouse Electric Corp. v. Gulf Oil Corp.*, 588 F.2d 221 (7th Cir. 1978).

D. PROSPECTIVE CLIENT CONFLICTS

As a practical matter, you will conduct initial interviews with prospective clients. Your duties to a prospective client are analogous to your responsibilities to an actual client: (1) treating information from the prospective client as confidential, (2) taking care of property that she entrusts to you, (3) giving competent advice, (4) keeping a promise to check on something about her case by acting competently, and (5) checking for possible conflicts of interest between her case and your past or current clients, per Rule 1.7.

1. Identifying a Prospective Client

Rule 1.18 explicitly recognizes a duty to a prospective client, even though you may not talk to her for very long or in much depth about her case and even if you end up not representing her. A "prospective client" is a "person who discusses with a lawyer the possibility of forming a client-lawyer relationship with respect to a mater." Rule 1.18(a). Comment 2 limits this broad definition. Unilaterally giving information to the lawyer does not guarantee that there is a client-lawyer relationship. Instead, it is your willingness to discuss the possibility of forming a client-lawyer relationship that determines whether the client has a "reasonable expectation" of becoming a client.

What is "reasonable" is measured from the client's expectations. A person who contacts you as part of a deception to disqualify you from representing another party to the dispute has no "reasonable expectation" of becoming a client. ABA Formal Opinion 90–358 (1990). She has provided information to you for the sole purpose of creating a conflict of interest for you. Because she would not be a prospective client, you have no duty of confidentiality to her, and you could proceed to represent that other party because there would be no conflict of interest.

2. Duties to the Prospective Client

Confidentiality. You have a duty of confidentiality to the prospective client while deciding whether to represent her, no matter how brief was your initial conference. Rule 1.18(b). The confidential information obtained from her cannot be disclosed unless she agrees in writing that the content of the conversations are not to be treated as confidential. If you decline the representation, the Rules treat her as a former client regarding the confidential information she disclosed to you, and you cannot use that information to her disadvantage. Rule 1.9; Rule 1.18. The exception to that standard applies when the information becomes generally known or if a Rule like 1.6 or 3.3 requires disclosure. Rule 1.9.

Loyalty. If the prospective client never becomes a client, generally you cannot represent another client who has interests "materially adverse to those of a prospective client in the same or substantially related matter if the lawyer received information from the prospective client that could be significantly harmful to that person in the matter." Rule 1.18(c).

While Rule 1.18 provides your prospective client with some protection from conflicts with your other clients, that protection is not as extensive as with your actual clients. The test is similar but not precisely the same as previously discussed for other former clients. Under Rule 1.9, you cannot later represent someone against a former client in the same or substantially related matter if their interests are "materially adverse" and you had acquired material confidential information.

Under Rule 1.18, there is a higher standard than under Rule 1.9 for which information is disqualifying. The Rule 1.18 test is the same as for the former client, *plus* you could represent the new client only if the confidential information from the former prospective client could not be "significantly harmful" to her. In other words, you could not represent the new client if the confidential information you learned from the former prospective client was "significantly harmful" to her. Rule 1.18, Comment 6.

You can limit the scope of the information that you learn during the initial interview by asking only for information that helps to decide whether to represent the new client, such as factual information about the client and the adversary, along with the general nature of the dispute.

E.   IMPUTED CONFLICTS

When you are disqualified from representing a client, generally none of the lawyers with whom you are affiliated can represent that client either. The rationale for the principle is that a lawyer uses all the resources of his firm in representing a client, including sharing confidential information with his colleagues. All lawyers with whom you are affiliated owe a duty of loyalty to their clients. A law "firm" includes private firms, corporate law departments, legal services organizations, lawyers who share office space but hold themselves out to the public that they are a partnership, and co-counsel who represent the same party and have exchanged confidential information. Rule 1.0(c).

1.   Imputed Conflicts for Lawyers Currently Associated in Same Firm

Rule 1.10(a) applies imputed disqualification to the principles of Rules 1.7 and 1.9. If you are disqualified from representing a client under Rule 1.7 or 1.9, under Rule 1.10(a) your law partner cannot represent her. The motion to disqualify you would be based on Rule 1.7, and the motion to disqualify your law partner would be based on Rule 1.10(a).

The major exception to the imputed disqualification requirement is that a personal interest that required your disqualification is not imputed to your colleagues. Rule 1.10(a). Suppose that your personal belief against representing a client which manufactures firearms threatens your ability to render competent representation. Although you cannot represent that client, your colleagues may.

2.   Imputed Conflicts When a Lawyer Changes Firms

Rule 1.10(a) is not applicable to situations where one lawyer, either the one with the actual disqualification or another lawyer with the imputed disqualification, leaves the first law firm and joins another firm. Rules 1.10(b) and 1.9(b) govern those situations. If you leave your law firm without knowing any confidential information about Client A, you would not be disqualified from representing Client B, the adversary of Client A, at your new firm. Your representation of Client B does not breach any expectation of loyalty from your old firm. Because you are not disqualified, no one in your new firm is disqualified. Rule 1.9(b). You had no confidential information about Client A; you had only imputed knowledge from your old firm. Your imputed knowledge cannot be imputed to your new law firm. Disqualification here would unduly restrict mobility in the legal profession.

If you change law firms knowing confidential information about Client A, you cannot represent Client B in the same or a substantially related matter if your old firm had previously represented Client A whose interests are materially adverse to Client B and you have confidential information about Client A. Rule 1.9(b).

If you leave your law firm after having represented Client A, your old firm may represent Client B whose interests are materially adverse to Client A, as long as Client B's case is not the same or a substantially related matter as the one for which the firm had represented Client A *and* no one remaining with the old firm has confidential information from Client A. Rule 1.10(b). If everyone who had confidential information about Client A has left the old firm, it can represent Client B.

3.   Imputed Conflicts and the Prospective Client

Rule 1.18 differs from the other Rules for imputed disqualification. Whereas Rule 1.10 attributes your conflict of interest to all the lawyers with whom you practice, Rule 1.18(d)(1) is not as broad. Unless you have information that "could be significantly harmful" to your formerly prospective client, anyone with whom you practice can represent someone else in the matter. Rule 1.18(c). Even if your colleagues are subject to disqualification, however, they may obtain informed consent waivers from both their new client and your former prospective client in order to represent the new client. Rule 1.18(d)(1).

4. Waiver of Imputed Conflict

A client affected by imputed disqualification principles may waive its protections if (1) each client gives informed consent confirmed in writing, and (2) each lawyer reasonably believes that she will be able to provide competent and diligent representation. Rule 1.10(c); Rule 1.0(e).

5. Screening of Disqualified Lawyers

A screen may suffice to remove the imputation of disqualification, by walling off the disqualified lawyer and permitting his colleagues to proceed with the representation. Screening "denotes the isolation of a lawyer from any participation in a matter through the timely imposition of procedures within a firm that are reasonably adequate under the circumstances to protect information that the isolated lawyer is obligated to protect under these Rules or other law." Rule 1.0(k). Screening has been approved in the case law, in some state disciplinary codes, in the Restatement, and in Rules 1.11, 1.12, and 1.18.

Prospective clients. If the new client and the former prospective client *both* do not waive the conflict of interest, Rule 1.18(d)(2) nevertheless permits you to be screened from your colleagues in order for them to represent the new client. Screening is possible only if your colleagues "took reasonable measures to avoid exposure to more disqualifying information than was reasonably necessary to determine whether to represent the [former] prospective client." Rule 1.18(d)(2).

Several steps are necessary for an effective screen when you are disqualified. First, it must be set up in a timely manner, ideally before anyone else raises the issue. Second, your colleagues must promptly inform your former prospective client in writing. Third, they must notify the new client, describing the subject about which you consulted the former prospective client as well as the screening methods to be used. Rule 1.18, Comment 8. Finally, you cannot receive any part of the fee paid to the new client.

Any effort by a law firm to screen you from the new client's case should attempt to insure that none of the confidential information you possess would be used to the new client's disadvantage. The firm should take action before any sharing of information occurred and certainly before any motion is made by the opposition to disqualify the entire firm. In addition, the firm should deny you access to the files in the new client's case, and admonish you and all other firm personnel not to discuss the new client's case when you are present. As to compensation, if you are a salaried attorney, you may continue to receive your regular compensation. If you are a partner, you should not share in the profit from the client's representation.

Lawyers changing firms. Screening also may be used when you change firms. In early 2009 the ABA amended Rule 1.10(a). When you move from private practice in one office to a law firm or corporate law office that represents a client with interests adverse to your former client, your new firm can use an ethics screen and avoid imputed disqualification without obtaining or asking for the consent of your former client. Your new firm must provide written notice of the screen to your former client. The notice must (1) describe the screening procedures, (2) promise that both your new firm and you will comply with the MRPC, (3) state that judicial review of the screen is available, and (4) include an agreement that responds to your former client's concerns. Upon written request of your former client, you and a partner at your new firm periodically must certify compliance with the screening procedure.

A proposal for further amending Rule 1.10 was recommended by the ABA Standing Committee on Professional Responsibility to the House of Delegates at the August 2009 meeting. This amendment would change the introductory phrase of Rule 1.10(a)(2) to read "the prohibition is based upon Rule 1.9(a) or (b) *and arises out of the disqualified lawyer's association with a prior firm.*" (proposed language in italics) The amendment would clarify that the earlier 2009 amendment is intended to limit screening to lawyers who move between private firms or entities.

6. Imputed Conflicts for Most Rule 1.8 Violations

Except for sexual relations with a client, all Rule 1.8 conflicts between you and your client are imputed to other lawyers in your firm. Rule 1.8(k). If your conflict with a client relates to having sexual relations with your client since the start of the lawyer-client relationship, you still can send that client to your law partner to handle the client's case. For other violations of Rule 1.8, your law partners are imputed with your violation and are likewise disqualified.

F. ACQUIRING AN INTEREST IN LITIGATION

1. Acquiring an Interest in the Client's Claim

If you acquire a financial interest in your client's litigation, there is a risk that your independent professional judgment will be affected by your interest. Your client may believe that you are more objective about the transaction than you really are, and you may be tempted to use her confidential information to her disadvantage. Therefore, you cannot acquire a proprietary interest in a claim for relief or the subject matter of a litigation. (The Rule is inapplicable to a pre-existing interest held by you before your representation begins, but Rule 1.7 would apply.) Most of the interest in Rule 1.8(i) focuses on its two exceptions. First, you can obtain a proprietary interest in your client's case through a reasonable contingent fee in civil cases. Rule 1.8(i)(2).

The other Rule 1.8(i) exception permits you to acquire a contractual lien to secure your fee or expenses as long as the lien satisfies state law. Rule 1.8(i); ABA Formal Opinion 02–427. Acquisition of liens on a client's property constitute a business transaction with a client and must also comply with Rule 1.8(a). A charging lien or a retaining lien may be used. (Retaining liens, which give you an interest in your client's papers and funds in your possession to secure your fee, are not favored. Restatement, § 43.) Charging liens give you the right to apply any recovery to the payment of your fees, after notifying the person who will be paying the settlement. If the person paying the recovery pays it directly to your client, that person is liable to you for your fee. That is the reason why settlement checks are made out to both you and your client. Your client must agree in writing to the use of a charging lien, thereby making the lien consensual.

2. Publication Rights

You cannot negotiate with your client for literary or media rights to a particular matter while you are still working for her on that case. Rule 1.8(d). The Rule protects both your client from your potential overreaching and the judicial system from being used for your benefit. You should not be tempted to practice your case in a manner that increases the publicity value of the media rights. For example, you should not reject a plea offer ending your client's case to her benefit because going to trial instead would increase the market value of a book or movie about her case. *After* the representation concludes, you have no advantage over a literary agent in obtaining the rights to your (possibly now former) client's story.

By the Rule, you still could represent someone on a contract to publish her story about a case handled by a lawyer other than you or someone in your firm. It also does not cover the situation where you represent your client in a dispute about her intellectual property rights such as a copyright claim, for which you may charge a reasonable contingent fee. Rule 1.8, Comment 9.

3. Advancing Money to Clients

You cannot support your client financially by giving her money for her living expenses or medical bills. Financial assistance of this kind "would encourage clients to pursue lawsuits that might not otherwise be brought and because such assistance gives lawyers too great a financial stake in the litigation." Rule 1.8, Comment 10. You are likely to do a better job as your client's lawyer if you are not also her creditor.

You can advance or even guarantee your client's litigation expenses and court costs without her being ultimately responsible for paying them. Rule 1.8(e). Litigation expenses include payments for expert witnesses or expenditures for your client to travel to a deposition. Court costs include filing fees and copying costs. If your client is not indigent, you must incorporate any advance of expenses in the fee agreement, providing that they must be paid from the proceeds of any recovery. If she is indigent, you are allowed to pay them and not make them payable from any proceeds.

G. BUSINESS TRANSACTIONS WITH CLIENTS

As a fiduciary of your client, you have duties toward your client that fall outside the lawyer-client relationship. You may be involved in business dealings with other people that may affect your ability to represent your client. The significance and materiality of that dealing may affect your judgment and require that you decline the case. Unless you reasonably believe that your representation will not be adversely affected by that dealing and your client gives an informed consent, you should not begin to represent your client. The focus of the MRPC is on whether the transaction is fair and reasonable to the client, i.e., that you do not abuse your position of trust.

You can knowingly acquire a pecuniary interest adverse to a current client if: (1) the transaction is fair and reasonable to your client, including your role, (2) the terms of the transaction are given to her in writing in clear language so that she can understand the terms, (3) she is advised in writing that she can consult another lawyer, and (4) she gives informed consent in writing. Rule 1.8(a). It is your duty to bring the situation to your client's attention and to explain to her the significance of what is happening, including the risk that you will favor yourself in the transaction. You must be clear in the writing to indicate whether you represent the client in the transaction. Rule 1.8(a)(3).

On the other hand, you can purchase an automobile from your client without the need to comply with Rule 1.8(a). Because the transaction is available on the same terms to the general public, you have no duty to your client.

Ordinary lawyer-client fee agreements providing for hourly, lump-sum, or contingent fees are not regarded as business transactions with the client. Restatement, § 126. But modification of a fee agreement is a business transaction, subject to Rule 1.8(a).

When you accept an ownership interest such as stock in your client's business as the fee for legal services, your fee constitutes a business transaction with your client and your total fee must be reasonable. ABA Formal Opinion 00–418. The value of the stock and the fee's reasonableness are determined at that time and put in writing. Written details reinforce the significance of your client's understanding about both the transaction and a waiver he will sign, but you "bear[ ] the risk of omitting a term that seems unimportant at the time." ABA Formal Opinion 00–418. Your ongoing legal representation raises potential conflicts of interest, because you will be asked to provide independent judgment on issues that can have an immediate effect on the business. You also have potential malpractice exposure when someone complains that you should have taken some action as counsel for the business that might have had a short term adverse effect on the business.

H. THIRD PARTY COMPENSATION AND IN-FLUENCE

1. Compensation From Third Parties

When you represent a teenager charged in juvenile court, her parents probably will pay your fee. The parents' interests may vary from your client's. Because your obligations are to your client, you cannot allow her parents to interfere with or influence your exercise of independent professional judgment. You must inform your client that someone is paying your fee and obtain her informed consent to that fee arrangement, part of which relates to respect for your client's confidentiality rights. Rule 1.8(f)(2)–(3). Unless she consents, you cannot disclose confidential information about her case to the payer, nor can that third party influence the manner in which you practice the case. In another context, when an insurance company pays you to represent its insured, the insured is your client. Rule 1.8, Comment 11.

2. Aggregate Settlements

In representing multiple clients, you may negotiate an aggregate settlement of their civil claims or plea bargains of their criminal charges. Rule 1.8(g). An "aggregate settlement" occurs when two or more clients consent to have their matters resolved together. In aggregate settlement situations, you may be tempted not to investigate the cases individually and you may be tempted to close the cases too soon.

Each such client must consent in writing after consultation, which must include "disclosure of the existence and nature of all the claims involved and of the participation of each person in the settlement." Rule 1.8(g). Because of the importance of what the client is doing, this writing requirement is more demanding than the general conflict of interest Rules. Specifically, the following information must be disclosed: (1) the total amount of the aggregate settlement or the result of the aggregate agreement, (2) details of every client's participation in the aggregate settlement of agreement, (3) the total fees and costs to be paid to you as a result of the aggregate settlement, if they are to be paid from the settlement's proceeds or by an opposing party, (4) the method by which costs are to be apportioned among the clients, and (5) the existence and nature of all claims, defenses, or pleas involved in the aggregate settlement. ABA Formal Opinion 06–438.

Rule 1.8(g) applies to class actions if you have a lawyer-client relationship with two or more class members. Rule 1.8(g), Comment 13. While disclosure must include the settlement offered to other clients, this Rule is not applicable when a settlement offer is made to only one of your clients at a time. Rule 1.7 might still apply, though, because failing to tell the other class members limits your representation of the client who lacks information about offers made to your other clients.

I.   LAWYERS CURRENTLY OR FORMERLY IN GOVERNMENT SERVICE

The revolving door. Lawyers who leave either a government position to join a private law firm or a private firm to join the government have special conflict of interest standards to address their "revolving door" status. The MRPC and federal statutes attempt to limit potential abuses of confidential information without unduly restricting the government's ability to attract lawyers. If the mobility of lawyers who work for the government is unnecessarily limited, they might choose to bypass government employment completely and the government's recruitment of new or experienced lawyers would suffer.

1.   Lawyers Moving From Government Employment to the Private Sector

After you leave government employment, you can never represent a client in connection with a matter in which you participated personally and substantially as a government employee, unless the appropriate government agency consents in writing. Rule 1.11(a)(2).

Matter. A "matter" is "any judicial or other proceeding, application, request for a ruling or other determination, contract, claim, controversy, investigation, charge, accusation, arrest or other particular matter involving a specific party or parties." Rule 1.11(e)(1). Two situations involving the same parties and facts are likely to be considered the same matter. Restatement, § 133. If you leave government employment while suing a large oil company and become counsel in private practice defending that oil company in the same lawsuit, that is the same "matter."

By contrast, suppose as a government employee you help to draft a law to govern conduct by all oil companies. After you leave, you may become counsel for one of the oil companies in a case involving the law you helped to draft. Those two representations are not considered the same "matter," because the legal drafting did not involve a transaction between identifiable parties in a particular situation.

Personally and substantially. You lack substantial responsibility over a matter if you give it only superficial approval. You must have "had such a heavy responsibility for the matter in question that it is likely [you] became personally and substantially involved in the investigative or deliberative processes regarding that matter." ABA Formal Opinion 342 (1975).

Federal statutes. In contrast to the MRPC, 18 U.S.C. § 207 restricts senior personnel of the federal executive branch and federal agencies even after they have left government service. That statute does not preempt state versions of the MRPC, but it is broader than the MRPC because it applies to former government officials even if they are not lawyers. The sanctions for violating § 207 are criminal rather than disciplinary. The federal statute uses three reference points to decide whether a person who acted personally and substantially as a government official may later act for a private party: (1) the United States government must be a party or have a direct and substantial interest in the matter, (2) the former official must have participated as an officer or employee by making a decision, giving advice, investigating or taking other action, and (3) the matter must have involved a specific party at the time of participation, rather than being familiar with or approving procedures.

The federal statute imposes a lifetime ban for appearing in connection with a particular matter if the government official participated personally and substantially in working on the matter. There is a two-year ban if the matter was merely under the person's "official responsibility." Finally, there is a one-year ban which precludes the former official from contacting her former agency with the intent to influence any agency action.

Confidential information. As a former government lawyer, you cannot use confidential information about a person to that person's "material disadvantage" Rule 1.11(c). Confidential government information is information obtained by you pursuant to government authority and not available to the public. Rule 1.11(b). Any government information known only by other government officials is not imputed to you. As a former government lawyer, if your representation of a private client would require you to use your confidential government information, you cannot represent her. However, other members of your firm may represent her if you are properly screened from the matter as described in the next subsection.

Imputation. If the imputation rules were strict, private clients' counsel choices would be limited when they want to employ a former government lawyer with significant experience and knowledge about how government works. If you are disqualified from representing a private client under Rule 1.11, every other lawyer in your new firm is not disqualified. They may represent your client if you are "screened" from any participation in the matter and you receive no part of the fee from that matter. Rule 1.11(a). No governmental consent to screening is required. Your law firm must "promptly" notify the governmental agency in writing about the conflict and the screening so that it can be certain that the screening is effective. Rule 1.11(a)(2). While you cannot receive any apportioned part of the specific fee from your law firm's representation, you still are entitled to receive "a salary or partnership share established by a prior agreement." Rule 1.11, Comment 6. The Comment's effect is that you can continue to receive your partnership share even though it includes proceeds from the case in which you were disqualified.

Negotiating for private employment. While you are working for the government, you cannot negotiate for private work with a party who is involved in a matter in which you are then participating personally and substantially. Rule 1.11(d)(2). The notable exception to this Rule applies to a law clerk for a judge. Under the circumstances described, she may negotiate for private employment as long as she first notifies the judge for whom she works. Rule 1.12(b).

2. Lawyers Moving From the Private Sector to Government Employment

If you personally and substantially worked on a matter while in nongovernmental employment and then began working for the government (regardless of whether your former client's work is now adverse or involves confidential information), you are disqualified from working on that same matter unless the government agency consents in writing. Rule 1.11(d)(2)(i). You should not be switching sides in the same matter. Because you probably learned confidential information from the private client, you cannot use that information to the detriment of your former client.

Imputation. The disqualification imposed on you as a former private practitioner now employed by the government is not imputed to any other lawyer in the government. From a financial perspective, as a salaried government lawyer you lack the monetary interest in the success of your governmental representation that is assumed to be inherent in private practice. ABA Formal Opinion 342 (1975). Even if your disqualification is not imputed to your colleagues, "ordinarily it would be prudent to screen such lawyers." Rule 1.11, Comment 2.

J. FORMER JUDGE, ARBITRATOR, MEDIATOR OR OTHER THIRD PARTY NEUTRAL

The MRPC address the related issues of former judicial officers who are: (1) negotiating for future employment, or (2) disqualified from representing anyone connected with a case in which they had acted as an adjudicative official.

Disqualification from representing former litigants. Any lawyer, who participated personally and substantially on the merits as a judge, other adjudicative officer, arbitrator, mediator, or third-party neutral, cannot accept private employment in a matter in which she acted in a judicial capacity. Rule 1.12. She cannot exploit her office for personal advantage. An exception permits representation if all parties to the former proceeding consent in writing.

Negotiating for future employment. In a matter in which she is working personally and substantially, a judge or other adjudicative official cannot negotiate for employment with anyone involved as a party or the lawyer for a party. Rule 1.12(b). The standard applies to both trial judges and appellate judges.

Judge's law clerks. As long as she *first* notifies the judge for whom she works, while working for the government, a judicial law clerk may negotiate for private work with a party who is involved in a matter in which the clerk participated personally and substantially. Rule 1.12(b). A former judicial law clerk is disqualified from later representing anyone in a matter on which she worked with the judge personally and substantially on the merits. Rule 1.12(a).

Imputation. Any disqualification of a former judicial official under Rule 1.12 is *not* imputed to any lawyer in her new law firm if the same two conditions discussed above (and repeated in Rule 1.11) are met. First, the former official is screened from the disqualifying matter, and is apportioned no fee from that case. Second, the law firm must promptly notify in writing the appropriate tribunal which can decide the sufficiency of the screening. Rule 1.12(c).

CONFLICTS OF INTEREST CHECKLIST

A. Current Client Conflicts

   1. The rationales for standards for concurrent client conflicts

      a. The duty to protect your client's confidential information

      b. The duty to be loyal to your client.

   2. "Directly adverse" conflict

      a. Rule 1.7(a)(1) prohibits you from representing a client if that representation "will be directly adverse to another client."

      b. Examples

         1. Representing plaintiff and defendant in the same lawsuit.

         2. Representing buyer in negotiating for the sale of property when the seller is also your client, even in a different matter.

   3. "Materially limited" conflict

      a. Rule 1.7(a)(2) prohibits representation if there is a significant risk that the representation will be "materially limited" by your responsibilities to another, whether that client is a current client, a former client, a third person, or even yourself.

      b. Examples

         1. In a class action where you represent the plaintiff class, you have a materially limited conflict if one of the potential defendants for the class is also a current client.

         2. If you represent several people who are forming a business, you cannot permit any responsibility to one of

those clients to materially limit your responsibilities in representing the others.

4. Method for resolving conflicts of interest

    a. Independently decide whether you can competently and diligently represent all the affected clients,

    b. Decide whether some other law precludes you from accepting the representation,

    c. You must not represent one client against another client "in the same litigation."

    d. Each affected clients must give you "informed consent, confirmed in writing."

5. Concurrent representation in unrelated matters

    a. General rule: you cannot sue Client B on behalf of Client A, while you represent Client B on an unrelated matter.

    b. Generally, if you represent two directly adverse clients in different lawsuits, if they do not consent to the conflict, you usually must withdraw from representing both parties in the two cases.

6. Waiver

    a. Rule 1.7 permits a written client waiver, which initially requires you to have a reasonable belief that you can provide competent and diligent representation to the affected clients, despite the conflict that you have identified. Where you represent both sides of the same lawsuit, the conflict is so serious that it cannot be cured by the consent of the parties.

    b. You must make a full disclosure to your clients, by explaining to them the relevant circumstances that created the conflict and the risks and benefits of one lawyer representing all of them as opposed to each of them having separate lawyers.

    c.   Outside the litigation context, you may be able to represent adverse parties, such as the buyer and seller of real estate by following the aforementioned steps for a valid informed consent.

7.   Examples of concurrent representation

    a.   Multiple representation in criminal cases. It is reversible error if the trial judge requires that defendants be tried together, over the defendant's timely objection. The joint representation is presumed prejudicial. ***Holloway v. Arkansas***, 435 U.S. 475 (1978).

    b.   If you negotiate for a new job with an opposing party or that party's lawyer, there is a "materially limited" conflict.

    c.   The Rule 1.7 analysis applies to lawyers who are related or married to each other and who are on opposite sides of the same case. The two lawyers should obtain both clients' consent before representing the clients. The conflict is not imputed to others in your firm.

    d.   When a lawyer from another firm retains you to represent her, you may have a conflict of interest if the two of you concurrently represent clients who are adverse to each other in a separate case.

    e.   Insured and insurer. Conflicts of interest may arise when the insured is sued for more than the policy limits and she wants to settle for an amount less than the policy limits.

    f.   A positional conflict exists when you represent a client in one matter seeking a particular result, and at the same time you represent another client in a different case in which you are taking a contrary *legal* position.

B. Current Client Conflicts—Lawyer's Personal Interest or Duties

1.   Sexual relations with your client. You cannot have a sexual relationship with a client, unless that consensual

relationship existed prior to the beginning of the lawyer-client relationship.

2. Accepting gifts from clients.

    a. No matter how large the gift, the MRPC do not prohibit gifts from your client to you, as long as the gifting does not require you to draft a legal instrument.

    b. Exceptions to the Rule's operation. If you cannot accept a gift, no one related to you can accept the gift, unless you or the other gift recipient is related to the client. Rule 1.8(c). The Rule does not prohibit you from seeking an appointment as executor of your client's estate.

C. Former Client Conflicts

1. If you formerly represented a client in a matter, you cannot represent a new client in the same or substantially related matter if your new client has interests that are "materially adverse" to your old client.

2. Definition of a "matter." A "matter" is not limited to lawsuits. "Substantially related" matter includes the "same transaction or legal dispute" or "if there otherwise is a substantial risk that confidential factual information that normally has been obtained in the prior representation would materially advance the client's position in the subsequent matter."

3. Examples of successive representation

    a. You represent the seller in the sale of a business, but later you represent the buyer of that business and tell him to stop making payments to the seller who has not complied with the terms of the deal. Your advice to the buyer breached your continuing duty of loyalty to the prior client, the seller, even in the absence of any showing that the seller's confidential information was disclosed to the buyer.

b. If you previously represented a witness for the opponent, you should disqualify yourself if confidential information you gained when you represented the prior client in the prior case would enable you to examine and impeach your prior client more effectively.

c. Your old firm represented Client A in a lawsuit against a defendant, though you were not involved in representing Client A and received no confidential information about her case. If you leave your firm and join the firm that represents the defendant in that same lawsuit, you may still represent that defendant because you have no actual knowledge of plaintiff's confidential information.

4. Waiver of successive conflict. Rules 1.9(a) and 1.9(b) permit the prior client to waive the conflict of interest. The otherwise disqualified lawyer may represent a new client against the prior client who gives informed consent in writing.

D. Prospective Client Conflicts

1. A "prospective client" is a "person who discusses with a lawyer the possibility of forming a client-lawyer relationship with respect to a matter." Your willingness to discuss the possibility of forming a client-lawyer relationship determines whether the client has a "reasonable expectation" of becoming a client. What is "reasonable" is measured from the client's expectations. A person who contacts you as part of a deception to disqualify you from representing another party to the dispute has no reasonable expectation of becoming your client.

2. Duties to the prospective client

a. You have a duty of confidentiality to the prospective client, in order to decide whether to represent a client, no matter how brief your initial conference was.

  b. If the prospective client never becomes a client, generally you cannot represent another client who has interests "materially adverse" to her "in the same or substantially related matter if the lawyer received information from the prospective client that could be significantly harmful to that person in the matter."

E. Imputed Conflicts

 1. When you are disqualified from representing a client, generally none of the lawyers with whom you are affiliated can represent that client.

 2. Imputed disqualification for lawyers currently associated in same firm. If you are disqualified under Rule 1.7 or Rule 1.9, the lawyers in your firm are disqualified under Rule 1.10(a).

 3. Imputed disqualification when lawyer changes firms

  a. Rule 1.10(a) applies where one lawyer, either the one with the actual disqualification or another lawyer with the imputed disqualification, leaves the first law firm and joins another.

  b. Rule 1.10(b) and 1.9(b) situations when a lawyer changes firms

   1. If you leave your law firm without knowing any confidential information about a Client A, you would not be disqualified from representing Client B, the adversary of Client A, at your new firm. Your imputed knowledge cannot be imputed to your new law firm.

   2. If you change law firms knowing confidential information about Client A, you cannot represent Client B in the same or a substantially related matter if your old firm had previously represented Client A whose interests are materially adverse to Cli-

ent B and you have confidential information about Client A.

3. If you leave your law firm after having represented Client A, your old firm may represent Client B whose interests are materially adverse to Client A, as long as Client B's case is not the same or a substantially related matter as the one for which the firm had represented Client A *and* no one remaining with the old firm has confidential information from Client A.

4. Waiving imputed disqualification. A client affected by imputed disqualification principles may waive its protections if each client gives informed consent in writing, and each lawyer reasonably believes that she will be able to provide competent and diligent representation.

5. Screening disqualified lawyers. A screen may suffice to remove the imputation of the disqualification, by walling off the disqualified lawyer and permitting his colleagues to proceed with the representation. Rule 1.10(a) provides for screening as a method of curing the disqualification when you leave one firm and go to another firm, in order to avoid the firm's imputed disqualification based on your individual conflict of interest.

6. Imputed disqualification for most Rule 1.8 violations. Except for sexual relations (a personal, not professional, conflict with a client), all Rule 1.8 conflicts between you and your client are imputed to other lawyers in your firm.

F. **Acquiring an Interest in Litigation**

1. Proprietary interest in client's claim

    a. You cannot acquire a financial interest in your client's litigation. You may acquire a charging lien to secure your fee or expenses, as long as the lien satisfies state law. It constitutes a busi-

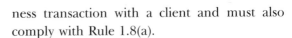

ness transaction with a client and must also comply with Rule 1.8(a).

b. The second exception allowing you to obtain a proprietary interest in your client's case is a reasonable contingent fee in civil cases.

2. Publication rights

a. You cannot negotiate with your client for literary or media rights to a particular matter while you are still working for her on that case.

b. You still could represent someone on a contract to publish her story about a case handled by a lawyer other than you or someone in your firm.

3. Advancing money

a. You cannot support your client financially by giving her money for her living expenses or medical bills.

b. You may advance or even guarantee litigation expenses and court costs without your client being ultimately responsible for paying them.

G. Business Transactions with Clients

1. You may conduct a business transaction with your current client if:

a. The transaction is fair and reasonable to your client.

b. The terms of the transaction are given to her in writing in clear language so that she can understand the terms.

c. She is advised in writing that she can consult another lawyer.

d. She consents in writing.

2. Investing in your client's business. When you accept stock in your client's business as the fee for legal services, your fee constitutes a business transaction with your client and your total fee must be reasonable.

H. Third Party Compensation and Influence

1. Compensation from third parties

   a. Because your obligations are to your client, you cannot allow the third party payer to interfere with your exercise of professional judgment.

   b. You must inform your client that someone else is paying your fee and obtain her consent to that fee arrangement, part of which relates to respect for your client's confidentiality rights.

2. Aggregate settlements

   a. An "aggregate settlement" occurs when two or more clients consent to have their matters resolved together.

   b. Each client must consent to an aggregate settlement in writing after consultation.

I. Lawyers Currently or Formerly in Government Service

1. Lawyers moving from government employment to the private sector

   a. After you leave government employment, you can never represent a client in connection with a matter in which you participated personally and substantially as a government employee, unless the appropriate government agency consents in writing.

   b. In contrast to the MRPC, 18 U.S.C. § 207 restricts senior personnel of the federal executive branch and federal agencies even after they have left government service.

   c. Your disqualification is not imputed to the other lawyers in your new firm. They may represent your client if you are "screened" from any participation in the matter and you receive no part of the fee from that matter. No governmental consent to screening is required.

   d. As a former government lawyer, you cannot use confidential information about a person to that person's "material disadvantage."

    e.   While working for the government, you cannot negotiate for private work with a party who is involved in a matter in which you are then participating personally and substantially.

  2. Lawyers moving from the private sector to government employment. If you personally and substantially worked on a matter while in nongovernmental employment and then began working for the government, you are disqualified from working on that same matter unless the government agency consents in writing.

J. Former judges moving to the private sector

  1. Any lawyer who participated personally and substantially on the merits as a judge or other adjudicative officer cannot accept private employment in a matter in which she acted in a judicial capacity. An exception permits representation if all parties to the former proceeding consent in writing.

  2. In a matter in which she is working personally and substantially, a judge or other adjudicative official cannot negotiate for employment with anyone involved as a party or the lawyer for a party.

  3. As long as she first notifies the judge for whom she works, a law clerk may negotiate for private work with a party who is involved in a matter in which the clerk participated personally and substantially. Later she is disqualified from representing anyone in a matter on which she worked with the judge personally and substantially on the merits.

  4. Any disqualification of a former judicial official under Rule 1.12 is not imputed to any lawyer in her new law firm if the following two conditions are met.

    a. The former official is screened from the disqualifying matter and is apportioned no fee from that case.

    b. The law firm must promptly notify in writing the appropriate tribunal which can decide the sufficiency of the screening.

ILLUSTRATIVE PROBLEMS

■ PROBLEM 4.1 CURRENT CLIENT CONFLICT ■

Janet Dean is a Ph.D. biologist whose law degree has given her the opportunity over time to represent many clients in environmental litigation. Five clients have consulted with her during the past month about representing them in conjunction with the release and threatened release of hazardous substances at the Tri–County Disposal site near Hartford. The possible corrective action by the United States Environmental Protection Agency may be taken under the provisions of the Comprehensive Environmental Response, Compensation and Liability Act of 1980 (CERCLA), which makes current and past owners, operators, and others associated with real property responsible for removing hazardous substances from the site. Each of the five clients has been notified that it is a potentially responsible party (PRP) for the total cost of cleaning the disposal site. The five are current and former owners and operators of the disposal site, producers of the disposed hazardous substances, and transporters of the substances at the site. Can Janet Dean ethically represent the five PRPs? If she can represent all of the PRPs, what is the nature of the consent which must be acquired from each of them?

Analysis

Rule 1.7 prohibits a lawyer from concurrently representing clients whose interests are "directly adverse to another client," or "there is a significant risk that the representation of one or more clients will be materially limited by the lawyer's responsibilities to" other clients. Despite the presence of a conflict of interest, the lawyer may represent multiple clients if he "reasonably believes" that he "will be able to provide competent and diligent representation to each affected client" and each of the represented clients consents in writing after being informed of the conflict by the lawyer.

The first issue to be addressed is whether Janet Dean's clients' interests are in conflict. The nature of the CERCLA investigation and the potential liability of each client for the entirety of the cleanup of the hazardous substances at the disposal site clearly indicates conflicts among their respective interests. Even if the CERCLA case law suggests that the different functions performed by the various PRPs dictates a percentage range of their respective liabilities, there may be significant conflicts between the PRPs as to whether each client is liable and whether each is liable on the high or low side of the damage range for the cleanup.

To represent these PRPs at the same time, Janet Dean or another lawyer should provide each of them with adequate information so that each can make an informed decision about whether to consent to the concurrent representation or to seek another attorney. Included within this information should be the nature and scope of the conflicting interests as well as the fact that Janet Dean may have to withdraw from representing one or more, if not all, of the PRPs at some later time. This advice should include full disclosure of the circumstances and advice about any actual or reasonably foreseeable adverse effects of those circumstances upon the representation.

The scope of the consent which Janet Dean should obtain from each client is two-fold, dealing with 1) consent to the representation of their conflicting interests, and 2) the consent to the disclosure of each client's confidential information to the other clients. Even if the clients consent to her representation of their conflicting interests, it is important for her to seek from them an additional consent that she can share the confidential information of each with the rest of the clients.

■ PROBLEM 4.2 FORMER CLIENT CONFLICT ■

Larry Lawyer has practiced law for four years. LaVerne Smith comes to his office to tell him about concerns she has about her job situation. Last summer, she became the assistant women's basketball coach at New State College, a highly successful program. Since her arrival, LaVerne has overheard several of the older players refer to tardy financial payments that they were expecting from boosters of the basketball program. Because such payments violate the rules of the National Collegiate Athletic Association (NCAA), LaVerne believes that she should talk to the NCAA compliance officer at the college. She asks whether it would be better if Larry contacted the compliance officer, Shirley Crane, so that LaVerne is not perceived as a whistle-blower which she fears could result in the loss of her job. As Larry interviews LaVerne, he realizes that two years ago he represented Shirley Crane when she divorced her first husband. That representation has concluded.

Analysis

Under Rule 1.9(a), a lawyer who has previously represented a client must not represent another person in the same or a substantially related matter in which that person's interests are materially adverse to the interests of the prior client. Under Rule 1.9(c), a lawyer cannot use information relating to the former representation for the disadvantage of the former client. Larry represented the college's compliance officer two years ago in her divorce. Because LaVerne is asking Larry to discuss her job situation with Shirley, there does not appear to be any possibility that the current representation relates to the same or a substantially related matter under Rule 1.9(a) as Shirley's divorce action. On the other hand, Larry may be aware of confidential information about Shirley or her divorce action that he may want to raise with Shirley in his discussions with Shirley about LaVerne's problem.

Under Rule 1.9, Larry can represent LaVerne: 1) because her case is factually different from Shirley's earlier divorce case, and 2) if Larry does not use information relating to his former representation of Shirley to her disadvantage.

■ PROBLEM 4.3 FORMER CLIENT CONFLICT AND IMPUTED DISQUALIFICATION ■

A lawsuit was filed recently by First National Bank against Paul Sims, in which Smith and Jones represents the plaintiff. The suit alleges that prior to leaving the bank's employ in 2005, Sims made fraudulent loans to himself through several fictitious accounts. Prior to attending law school, an associate attorney at Smith and Jones, Bill Travis, worked at First National Bank as a loan officer assigned to Sims's loan area but does not recall working on any of Sims's personal accounts. Travis also recently came to work for Smith and Jones after working for three years at the law firm of Wilson and Craig, which just completed the representation of Sims in connection with a lawsuit over a 2006 business dispute between Sims and a business partner. However, Travis is unaware of any information about that case. Can the firm be disqualified from representing First National Bank by virtue of Bill Travis's prior employment at Wilson and Craig while that firm represented Sims in a lawsuit?

Analysis

Smith and Jones cannot be disqualified under imputed disqualification. Imputed disqualification is relevant because Travis recently went to work for Smith and Jones after practicing at Wilson and Craig. Rule 1.10 prescribes standards by which an entire firm can be disqualified due to a conflict of interest attributable to one lawyer in that firm. No Smith and Jones lawyer is disqualifiable under Rule 1.10(a). Smith and Jones cannot represent First National Bank if Wilson and Craig represented Sims (while Travis was at Wilson and Craig) on the same or a substantially related matter as the current case, and during that time Travis acquired confidential information that is material to the *First National Bank* case.

Travis worked at Wilson and Craig, but he did no work on on any matter where Sims was involved, as a bank officer or personally.

Travis's only recollection about Sims's representation by Wilson and Craig dealt with a matter where other attorneys there represented Sims in a dispute with his business partner. That dispute was a 2006 breach of contract action against Sims. However, the *First National Bank* case deals with defrauding the bank in 2005. The two matters are not factually the same or even substantially related. Even if those matters were substantially related, Travis acquired no confidential information whatsoever about Sims's breach of contract case while at Wilson and Craig, much less any information which would be material to the *First National Bank* case. Because there does not appear to be any violation of CRPC 1.9, Smith and Jones may continue to represent First National Bank in its lawsuit against Sims.

■ PROBLEM 4.4 PAYMENT OF FEE BY THIRD PARTY ■

In Problem 4.1, Milennial Industrial Services (MIS) is the largest and the wealthiest of the five PRPs. As such, it is interested in paying its own legal fees to Janet Dean as well as the fees of the other four PRPs. Under what circumstances can MIS pay Janet Dean's legal fees for representing all of the PRPs?

Analysis

Unless specific conditions are met, a third person (including another client) cannot compensate an attorney for representing a client. Because of the appearance that someone than the client or the attorney would be involved in making or influencing important decisions relating to the representation, Rule 1.8(f) prohibits an attorney from accepting compensation from a third person for representing a client unless specific conditions are met. First, the attorney must disclose to the client that a third party is compensating the attorney for representing the client, who must thereafter consent to such payment. Rule 1.8(f)(1). At a minimum, the disclosure by Janet Dean should inform the client that payment of the fee by another will not affect (1) the attorney's independent judgment; (2) the relationship between the attorney and the client; or (3) the duty of confidentiality owed by the attorney to the client. The client must then consent to the compensation of Janet Dean by someone other than the client. The second condition is that the payment will not interfere with the attorney's independent professional judgment or with the attorney-client relationship. Rule 1.8(f)(2). Only Janet Dean as the attorney in this case can make the determination to prevent such interference. Third, despite such payment by a third party, the attorney must preserve information relating to the representation. Rule 1.8(f)(3). This requirement merely reinforces the tradition that Janet Dean must preserve the confidentiality of information relating to the representation of any client.

■ PROBLEM 4.5 FORMER GOVERNMENT LAWYER ■

After leaving the Haven prosecutor's office, where she worked as a trial attorney for three years bringing state criminal cases for consumer fraud and other white collar crime, Stella Starks joined a small firm that does an extensive amount of criminal defense work. May Starks represent Grace Ewald, who is under indictment by Starks's former office for consumer fraud if the indictment was returned by a grand jury while Starks was still at her former job when Starks shared office space with Neil Page, the assistant prosecutor who conducted the investigation of Ewald and will try the case? Starks on several occasions heard Page talking with investigators and other assistant prosecutors about evidence in the case and litigation strategy.

Analysis

Under Rule 1.11, a former government attorney cannot represent a private client in connection with a matter in which the lawyer either participated personally and substantially as a government lawyer or has acquired confidential governmental information as a government attorney, unless the appropriate governmental agency consents after consultation. In addition, a lawyer with information that she knows is confidential government information about a person which she acquired as a public employee cannot represent a private client in a matter in which the information could be used to the material disadvantage of the government.

The first issue to be addressed is whether Stella Starks participated personally and substantially as a government attorney in the prosecution of Grace Ewald. Although Ewald was indicted while Starks worked as a public prosecutor and shared office space with the assistant prosecutor who conducted the Ewald investigation, Stella herself did not participate in the investigation of Ewald. She would not be disqualified under Rule 1.11(a).

There is another potential basis for Stella Starks's disqualification. The facts state that Starks on several occasions heard the prosecutor who is responsible for the Ewald investigation talking with investigators and other assistant prosecutors about evidence in the case and litigation strategy. That type of information probably qualifies as "confidential government information" under Rule 1.11(c), because Stella's knowledge about the Ewald case was gained by her "under government authority" and is not otherwise available to the public. The language of Rule 1.11(c) suggests that Stella cannot represent Ewald because she has information that she knows is confidential government information about the prosecutor's investigation and litigation strategy which could be used to the government's material disadvantage.

Even if a former government attorney is disqualified, a firm with which that attorney is associated may represent the private client if the disqualified lawyer is screened from any participation in the case and receives no part of the fee from the representation. The language of Rule 1.11(b) states that a law firm with which Stella is associated may represent Ewald in her case only if Stella is screened from any participation in the matter and is apportioned no part of the fee generated by the Ewald representation.

Any effort by the firm to screen Stella from the Ewald case should attempt to insure that none of the confidential government information she possesses would be used to the government's disadvantage. The most important aspect of the effort is that the firm took action before any sharing of information occurred and certainly before any motion is made by the prosecutor to disqualify the entire firm. In addition, the firm should deny Stella access to the files in the Ewald case, and admonish her and all other firm personnel not to discuss the case when Stella is present. As to compensation, if Stella is a salaried attorney, she may continue to receive her regular compensation. If she is a partner, she should not share in the profit from the Ewald representation.

POINTS TO REMEMBER

- Rule 1.7(a)(1) prohibits you from representing a client if that representation "will be directly adverse to another client." Examples include representing a buyer in negotiating for the sale of property when the seller is also your client, even in a different matter.

- Rule 1.7(a)(2) prohibits representation if there is a significant risk that the representation will be "materially limited" by your responsibilities to another, whether that client is a current client, a former client, a third person, or even yourself.

- If you have a reasonable belief that you can provide competent and diligent representation to the affected clients, despite the conflict that you have identified, each affected client must give you "informed consent, confirmed in writing." You must fully disclose to your clients the risks and benefits of representing all of them

- You cannot sue Client B on behalf of Client A, while you represent Client B on an unrelated matter. If the parties do not consent to the conflict, you usually must withdraw from representing both parties in the two cases.

- You cannot have a sexual relationship with a client, unless that consensual relationship already existed prior to the beginning of the lawyer-client relationship.

- Except for sexual relations, all Rule 1.8 conflicts between you and your client are imputed to other lawyers in your firm.

- No matter how large the gift, the Rules do not prohibit gifts from your client to you, if the gifting does not require you to draft a legal instrument.

- If you used to represent a client in a matter, you cannot represent a new client in the same or substantially related matter if your new client has interests that are "materially adverse" to your old client.

- Rules 1.9(a) and 1.9(b) permit the prior client to waive the conflict of interest; the disqualified lawyer may represent a new client against the prior client who gives informed consent in writing.

- A "prospective client" is a "person who discusses with a lawyer the possibility of forming a client-lawyer relationship with respect to a matter."

  - If the prospective client never becomes a client, generally you cannot represent another client who has interests "materially adverse to those of a prospective client in the same or substantially related matter." Rule 1.18(c).

  - You could represent the new client only if the confidential information from the former prospective client could not be "significantly harmful" to her.

- When you are disqualified from representing a client, generally none of the lawyers with whom you are affiliated can represent that client. If you are disqualified under Rule 1.7 or Rule 1.9, the lawyers in your firm are disqualified under Rule 1.10.

- If you leave your law firm without knowing any confidential information about a Client A, you would not be disqualified from representing Client B, the adversary of Client A at your new firm. Your imputed knowledge cannot be imputed to your new law firm.

  - However, if you change law firms knowing confidential information about Client A, you cannot represent Client B in the same or a substantially related matter if your old firm had previously represented Client A whose interests are materially adverse to Client B and you have confidential information about Client A. Rule 1.9(b).

- If you leave your law firm after having represented Client A, your old firm may represent Client B whose interests are materially adverse to Client A, as long as the Client B's case is not the same or a substantially related matter as the one for which the firm had represented Client A *and* no one remaining with the old firm has confidential information from Client A. Rule 1.10(b).

- A client affected by imputed disqualification principles may waive its protections if each client gives informed consent in writing, and each lawyer reasonably believes that she will be able to provide competent and diligent representation. Rule 1.10(c).

- Unless you have information that "could be significantly harmful" to your formerly prospective client, anyone with whom you practice can represent someone else in the matter. Rule 1.18(c).

- A screen may suffice to remove the imputation of the disqualification, by walling off the disqualified lawyer and permitting his colleagues to proceed with the representation. Rule 1.10(a) provides for screening as a method of curing the disqualification when you change firms, in order to avoid your new firm's disqualification based on your individual conflict of interest.

- You cannot acquire a financial interest in your client's litigation.

  - But you may acquire a contractual lien to secure your fee or expenses, as long as the lien satisfies state law. Acquisition of liens on a client's property constitute a business transaction with a client and must also comply with Rule 1.8(a).

  - You may obtain a proprietary interest in your client's case with a reasonable contingent fee in civil cases.

- You cannot negotiate with your client for literary or media rights to a particular matter while you are still working for her on that case.

- You cannot support your client financially by giving her money for her living expenses or medical bills. You can advance or even guarantee litigation expenses and court costs without your client being ultimately responsible for paying them.

- You can conduct a business transaction with your current client if the transaction is fair and reasonable to your client, the terms of the transaction are given to her in writing in clear language so that she can understand the terms, she is advised in writing that she can consult another lawyer, and she consents in writing.

- An attorney cannot accept compensation from a third person for representing a client unless specific conditions are met:

  - The attorney must disclose to the client that a third party is compensating the attorney for representing the client, who must thereafter consent to such payment,

  - The payment will not interfere with the attorney's independent professional judgment or with the attorney-client relationship, and

  - The attorney must preserve information relating to the representation.

- In representing multiple clients, you may negotiate an aggregate settlement of their civil claims or plea bargains of their criminal charges. Each such client must consent to that structure in writing after consultation, which must include "disclosure of the existence and nature of all the claims involved and of the participation of each person in the settlement."

- After you leave government employment, you can never represent a client in connection with a matter in which you participated personally and substantially as a government employee, unless the appropriate government agency consents in writing.

- While you are working for the government, you cannot negotiate for private work with a party who is involved in a matter in which you are then participating personally and substantially.

- If you personally and substantially worked on a matter while in nongovernmental employment and then began working for the government, you are disqualified from working on that same matter unless the government agency consents in writing.

- Any lawyer, who participated personally and substantially on the merits as a judge cannot accept private employment in a matter in which she acted in a judicial capacity. An exception permits representation if all parties to the former proceeding consent in writing.

- In a matter in which she is working personally and substantially, a judge or other adjudicative official cannot negotiate for employment with anyone involved as a party or the lawyer for a party.

- As long as she first notifies the judge for whom she works, while working for the government, a law clerk may negotiate for private work with a party who is involved in a matter in which the clerk participated personally and substantially

- Any disqualification of a former judicial official under Rule 1.12 is not imputed to any lawyer in her new law firm if the former official is screened from the disqualifying matter and is apportioned no fee from that case and the law firm promptly notifies in writing the appropriate tribunal which can decide the sufficiency of the screening.

CHAPTER 5

Competence and Legal Malpractice

A. COMPETENCE NECESSARY TO UNDER-TAKE REPRESENTATION

You are a competent lawyer if you have "the legal knowledge, skill, thoroughness and preparation reasonably necessary for the representation." Rule 1.1. Your skills must include the ability to research, write, advocate, and negotiate. Acquisition of these attributes are reasonably necessary to representing your client, which means that you can be or become competent without causing unreasonable delays or expenses for your client. Your failure to provide competent representation may result in discipline, malpractice liability, or an ineffective assistance of counsel claim.

You may take a type of case with which you are unfamiliar. Rule 1.1, Comment 2. That makes sense, because everybody has a first case of a particular kind. Otherwise, how would you become experienced in any type of case? By studying or talking to other lawyers, you become knowledgeable even if you lacked the requisite knowledge when you began the representation. Rule 1.1, Comment 2. Through your knowledge, you also become thorough and prepared to represent your clients.

Competence is a function of what is reasonable under the circumstances. In an emergency where it is impractical for a person to contact another lawyer, you may enter a limited relationship with a client to protect her interests caused by the situation. Rule 1.1, Comment 3. Even if you outsource legal or nonlegal services to others as independent contractors, you are ultimately responsible for providing competent service to your client. ABA Formal Opinion 08–451.

Ineffective Assistance of Counsel. General claims of ineffective assistance of counsel under the Sixth Amendment are controlled by *Strickland v. Washington*, 466 U.S. 668 (1984). For a criminal conviction to be reversed, the defendant must show that her lawyer's performance was "outside the wide range of professionally competent assistance" and that his ineffectiveness caused "actual prejudice." As for your performance, ineffective assistance claims that involve the exercise of strategic judgment are usually unsuccessful, unless your judgment was outside the range of reasonable lawyer assistance. A failure to investigate the facts or the applicable law may constitute ineffective assistance if a reasonable lawyer would have conducted the investigation or research. As for prejudice to the client as a result of your ineffectiveness, it is insufficient to show that the your errors had some effect on the outcome of the case. The former client must show that, without your failed performance, the result of the proceeding would have been different. In rare instances, prejudice will be presumed. Examples of presumed prejudice include situations when you as counsel were not present at the trial, when the government interferes with your assistance by denying access to information, or when you were representing conflicting interests during the representation.

B.   MAINTAINING COMPETENCE

New lawyers become competent before becoming experienced. Law school has trained you to think about issues and analyze facts and legal precedent. You may enhance your competence by working with experienced lawyers to develop specific skills like drafting or examining witnesses. You also may become more competent by associating with a more experienced lawyer from outside your law firm, usually with your client's consent.

Becoming competent includes remaining competent, as for example by involvement in continuing legal education [CLE]. Your duty of competence includes the duty to attend CLE courses. More than forty states have mandatory CLE requirements, and lawyers who fail to comply with those standards are disciplined. Rule 1.1, Comment 6.

C. EXERCISING DILIGENCE AND CARE

When you represent a client, you must act with reasonable diligence. Diligence includes a vigorous lawful and ethical commitment to accomplish your client's objectives "despite opposition, obstruction, or personal inconvenience" to you. Your duty "does not require the use of offensive tactics or preclude the treating of all persons involved in the legal process with courtesy and respect." Rule 1.3, Comment 1. Your client cannot waive the duty of diligence that you owe to her.

Reasonable diligence requires that you assess the work that needs to be done on her behalf and to exercise reasonable promptness in completing that work. A statute of limitation, a rule of procedure, or your client's schedule may affect your timetable for completing your work. Delays happen in law practice. You may agree "to a reasonable request for a postponement that will not prejudice" your client. Rule 1.3, Comment 3. You are subject to legal discipline for neglect only when there is a pattern of action or inaction. Your heavy workload does not excuse your neglect of the cases for which you have assumed responsibility.

Lawyers who represent indigent defendants often have excessive caseloads which adversely affect their duties of diligence and competence. You must control your workload to avoid impairment of the obligations you owe to your existing clients. ABA Formal Opinion 06–441. Likewise, if your workload begins to affect those duties, you must find assistance or reduce your workload. If your supervisor fails to provide relief for you, you should move up the chain of command within your organization and then seek relief from the court with jurisdiction over the case. If no one can offer relief, you must continue to represent your clients to the best of your ability.

D. CIVIL LIABILITY TO CLIENTS, INCLUD-ING MALPRACTICE

Suppose that you are not diligent in your representation. You may be subject to discipline for having performed your legal work incompetently or negligently. In addition, you may be liable for monetary damages to a former client or to a nonclient for malpractice committed by you or your employee. Even if you have already been disciplined by your state bar association for incompetence, you are not automatically liable for malpractice. The finding of an ethics violation against you, however, is likely to be viewed as relevant to your malpractice liability.

Several legal theories may be the basis of a malpractice allegation against you: (1) breach of contract, for violating your agreement with your client to use you skill to protect her interests, (2) breach of fiduciary duty, for having violated your duties of loyalty, confidentiality, and honesty, (3) intentional tort liability for claims such as fraud, abuse of process, or conversion, and (4) unintentional tort liability for negligence in violating your duty of care toward your client. Negligence is the most common civil claim brought by former clients against their lawyers. Because former clients frequently bring legal malpractice claims, many lawyers carry legal malpractice insurance.

Under the tort of negligence, you may be liable for either a single instance of neglect or a pattern of negligent activities. To recover damages for malpractice, your former client must prove that (1) you owed her a duty of care, see Section A, above, (2) you breached that duty, (3) the breach caused injury to her in the form of damages, and (4) without your negligence she would have been more successful in the underlying matter. You owe a duty of care to any person who reasonably believes that you represent her. The standard of care you owe is a level of diligence and competence to be exercised by a reasonable lawyer in similar circumstances. Restatement, § 52. You do not commit malpractice when you exercise your judgment to make strategic decisions such as deciding which witnesses will testify at trial. If you hold yourself out to the public as a specialist, you may be held to a higher standard of care.

If your former client can prove that you negligently practiced her case, she can recover a monetary amount representing the difference between the outcome of her case with your representation and the outcome she would have realized without your negligence. She also may be able to recover the fees she had paid to you as well as the fees she is paying to your replacement. Your former client must also prove that without your negligence, she would have been more successful. In other words, she must show that your negligence caused a less favorable result and that the original case otherwise would have ended more favorably. In criminal cases, many courts require the defendant to establish his factual innocence to win a malpractice verdict.

Although you generally do not owe a duty of care to nonclients, your mistake on behalf of a client may harm a nonclient. You do owe a duty of care to the nonclient as well as to your client, if your work for a client is intended to provide an advantage to a nonclient, as when the nonclient is the beneficiary of a will you wrote for a client. Or, if your client is a trustee, you owe a duty of care to the beneficiary of the trust.

E.   LIMITING LIABILITY FOR MALPRACTICE

Generally, clients cannot prospectively waive the duty of competence owed to them. Rule 1.2, Comment 5. You cannot ask your client to agree to your incompetent representation. You *may* make an agreement with her that prospectively limits your liability to her for malpractice, but only if she is independently represented by counsel. Rule 1.8(h)(1). For example, a corporation with its own lawyer to hire outside lawyers to represent the corporation may choose to waive malpractice liability claims against the outside lawyers. The Rule allows a corporation to control its legal costs.

Limited liability companies (LLC) or limited liability partnerships (LLP) purport to shield lawyers from vicarious liability for the malpractice of other lawyers in the firm. If you are a lawyer in such a company or partnership recognized by the law to have that purpose, you may limit your imputed liability for your colleagues' malpractice. ABA Formal Opinion 96–401. Your law firm, though, must still comply with the duty to supervise subordinate lawyers and nonlawyers in the organization.

Arbitration agreements, which provide a different forum to determine lawyer-client disputes, address remedy issues and therefore do not conflict with Rule 1.8(h). ABA Formal Opinion 02–425 requires that your client (1) be advised about the advantages and disadvantages of arbitration, such as waiver of jury trial and waiver of appeal, (2) give informed consent, and (3) not be prevented from suing you which she has a right to pursue under existing law. Under those circumstances, you may include an arbitration clause in a fee agreement without violating your fiduciary duties.

If your disgruntled client is pursuing a malpractice claim against you and is not represented by counsel, Rule 1.8(h) requires that you advise her in writing to seek independent representation before settling a malpractice claim against you. You must give her a reasonable opportunity to obtain such advice.

LAWYER–CLIENT RELATIONSHIP BASICS CHECKLIST

A. **Competence**

   1. You are a competent lawyer if you have "the legal knowledge, skill, thoroughness and preparation reasonably necessary for the representation."

      a. Your skills must include the ability to research, write, advocate, and negotiate.

      b. You may take a type of case with which you are unfamiliar.

      c. Competence is a function of what is reasonable under the circumstances.

2. General claims of ineffective assistance of counsel under the Sixth Amendment are controlled by ***Strickland v. Washington***, 466 U.S. 668 (1984).

    a. The defendant must show that his lawyer's acts or omissions were "outside the wide range of professionally competent assistance."

    b. The defendant must also show that ineffectiveness caused "actual prejudice."

B. **Maintaining Competence**

1. Becoming competent includes remaining competent, such as complying with CLE requirements.

2. Lawyers must control their workload to avoid impairment of the obligations you owe to your existing clients.

C. **Exercising Diligence and Care**

1. You must act with reasonable diligence.

    a. Your duty to your client includes a lawful and ethical commitment to accomplish her objectives "despite opposition, obstruction, or personal inconvenience" to you.

    b. Your client cannot waive the duty of diligence that you owe to her.

2. Reasonable diligence requires that you assess the work that needs to be done on her behalf and to exercise reasonable promptness in completing that work.

D. **Civil Liability to Clients, Including Malpractice**.

1. You may be subject to discipline for having performed your legal work incompetently or negligently, and you may be liable for monetary damages to a former client or to a nonclient for malpractice committed by you or your employee.

2. In a professional malpractice claim based on negligence, your former client must prove that:

    a. You owed her a duty of care, and breached that duty.

    b.   The breach caused injury to your client in the form of damages.

    c.   Without your negligence, your client would have been more successful in the underlying matter.

E. **Limiting Liability for Malpractice**.

    a.   You can make an agreement with your client that prospectively limits your liability to her for malpractice if she is independently represented by counsel.

    b.   Limited liability companies (LLC) or limited liability partnerships (LLP) shield lawyers from vicarious liability for the malpractice of other lawyers in the firm.

ILLUSTRATIVE PROBLEM

After passing the state bar examination, Bill Bigelow recently began a solo practice in a shopping mall office on the edge of a large city. Because of the need to pay his monthly rent, Bill felt increasing pressure to represent lots of shoppers who would visit his office for legal advice at very low rates. Bill could not afford to buy books for his law library or subscribe to an online data base, and the county law library was twenty miles away with daytime hours only. After three slow months of law practice, Bill worries so much about his economic situation that he is not prepared for his court appearances and fails to prepare documents he has promised to clients upon their return to his office. Does Bill have an ethical problem?

Analysis

Bill has competence and diligence problems. Competence under Rule 1.1 requires thoroughness and preparation. His economic or other worries cannot affect his preparation to perform the legal services requested by his clients. Even if his cases do not require specialized skill, he still had a duty to prepare reasonably for his court appearances. A lawyer can prepare for court appearance or other legal tasks by having a law library for research or by seeking the advice of another lawyer.

Diligence under Rule 1.3 requires Bill to be prompt in meeting deadlines for or on behalf of his clients. When Bill promises to handle a matter for a client, he must complete it. Just as Bill's reputation with the local courts will suffer when he fails to prepare for his court appearances, his clients will not have a high regard for him if he cannot keep the obligations he incurred to his clients to prepare documents or perform other tasks.

POINTS TO REMEMBER

- You are a competent lawyer if you have "the legal knowledge, skill, thoroughness and preparation reasonably necessary for the representation." Rule 1.1.

    - Your skills must include the ability to research, write, advocate, and negotiate.

    - Competence is a function of what is reasonable under the circumstances.

- General claims of ineffective assistance of counsel under the Sixth Amendment require a showing that his lawyer's acts or omissions were "outside the wide range of professionally competent assistance" and that the ineffectiveness caused "actual prejudice." *Strickland v. Washington*, 466 U.S. 668 (1984).

- Your duty of diligence includes a lawful and ethical commitment to accomplish your client's objectives "despite opposition, obstruction, or personal inconvenience" to you.

- In a professional malpractice case based on your negligence, your former client must prove that you owed her a duty of care, that you breached that duty, and that the breach caused injury to her in the form of damages.

- You may limit your liability for malpractice if your client is independently represented by counsel.

*

CHAPTER 6

Litigation and Other Forms of Advocacy

A. MERITORIOUS CLAIMS

When you are the advocate for you client, you may present any nonfrivolous interpretation of the law that favors her. You cannot present frivolous claims, defenses, or motions. Rule 3.1. You do not have to make a complete factual or legal investigation before asserting a claim, defense, or motion, but you are acting frivolously when you knowingly put forth a position unsupported by the facts and the law. (You also cannot present frivolous discovery requests, under Rule 3.4(a), discussed later in this Chapter.) Any good faith argument for extending, modifying, or reversing existing law is permitted. While the line between frivolous and nonfrivolous advocacy may be difficult to identify, courts generally try not to chill lawsuits based on novel legal theories.

A court's inherent powers provide methods to deal with frivolous advocacy. For example, 28 U.S.C. § 1927 prohibits a lawyer in federal court from unduly multiplying proceedings "unreasonably and vexatiously." Courts also have the inherent power to hold lawyers in contempt to control lawyer advocacy.

The procedural rules also determine the level of necessary factual investigation and legal research. FRCP 11 provides that every pleading and motion must be signed by a lawyer. That signature certifies that it is well grounded in fact and is warranted by existing law or a good faith argument to extend, modify or reverse existing law, and that it is not filed for an improper purpose. The court may sanction the party or her lawyer for violating Rule 11. Rule 11 also provides a safe harbor so that if a challenged position is withdrawn or corrected, sanctions will not be sought. Deterrence is the rationale for the Federal Rule.

The fact that a lawsuit or a motion is unsuccessful does not mean that it is frivolous. In *BE & K Construction Co. v. National Labor Relations Board*, 536 U.S. 516 (2002), the Court defined sham litigation as subjectively brought with a bad motive and "objectively baseless." If a litigant's "purpose is to stop conduct that he reasonably believes is illegal, petitioning is genuine both objectively and subjectively." *Id.* at 534.

If you assert a frivolous position, you may be sued for damages in tort for abuse of process or for malicious prosecution. Abuse of process occurs when a person uses the legal process to accomplish a purpose for which it was not designed. Proof of malicious prosecution requires that you brought a civil case: (1) without probable cause to pursue your client's civil remedy, (2) with a primary purpose other than the proper resolution of the claim, and (3) which ended in your favor.

In criminal cases, both prosecutors and defense counsel have special duties. The prosecutor's obligation is not to bring charges if she knows that they are not supported by probable cause. Rule 3.8(a). For defense counsel, advocating your client's position so as to put the prosecution to its burden of proof is not frivolous advocacy. Your duty is to ensure that the prosecutor proves every element of the case against your client, even if you choose not to advance any legal or factual defenses. On appeal, you have a duty to file a brief explaining that there are no nonfrivolous grounds for appeal. *Anders v. California*, 386 U.S. 738 (1967).

B.   EXPEDITING LITIGATION

You must make "reasonable efforts to expedite litigation" that are "consistent with the interests of the client." Rule 3.2. "The question is whether a competent lawyer acting in good faith would regard the course of action as having some substantial purpose other than delay. Realizing financial or other benefit from otherwise improper delay in litigation is not a legitimate interest of the client." Rule 3.2, Comment. It is not proper for you to routinely fail to expedite litigation solely for *your* convenience. Rule 3.2, Comment. If delay may harm your client's interests, you should inform your client about your need for that delay.

C.   CANDOR TOWARD THE TRIBUNAL

The duty of candor to a tribunal first requires defining a "tribunal," which is any legal body or entity acting in an adjudicative capacity. Rule 1.0(m). An arbitration is a tribunal but a mediation where a person tries to encourage the parties to reach an agreement is not. The duty of candor also applies outside the courtroom and beyond adjudicative contexts. It applies also to any "ancillary proceeding conducted pursuant to the tribunal's adjudicative authority, such as a deposition." Rule 3.3, Comment 1. It also applies to nonadjudicative proceedings, per Rule 3.9.

Statements of law and disclosure of adverse authority. You cannot knowingly make a false statement of law to a tribunal, in a filed document or in open court. If you happen to make a false statement which you discover was false, you must correct it if it was a materially false statement. Rule 3.3(a)(1). A tribunal has to be able to trust what you say. You cannot manipulate quotations from cases to make them appear more favorable.

You also have a duty to voluntarily disclose to the tribunal any legal authority in the controlling jurisdiction that you know is directly adverse to your client's position and which your adversary has not disclosed. Rule 3.3(a)(2). A case directly on point from an adjacent state does not have to be disclosed. Because you must be aware of the adverse legal authority before you can be disciplined, the Rule does not punish the inept researcher. A competent researcher must ask whether any judicial decision that "opposing counsel has overlooked [is] one which the court should clearly consider in deciding the case". ABA Formal Opinion 280 (1949). A good advocate will distinguish any case precedent, argue that it should be overruled, or challenge the soundness of the precedent's reasoning. As with any of the duties under Rule 3.3(a)–(b), your duty extends to the conclusion of the proceedings, "even if compliance requires disclosure of information otherwise protected by" the Rules on confidentiality. Rule 3.3(c).

Statements of fact. As with statements of law, you cannot make false statements of fact to a tribunal, and you must correct any statement of fact that you learn was both false and material to the proceeding. Rule 3.3(a)(1). While you do not testify to a tribunal, any factual assertions to the tribunal ("my client is ill") must be based on your knowledge that you know is true or believe to be true on the basis of a reasonably diligent inquiry. Rule 3.3, Comment 3. The "failure to make a disclosure is the equivalent of an affirmative misrepresentation." Rule 3.3, Comment 3.

Offering evidence to a tribunal. There is no constitutional right for a party to lie or for you to assist in that perjury. *Nix v. Whiteside*, 475 U.S. 157 (1986). You must not offer evidence that you know is false. Rule 3.3(a)(3). As an officer of the court, you cannot participate in misleading the court even when your client insists. (If other law requires you to keep silent or permits your client to present false testimony through a narrative approach, that law supersedes the MRPC. Rule 3.3, Comment 7.)

If your client tells you that she fabricated a document or found a witness who will testify falsely, your duty of candor requires that you not use the document or call that witness. You *may*, on the other hand, offer evidence showing that the opposing party has contradicted herself. Rule 3.3, Comment 5. If you reasonably believe but do not "know" that a piece of evidence is false, you may refuse to offer it. Thus, you may refuse to call your client as a witness, although in criminal cases she has a constitutional right to testify (but not falsely). If your client nevertheless wants you to present the evidence, either you or she may prefer to terminate the lawyer-client relationship. For cases already before a tribunal, you or your client must obtain the court's permission to withdraw as counsel. Rule 1.16(a).

If you learn before the conclusion of the proceedings that a piece of "material evidence" you offered was false when admitted, you must take reasonable remedial measures. Rule 3.3(a)(3). Your first attempt should be to convince your client or the witness to correct the false evidence. If your efforts are not successful, you must consider withdrawing from the representation. Your duty to take reasonable remedial measures supersedes any duty of confidentiality to your client under Rule 1.6. If withdrawal is not possible or if it will not reverse the effect of the false evidence, you must disclose the false information to the tribunal which then must decide how to proceed—to inform the factfinder, to declare a mistrial, or to do nothing. Rule 3.3, Comment 10. If your client disputes the perjury allegation, you cannot represent her any longer because you will be a witness with a view of the facts contrary to hers. If you learn that your client intends to engage or has engaged in fraudulent or criminal conduct such as bribery or intimidation of a witness, juror, or court official, you must take reasonable remedial measures, including disclosure to the court. Rule 3.3(b).

Your duty lasts until the conclusion of the proceedings. In a criminal case, the duty applies until an acquittal has occurred. In either a criminal or civil case, the proceedings conclude when "a final judgment . . . has been affirmed on appeal or the time for review has passed." Rule 3.3, Comment 13.

In preparation for trial, you may interview witnesses and prepare them for their testimony. However, you cannot suggest to a client or a witness that she testify falsely. Rule 3.4(b). Even if your suggestion does not amount to suborning perjury, your ethical responsibilities preclude you from coaching your client or witness to testify falsely.

Candor in an *ex parte* proceeding. In an *ex parte* proceeding, you must disclose *all* material facts, adverse or otherwise, and all applicable law to the tribunal so that it can make an informed decision. Rule 3.3(d). Your increased duty of disclosure is necessary to offset the absence of an adversary position presented by the other side. Rule 3.3, Comment 14. An example of an *ex part* proceeding would be an application to a court for a temporary restraining order.

D. FAIRNESS TO OPPOSING PARTY AND COUNSEL

You cannot unlawfully obstruct access to, alter, or conceal evidence or witnesses, and you cannot encourage a witness to testify falsely. Rule 3.4(a)–(b). If your client asks you to take possession of physical evidence of a crime, you may do so for a reasonable amount of time in order to look at it. However, you must not alter or destroy it, *and* after you have had the opportunity to examine the evidence, you must either return it to the site where it was or notify the prosecutor that you have the evidence. Restatement, § 119.

While you cannot pay a witness for the content of her testimony, you may pay a non-expert witness reasonable compensation for her loss of time in preparing or attending a trial or deposition in order to testify. ABA Formal Opinion 96–402. You have to decide the value of your witness's time. In criminal cases, a prosecutor's offer of immunity or a reduced sentence in return for testimony is regarded as a method of seeking truthful testimony rather than an improper incentive to testify under Rule 3.4(b).

You cannot disobey the rules of a tribunal, which include the court's local rules. However, you may disobey them by an open refusal based on your advocacy that no valid obligation exists to comply with the rule, e.g., by asking the court's permission to violate its order of document disclosure because the documents are privileged. Rule 3.4(c). The MRPC further forbid unlawful methods to disobey a court's order which disrupts a court proceeding. Rule 3.5(d).

You may advise your client and certain nonclients not to volunteer any information to the opponent, without obstructing the opponent's ability to gather evidence. Rule 3.4(a). As to your client, for example, you want to review documents before turning them over in order to avoid accidental waivers of privileged information. For nonclients, you may request that an unrepresented nonclient refuse to volunteer information *if* she is your client's relative, employee or agent and her interests will not be adversely affected if your request is honored. Rule 3.4(f).

Under Rule 3.4(d), you cannot make a frivolous discovery request, which is probably evaluated by the Rule 3.1 standards about what is frivolous. In addition, under Rule 3.4(d) you must make a reasonably diligent effort to comply with a legally proper pretrial discovery request by an opposing party.

During trial, you may allude only to matters that you reasonably believe are relevant or admissible. For example, you cannot ask a clearly prohibited question. You cannot assert your personal opinion or personal knowledge about the facts, as by asserting that a witness is lying, unless you are testifying as a witness. Rule 3.4(e).

Mary Carter agreements. A forbidden "Mary Carter" agreement exists if a defendant secretly settles with a plaintiff and the settling defendant retains a financial stake in the plaintiff's recovery while not withdrawing from the trial as a defendant. *Booth v. Mary Carter Paint Co.*, 202 So.2d 8 (Fla.App. 1967). The agreement is that the secretly settling defendant's maximum liability is fixed, and that the payment she must make to the plaintiff will be reduced proportionately by the liability of the non-settling defendant. If the defendant stays in the case, she will receive money in the form of a reduced settlement obligation based on the content of her testimony, i.e., by shifting the blame to the other defendant. These agreements violate the MRPC prohibition on offering a witness an inducement to testify falsely, because once the defendant settles, she is testifying as a non-party witness. Rule 3.4(b).

E. IMPROPER CONTACTS WITH JUDGE, JURORS AND OTHER OFFICIALS

You cannot attempt to influence a judge, juror, prospective juror, or other official by illegal means such as bribery. Rule 3.5(a). Similarly, there cannot be *ex parte* communications with these people during the proceedings, unless a law or court order specifically permits it, e.g., *ex parte* communications with a judge for scheduling purposes. Rule 3.5(b). After the jury is discharged, you also cannot communicate with them if (1) the law prohibits such contact, (2) the court orders no contact, (3) the jurors request no contact, or (4) the communication involves "misrepresentation, coercion, duress or harassment." Rule 3.5(c).

F. TRIAL PUBLICITY

The MRPC forbid any communications by you that "will have a substantial likelihood of materially prejudicing an adjudicative proceeding in the matter." Rule 3.6(a). Anything you say about a witness's identity, her likely testimony, her credibility or prior criminal record, her pretrial statements or the absence of such statements, or your opinion about her guilt are examples of potentially prejudicial statements. The perspective for examining that standard is from the view of the reasonable lawyer making the statement, rather than the reasonable person. The statement in question must be one which you know or reasonably should know will be publicly disseminated, due to its possible influence on the fact-finder. Your statement may be less prejudicial if the fact-finder is a judge instead of a jury.

Despite the foregoing standard, you may make certain extra-judicial statements: information in a public record, a request for assistance in obtaining evidence, a warning of the danger about an individual if there is reason to believe such danger exists, scheduling or steps in the litigation, general scope of the investigation, and the identities of the accused as well as that of the arresting and investigating officers. Rule 3.6(b). You also may make statements that a reasonable lawyer would believe is required to protect a client from the "substantial undue prejudicial effect of recent publicity not initiated by" you or your client. Such statements must be limited to information that is necessary to mitigate that adverse publicity. Rule 3.6(c).

In addition to the restrictions on you as a participating counsel, anyone associated with you in a firm or governmental agency is likewise prohibited from making such statements. Rule 3.6(d). As a prosecutor, you must "exercise reasonable care" to prevent persons associated with you such as law enforcement personnel from making improper extrajudicial statements even if those persons are not under your direct supervision. Rule 3.8, Comment 6.

G.   LAWYER AS WITNESS

The MRPC addressing your conflicting roles as lawyer and witness are concerned about confusing the factfinder. One moment, you are acting as an advocate and in the next moment you are a witness. "It may not be clear whether a statement by an advocate-witness should be taken as proof or as an analysis of the proof." Rule 3.7, Comment 2. There is no provision for consent by your client or the opposing party.

Your ethical obligation is to withdraw as counsel if you are "likely to be called as a necessary witness." You are a "necessary" witness if your testimony is not cumulative of other information and it is unobtainable elsewhere. If another witness can testify about the same factual information, you are not "likely" to be a necessary witness and you would not have to withdraw. Even if you are a necessary witness, you have no duty to withdraw if (1) your testimony relates to an uncontested issue (e.g., factual information about dates and times), (2) your testimony relates to the nature and value of your legal services in that case, or (3) your withdrawal would work a "substantial hardship on" your client. Rule 3.7(a)(1)–(3). The latter exception may apply if you have superior knowledge about your client due to your prolonged involvement.

If you have to withdraw, you may consult with your substitute counsel and assist in trial preparation. The Rule does not impute the prohibition about your testimony to those with whom you practice, probably because factfinder confusion would no longer be a problem. Your law partner who would ask you the questions at trial, though, could have a conflict of interest issue if your testimony is against your client's interests. Rules 1.7, 3.7(b).

LITIGATION AND OTHER FORMS OF ADVOCACY CHECKLIST

A. **Meritorious Claims**

1. When a client consults you to be her advocate, you may present any nonfrivolous interpretation of the law that favors her.
    a. You cannot present frivolous claims, defenses, or motions.
    b. You cannot present frivolous discovery requests or fail to make a reasonably diligent effort to comply with discovery requests.
    c. A good faith argument for extending, modifying, or reversing existing law is permitted.
2. A court's inherent powers and its procedural rules also provide methods to deal with frivolous advocacy.
    a. Courts have the inherent power to hold lawyers in contempt to control lawyer advocacy.
    b. FRCP 11 provides that every pleading and motion must be signed by a lawyer. Her signature certifies that it is well grounded in fact and is warranted by existing law or a good faith argument to extend, modify or reverse existing law, and that it is not filed for an improper purpose.
3. The fact that a lawsuit or a motion is unsuccessful does not mean that it is frivolous.
4. In criminal cases, both prosecutors and defense counsel have special duties.
    a. The prosecutor's obligation is not to bring charges if she knows that they are not supported by probable cause.
    b. For defense counsel, advocating your client's position so as to put the prosecution to its burden of proof is not frivolous advocacy.

B. Expediting Litigation

1. You must make "reasonable efforts to expedite litigation" that are "consistent with the interests of the client."

2. If delay may harm your client's interests, you should inform your client about your need for that delay.

C. Candor to the Tribunal

1. You cannot knowingly make a false statement of law to a tribunal, in a filed document or in open court. You have a duty to voluntarily disclose to the tribunal any legal authority in the controlling jurisdiction that you know is directly adverse to your client's position and which your adversary has not disclosed.

2. As with statements of law, you cannot make false statements of fact to a tribunal, and you must correct any statement of fact that you learn was both false and material to the proceeding.

3. There is no constitutional right for a party to lie or for you to assist in that perjury. *Nix v. Whiteside*, 475 U.S. 157 (1986).

4. You must not offer evidence that you know is false, even when your client insists.

5. If you learn before the conclusion of the proceedings that a piece of evidence you offered was false when admitted, you must take reasonable remedial measures.

    a. Your first attempt should be to convince your client or the witness to correct the false evidence.

    b. If your efforts are not successful, you must consider withdrawing from the representation.

    c. If withdrawal is not possible or if it will not reverse the effect of the false evidence, you must disclose the information to the tribunal which then must decide how to proceed.

6. If you learn that your client intends to engage or has engaged in fraud or bribery, you must take reasonable remedial measures, including disclosure to the court.

7. In an *ex parte* proceeding, you must disclose *all* material facts, adverse or otherwise, to the tribunal so that it can make an informed decision.

D. Fairness to Opposing Party and Counsel

1. You cannot unlawfully obstruct access to, alter, or conceal evidence or witnesses, and you cannot encourage a witness to testify falsely.

    a. If your client asks you to take possession of physical evidence of a crime, you may do so for a reasonable amount of time in order to look at it.

    b. However, you must not alter or destroy it, and after you have had the opportunity to examine the evidence, you must either return it to the site where it was or notify the prosecutor that you have the evidence.

2. You cannot disobey the rules of a tribunal, which include the court's local rules.

3. During trial, you may allude only to matters that you reasonably believe are relevant or admissible, e.g., asking a clearly prohibited question.

4. In closing argument, you cannot assert your personal opinion or knowledge about the facts, e.g., a witness is lying, unless you are testifying as a witness.

5. You may advise your client and certain nonclients not to volunteer any information to the opponent, without obstructing the opponent's ability to gather evidence.

    a. As to your client, for example, you want to be able to review documents before turning them over in order to avoid accidental waivers of privileged information.

    b. For nonclients, you may request that an unrepresented nonclient refuse to volunteer information if she is your client's relative, employee or agent and her interests will not be adversely affected if your request is honored.

6. A forbidden "Mary Carter" agreement exists if a defendant secretly settles with a plaintiff and the settling defendant retains a financial stake in the plaintiff's recovery while not withdrawing from the trial as a defendant. ***Booth v. Mary Carter Paint Co.***, 202 So.2d 8 (Fla.App. 1967).

E. **Improper Contact with Judge, Jurors and Other Officials**

1. You cannot attempt to influence a judge, juror, prospective juror, or other official by illegal means such as bribery.

2. There cannot be improper *ex parte* communications with jurors or prospective jurors during the proceedings.

F. **Trial Publicity**

1. The general standard is to restrict speech that "will have a substantial likelihood of materially prejudicing an adjudicative proceeding in the matter."

    a. The perspective for examining that standard is from the view of the reasonable lawyer making the statement, rather than the reasonable person.

    b. The statement in question must be one reasonably likely to affect the outcome of the proceeding.

2. You may make certain extrajudicial statements: information in a public record, a request for assistance in obtaining evidence, a warning of the danger about an individual if there is reason to such danger exists, scheduling or steps in the litigation, general scope of the investigation, and identities of the accused as well as that of the arresting and investigating officers.

3. You also may make statements that a reasonable lawyer would believe is required to protect your client from the "substantial undue prejudicial effect of recent publicity not initiated by" you or your client. Such statements must be limited to information that is necessary to mitigate that adverse publicity.

4. In addition to the restrictions imposed on you as a participating counsel, anyone associated with you in a firm or governmental agency is likewise prohibited from making such statements.

G. **Lawyer as Witness**

1. If you will be testifying in a case where you are counsel of record, you must withdraw as counsel, subject to several exceptions.

2. Exceptions
   a. The testimony relates to an uncontested issue,
   b. The testimony relates to the nature and value of the lawyer's legal services in that case, or
   c. Withdrawal would work a "substantial hardship on" the client.

3. No imputed disqualification applies to the disqualified lawyer's law firm.

ILLUSTRATIVE PROBLEMS

■ PROBLEM 6.1 LAWYER'S DUTY AS AN ADVOCATE ■

Arthur Kirkland represents plaintiffs in civil litigation. At a pretrial conference conducted prior to the settlement of a client's case, Arthur was opposing a summary judgment motion filed by the opposing party. In preparing to oppose the summary judgment motion, Arthur found several cases with dicta directly against his client's legal position but did not disclose the cases to the court or opposing counsel. Also, in preparing to oppose the same summary judgment motion, Arthur realizes that his client testified in his deposition about a fact important to the case that Arthur knows is false.

Analysis

Under Rule 3.3(a)(2), an attorney must "disclose to the tribunal legal authority in the controlling jurisdiction known to the lawyer to be directly adverse to the position of the client and not disclosed by opposing counsel." Although you believe that the language in the case is dicta, a court may disagree and believe instead that it is important to consider in deciding the case. Arthur should have disclosed the cases to the court either in his response to the opponent's summary judgment motion or no later than his oral argument at the pretrial conference. However, Arthur does not have to elaborate on the adverse implications of the cases for his client, and he instead may argue that the adverse cases were decided incorrectly or are distinguishable on their facts.

If a lawyer learns before the conclusion of the proceedings that a piece of evidence he offered was false when admitted, he must take reasonable remedial measures. Rule 3.3(a)(3). Although a deposition is not conducted in open court, it is part of a judicial proceeding. Because Arthur realizes that the Jones's deposition testimony concerned an important fact, he must take "reasonable remedial measures" such as trying to persuade Jones to tell the truth. If Jones is unwilling to tell the truth, Arthur must disclose the nature and extent of Jones's misleading testimony to the court.

■ PROBLEM 6.2 LAWYER'S DUTY AS AN ADVOCATE ■

Stanley Kussy filed a negligence action against the Minutia Delivery Corp. for injuries sustained in a collision between Kussy's client's auto and Minutia's delivery truck. During pretrial discovery, Minutia's counsel properly seeks information about the plaintiff's medical experts who would testify about the plaintiff's physical injuries sustained in the collision.

Kussy responds to the defendant's interrogatories that he has retained Dr. Cecil Doan, who will testify about the nature and extent of the plaintiff's physical injuries. He includes Dr. Doan's opinions and the reasons for those expert conclusions. Upon receiving those answers from Kussy, Minutia's counsel has the court clerk issue a subpoena for Dr. Doan's deposition. Although Dr.

Doan is properly served with the subpoena, he fails to appear for the scheduled deposition. Minutia immediately moves to have Dr. Doan held in contempt for his failure to appear.

Dr. Doan appears at a hearing to show cause why he should not be held in contempt, and testified as follows: he met Kussy at a party in Kussy's neighborhood, with Kussy telling Doan about the instant case that is set for trial next year. Dr. Doan denied (and brought along a credible corroborating witness) that he ever was retained as an expert witness by Kussy because he never received any money from Kussy. Further, he never agreed to testify for Kussy and he never expressed any opinion about Kussy's client's injuries. After hearing this testimony, should the trial judge refer Stanley Kussy to the State Bar Association for possible charges of unethical conduct?

Analysis

Rule 3.3(a)(1) prohibits an attorney from knowingly making a false statement of fact to a tribunal. In his interrogatory answer, Kussy stated that Dr. Doan would be testifying for his client at trial. Dr. Doan and a corroborating witness clearly testify that Dr. Doan never agreed to serve as an expert witness for Kussy.

Under Rule 3.4(c), an attorney shall not knowingly "disobey an obligation under the rules of a tribunal." If the jurisdiction has a rule which requires a litigant to answer interrogatories fairly and not falsely or in a manner calculated to mislead, Kussy failed to obey this rule's requirement to provide truthful disclosures when he signed the interrogatory response knowing that it falsely stated that Dr. Doan would be an expert witness in the case.

Under Rule 3.4(d), an attorney must make a reasonably diligent effort to comply with a legally proper discovery request by an opposing party. When counsel for Minutia sent an interrogatory to Kussy seeking information about expert witnesses for trial, Kussy had an obligation to comply with that request. Instead, the hearing testimony established that Kussy failed to make a diligent effort to determine if Dr. Doan had agreed to be his expert, as well as a failure to make diligent efforts to determine the content of Dr. Doan's purported testimony if he *were* called as Kussy's expert witness.

■ PROBLEM 6.3 LAWYER AS WITNESS ■

A lawsuit was filed recently by First Bank against Sims, in which Smith and Jones represents the plaintiff. The suit alleges that prior to leaving the bank's employ in 2007, Sims made fraudulent loans to himself through several fictitious accounts. Bill Travis, who is now an associate attorney at Smith and Jones and is assigned as counsel in *First Bank v. Sims*, worked at First Bank as a loan officer assigned to Sims's loan area. He worked on "one or two" of Sims's personal accounts. Can the firm be disqualified from representing First Bank by virtue of Bill Travis's testimony as a witness in *First Bank v. Sims*?

Analysis

In order for a lawyer to be disqualified when he will be a witness, he also must be acting as an advocate in the case. Travis is prohibited from acting as an advocate *and* witness. Because Travis likely will be a witness in the case, he will be disqualified under Rule 3.7.

The Rules also deal with the imputed disqualification consequences of the lawyer as witness. Even if Travis is a witness under Rule 3.7(a), Smith and Jones still could represent First Bank under Rule 3.7(b) as long as there is no conflict of interest under Rule 1.7 or 1.9. Rule 1.7 does not appear relevant, because it is phrased in the present tense, and Smith and Jones currently do not represent Sims in any matters. Moreover, 1.7(b)'s proscription relating to conflicts involving lawyers' personal interests is not an issue if no Smith and Jones attorney, current or past, has been involved with Sims on his deals, and he was not a "friend of the firm" or a referral source. Rule 1.9 is not relevant here because Travis was not an attorney at the time he worked as a loan officer and therefore was not in a position to have received confidential information from Sims. Thus, Rule 3.7(b) appears to present no ethical problem for the disqualification of the firm of Smith and Jones.

POINTS TO REMEMBER

- On behalf of a client, you cannot present frivolous claims, defenses, or motions, but you can make a good faith argument for extending, modifying or reversing existing law. Rule 3.1.

- You cannot present frivolous discovery requests or fail to make a reasonably diligent effort to comply with discovery requests. Rules 3.4(a), (d).

- When you seek an *ex parte* order from a tribunal, you must disclose both all applicable law and all material facts that you reasonably believe are necessary for the tribunal to make an informed decision. Rule 3.3(d).

- You cannot knowingly make a false statement of law to a tribunal, in a filed document or in open court. If you make false statement which you discover was false, you must correct it if it was a materially false statement. Rule 3.3(a)(1).

- You have a duty to voluntarily disclose to the tribunal any legal authority in the controlling jurisdiction that you know is directly adverse to your client's position and which your adversary has not disclosed. Rule 3.3(a)(2).

- There is no constitutional right for a party to lie or for you to assist in that perjury, *Nix v. Whiteside*, 475 U.S. 157 (1986), even when your client insists.

- If you learn before the conclusion of the proceedings that a piece of evidence you offered was false when admitted, you must take reasonable remedial measures: try to convince your client to correct it, consider withdrawal, or disclose the information to the tribunal. Rule 3.3(a)(3).

- You cannot unlawfully obstruct access to, alter, or conceal evidence or witnesses, and you cannot encourage a witness to testify falsely. Rule 3.4(a)–(b).

- During trial, you may allude only to matters that you reasonably believe are relevant or admissible, e.g., asking a clearly prohibited question. In closing argument you cannot assert your personal opinion or knowledge about the facts. Rule 3.4(e).

- There cannot be improper *ex parte* communications with jurors or prospective jurors during the proceedings. Rule 3.5(b).

- Extrajudicial speech is restricted when it "will have a substantial likelihood of materially prejudicing an adjudicative proceeding in the matter." Rule 3.6(a). The perspective for examining that standard is from the view of the reasonable lawyer making the statement, rather than the reasonable person.

- You may make statements that a reasonable lawyer would believe is required to protect your client from the "substantial undue prejudicial effect of recent publicity not initiated by" you or your client. Rule 3.6(c).

- If you will be testifying in a case where you are counsel of record, you must withdraw as counsel, subject to several exceptions: the testimony relates to an uncontested issue, the testimony relates to the nature and value of the lawyer's legal services in that case, and withdrawal would work a "substantial hardship on" the client.

*

CHAPTER 7

Communications With Non-Clients

A. TRUTHFULNESS IN STATEMENTS TO OTHERS

While you represent a client in either a litigation or a nonlitigation setting, you cannot knowingly "make a false statement of material law or fact to a third person." Rule 4.1(a). The Rule does not impose an obligation to volunteer relevant information to the opposition, but it is subject to procedural standards like discovery rules which require disclosure. When you do communicate with the opposition, your statements cannot be misleading or half-truths.

Your statements also cannot pass along false information provided by others if you know it is false. Rule 4.1, Comment 1. Your knowledge about the falsity of statements may come from your client, other people, or documents in your possession. If you are uncertain about the falsity of a statement, you do not violate Rule 4.1, but your negligence in making the statement may expose you to civil liability to the third person. Rule 4.1(a) applies to statements of material fact, not to opinions.

Unless prohibited by the Rule on confidentiality, you cannot knowingly fail to disclose a material fact to a third person when such disclosure is necessary to avoid assisting a criminal or fraudulent act by your client. Rule 4.1(b). Disclosure of material facts under Rule 4.1(b) is mandatory. When combined with Rule 4.1(b), the permissive disclosure provisions of Rules 1.6(b)(2)–(3) (discussed in Chapter 3) become mandatory provisions. Thus, disclosure to third persons is mandatory for financial crimes likely to cause substantial injury. If you fail to make the disclosure, you are participating in the fraud or crime by your client.

If you realize that your client is committing a crime or fraud against another person, you must inform her that you cannot participate further. Rule 1.2(d). If the fraud or crime is ongoing and you have provided legal services connected with the crime or fraud, you must withdraw if your client refuses to change her conduct, Rule 1.16(a), informing the opposing party of your withdrawal and disaffirming any false documents.

B. COMMUNICATIONS WITH REPRESENTED PERSONS

If you represent a client and you know that another person is represented by her own lawyer, you cannot communicate with that person about that matter, unless the other lawyer consents or the contact is authorized by law or court order. Per Rule 4.2, the represented person does not have to be a party or be adverse to your client, and the Rule applies even when the represented person first contacts you.

The Rule refers to communications relating only to the matter in which the person is represented. You can communicate with her about an unrelated topic without following the Rule's requirements. The rationale for the Rule is to prevent you from unduly influencing the other person. Your knowledge that another person is represented by counsel "may be inferred from the circumstances." Rule 4.2, Comment 8.

ABA Formal Opinion 06–443 addresses in-house counsel issues related to Rule 4.2. If an entity has outside counsel in a matter, the Rule does not prevent you from contacting the entity's in-house counsel about the subject of the representation. But the Rule does apply if either in-house counsel has her own independent lawyer in the matter, or if in-house counsel is a party in the matter regardless of whether she has separate counsel.

Statutes, regulations, constitutional provisions and judicial precedent may override the operation of Rule 4.2. Rule 4.2, Comment 4. Most courts regard Rule 4.2 as inapplicable to certain undercover operations like pre-indictment communications with represented parties, because those contacts are "authorized by law." The First Amendment right to petition the government for redress of grievances is another example of "other law" that modifies Rule 4.2. For example, if your client sues the government, you may contact government officials without going through the government lawyer. However, you must give the governmental lawyer notice of your intent to communicate with the officials so that she can discuss the planned contact. ABA Formal Opinion 97–408.

In criminal cases, Rule 4.2 does not apply in grand jury proceedings when prosecutors question witnesses outside their counsel's presence and without prior notice to counsel. Prosecutors have tried to avoid Rule 4.2's reach in other parts of their investigations, as when they covertly wire an undercover agent. But federal law now subjects federal prosecutors to the same ethical standards as other lawyers in each state. 28 U.S.C. § 530B.

Rule 4.2 does not prevent you from advising your client to contact the opposing party. Rule 4.2, Comment 1. Although you cannot direct your employee to contact a person known to have a lawyer, per Rule 8.4(a), you have a duty to your client to advise her that she can communicate with the adverse party. ABA Formal Opinion 92–362. While Rule 4.2 prevents you from contacting current employees of the opposing party, it is inapplicable to contacts with *former* employees of the opposing party. ABA Formal Opinion 91–359; Rule 4.2, Comment 7.

C. COMMUNICATIONS WITH UNREPRE-SENTED PERSONS

If a person has no lawyer, on behalf of your client you cannot state or imply that you are disinterested. Rule 4.3. If she misunderstands your role as a lawyer for someone else, you must make reasonable efforts to correct her misunderstanding. Otherwise, you do not have to disclose that you represent a client. You should not provide legal advice to an unrepresented person if you know or reasonably should know that the interests of your client and the unrepresented person have a "reasonable possibility of being in conflict." Rule 4.3. "Whether a lawyer is giving impermissible advice may depend on the experience and sophistication of the unrepresented person." Rule 4.3, Comment 2.

If you represent a defendant, you cannot contact putative members of an opposing class before the class has been certified. Until the class is certified, "putative class members are not represented parties" unless they employ separate counsel, in which case Rule 4.2 applies. ABA Formal Opinion 07–445.

D.   RESPECT FOR RIGHTS OF THIRD PERSONS

In representing a client, you cannot use means that serve no substantial purpose other than to "embarrass, delay, or burden a third person. . . . " Rule 4.4(a). Suppose you threaten to file a disciplinary complaint against opposing counsel to gain an advantage in a case or you agree not to report an ethical violation by that lawyer if a satisfactory settlement is made. Rule 8.3 requires that you report another lawyer's violation of the Rules, making it improper for you to threaten to report her but then agree not to report her if she agrees to a satisfactory settlement. Your conduct violates Rule 4.4 and may be prejudicial to the administration of justice. ABA Formal Opinion 94–383.

You also cannot use "methods of obtaining evidence that violate the legal rights of" another person. Rule 4.4(a). You cannot violate the law in order to obtain evidence or information for your client. The well-known example relates to a lawyer surreptitiously tape recording a conversation without the knowledge of the other party to the conversation. ABA Formal Opinion 01–422 stated that it was not longer inherently misleading under the MRPC for a lawyer to secretly record a conversation. However, such a secretive recording would violate the MRPC if it also violated the law where it occurred.

If you receive a document relating to a representation and you know or reasonably should know that the document was delivered to you inadvertently, you must inform the sender promptly. Rule 4.4(b). The same obligation applies when you receive a document that the sender may have obtained illegally. Either you or the sender thereafter may file motions in court and leave it to the judge to decide what should happen next. The Rule is inapplicable to documents sent intentionally. ABA Formal Opinion 06–442.

COMMUNICATIONS WITH NON—CLIENTS CHECKLIST

A. **Truthfulness in Statements to Others**

1. While representing a client in a litigation or a nonlitigation setting, you cannot knowingly "make a false statement of material law or fact to a third person."

    a. Your statements cannot pass along false information provided by others if you know that it is false.

    b. Rule 4.1(a) applies to statements of material fact, not to opinions.

2. Unless prohibited by Rule 1.6 on confidentiality, you cannot knowingly fail to disclose a material fact to a third person when such disclosure is necessary to avoid assisting a criminal or fraudulent act by your client.

    a. If you realize that your client is committing a crime or fraud against another person, you must inform her that you cannot participate further.

b. If the fraud or crime is ongoing and you have provided legal services connected with the crime of fraud, you must withdraw if your client refuses to change her conduct, informing the opposing party of your withdrawal as well as disaffirming any false documents.

B. Communications with Represented Persons

1. If you represent a client and you know that another person is represented by her own lawyer, you cannot communicate with that person about that matter, unless the other lawyer consents or the contact is authorized by law or court order.

   a. Statutes, regulations, constitutional provisions and judicial precedent may override the operation of Rule 4.2.

   b. The First Amendment right to petition the government for redress of grievances is an example of "other law" that overrides Rule 4.2. If your client sues the government, you may contact government officials without going through the government lawyer.

2. Rule 4.2 does not prevent you from advising your client to contact the opposing party.

3. Contacts with current and former employees of other persons. While the Rule 4.2 standard prevents you from contacting current employees of the opposing party, it is inapplicable to contacts with its former employees.

C. Communications with Unrepresented Persons

1. If a person has no lawyer, on behalf of your client you cannot state or imply that you are disinterested.

2. Ordinarily, you should not provide legal advice to an unrepresented person if you know or reasonably should know that the interests of your client and the unrepresented person have a "reasonable possibility of being in conflict."

D. **Respect for Rights of Third Persons**

    1. In representing a client, you must not use means that serve no substantial purpose other than to "embarrass, delay, or burden a third person."

    2. If you obtain evidence or information for your client, you cannot violate the law.

        a. You may secretly record a conversation as long as does not violate the law where it occurred.

        b. If you receive a document relating to a representation and you know or reasonably should know that the document was delivered to you inadvertently, you must inform the sender promptly.

ILLUSTRATIVE PROBLEM

Paula Prosecutor investigated possible criminal wrongdoing by Danny Defendant for over a year. Finally, she decided to indict him for one count of armed robbery and postpone action on any other charges. After a jury trial, Danny was acquitted, thanked his attorney Lawrence L. Lawyer for his help on the case, and told him that if he ever needed legal help, Lawrence would be his choice. Having overheard that conversation, Paula contacted Danny the next day to "discuss" other criminal offenses possibly committed by him. Was it proper for Paula to contact Danny?

Analysis

From the facts, it appears that the lawyer-client relationship between Danny and Lawrence ended after Danny's acquittal. Rule 4.2 requires a lawyer to obtain the consent of a person's lawyer if she knows that the person is represented by another lawyer in the matter. If, based on the conversation she heard, Paula had no reason to believe that Lawrence continued to represent Danny, there was no reason for her to comply with Rule 4.2. Because she did not think that Danny any longer had a lawyer "in the matter" (which arguably was broader than the one armed robbery charge and included the array of possible charges that Paula initially was considering against Danny), there was no reason for her to obtain the consent of Lawrence or any other lawyer before speaking to Danny on the day after the acquittal.

Even if Danny no longer employs a lawyer, Paula may have acted improperly under Rule 4.3. When Paula contacted Danny after the trial, even if she knew that he no longer had a lawyer to represent him, she could "not state or imply" that she was disinterested. After the acquittal she likely is interested in bringing other charges against him, although she previously indicted him for only one crime after considering other offenses. In her post-trial discussion with Danny, she must not indicate that she is disinterested. Rule 4.3 requires that Paula not give Danny any legal advice "other than the advice to secure counsel" when she knows that she is interested in possibly bringing additional criminal charges against Danny.

POINTS TO REMEMBER

- While you represent a client in a litigation or a nonlitigation setting, you cannot knowingly "make a false statement of material law or fact to a third person." Rule 4.1(a). The Rule applies to statements of material fact, not to opinions.

- Unless prohibited by the Rule on confidentiality, you must disclose a material fact to a third person in order to avoid assisting a criminal or fraudulent act by your client. Rule 4.1(b).

- If you represent a client and you know that another person is represented by her own lawyer, you cannot communicate with that person about that matter, unless the other lawyer consents or the contact is authorized by law or court order. Rule 4.2.

- You should not provide legal advice to an unrepresented person if you know or reasonably should know that the interests of your client and the unrepresented person have a "reasonable possibility of being in conflict." Rule 4.3.

- In representing a client, you must not use means that serve no substantial purpose other than to "embarrass, delay, or burden a third person. . . . " Rule 4.4(a).

CHAPTER 8

Different Roles
of the Lawyer

A. LAWYER AS ADVISOR

In your role as an advisor, you must exercise your independent professional judgment to give your client your realistic opinion about both what a court is likely to do in her case and the practical effects of the ruling. The exercise of your independent professional judgment refers to the advice to your client, free of biases created by other interests or parties. You also have a duty to tell your litigation clients about "forms of dispute resolution that might constitute reasonable alternatives to litigation." Rule 2.1, Comment 5. On the other hand, if your client tells you to confine your advice to legal matters or not to offer unsolicited advice, you should comply unless her inexperience suggests that you should say more to her. Rule 2.1, Comments 3 and 5.

The MRPC distinguish between your roles as advisor and as an evaluator. If your client asks you to conduct a title search for the benefit of the prospective buyer of a piece of property, you are an evaluator (per Rule 2.3) if your opinion is given to the buyer or is made public, but you are an advisor (per Rule 2.1) if your opinion is offered exclusively for the use of your client. Restatement, § 95.

B. LAWYER AS EVALUATOR

Your client may ask you to investigate a situation for or about her and report your findings to her or to a third party in a form known as an opinion letter. In this role of an evaluator, while your duty of loyalty is to your client, you also may have assumed obligations to third parties who will rely on your evaluation. If you give a negligent opinion that results in damage to the third party recipient of your opinion, the recipient can sue you even though she was not your client when you wrote the opinion letter.

The MRPC place several restrictions on your role as an evaluator. First, you must reasonably believe that doing the evaluation is compatible with other aspects of the lawyer-client relationship you have with her. Rule 2.3(a). Second, you first must obtain your client's informed consent if you know "or reasonably should know that the evaluation is likely to affect the client's interests materially and adversely." Rule 2.3(b). Your disclosure to her must include information about the effect of evaluating a matter for disclosure to a non-client. If the evaluation already is contemplated by your representation of the client and there is no significant risk of injury to her, you do not have to obtain her express consent to do the evaluation.

Your client may limit the scope of the evaluation that you do for a third party, such as excluding certain issues from the evaluation or setting deadlines for its completion. Whatever limits she imposes should be disclosed to the third party to avoid your evaluation from being misleading, and so the third party can decide whether to rely on the evaluation. Disclosure of the evaluation to a third party necessarily removes client confidentiality for information found in the evaluation. Other information, however, that relates to the evaluation but is not included in the evaluation remains confidential under Rule 1.6. Rule 2.3(c). To disclose such confidential information to the third party requires that you obtain your client's informed consent.

C. LAWYER AS NEGOTIATOR

As a litigator, you may negotiate a settlement of your client's case and avoid a trial. In nonlitigation situations such as real estate or business transactions, you also will negotiate. The MRPC prohibit you from making false statements of material fact but you do not have a duty to do any research for the other side of the litigation or transaction or to volunteer factual information that could weaken your client's position. Rule 4.1(a)

During a negotiation, you may exaggerate about facts and values. ABA Formal Opinion 06–439. If you state that your client will not settle for less than a certain amount when you know that is not true, your client's intentions "as to an acceptable settlement of a claim" are not considered to be a material fact. Rule 4.1, Comment 2. While posturing may be acceptable between counsel, a comparable statement to a judge during pretrial negotiations would violate Rule 4.1. ABA Formal Opinion 93–370.

D. LAWYER AS ARBITRATOR, MEDIATOR, OR OTHER THIRD–PARTY NEUTRAL

A third-party neutral does not represent either party to a dispute, but is seeking to promote the resolution of that dispute through the use of alternative dispute resolution (ADR) proceedings. Arbitrators and mediators are examples of third-party neutrals under the MRPC. The role of a lawyer who is a third-party neutral depends on the process "selected by the parties or mandated by the court." Rule 2.4, Comment 1. If you act as a third-party neutral, you must disclose to unrepresented parties that you are not representing them to remove potential confusion about your role. Rule 2.4(b). You must explain the differences between your role as a third-party neutral and your role when you represent a client. The disclosure is comparable to your duties when you represent a client against a party who has no counsel, although the third-party neutral is not acting in a representational capacity.

While you are serving as a third-party neutral, you cannot discuss future employment with either a party or lawyer representing a party in the matter. Rule 1.12(b). A party to that proceeding may ask you to represent her in a future proceeding related to the proceeding of the ADR process. You cannot represent a party in the same matter in which you "participated personally and substantially" as a third-party neutral, unless all of the parties to that proceeding give their informed consent, confirmed in writing. Rule 1.12(a). However, that Rule is inapplicable to you if you served as a lawyer-neutral on a multi-member arbitration panel. 1.12(d) would allow you to represent one of the litigants later in the same matter.

When you are disqualified from later representing one of the parties due to your prior status as a third-party neutral, no one in your law firm can represent any of the parties either, unless (1) you are screened in a timely manner from later representation in the matter, (2) you receive no part of the fee from the later representation, and (3) the parties and "any appropriate tribunal" receive notice in writing about the screen so that they can decide whether the first two requirements are being followed. Rule 1.12(c).

E. SPECIAL PROSECUTORIAL RESPONSIBILITIES

The MRPC refer to prosecutors as "ministers of justice." Rule 3.8, Comment 1. Prosecutors must provide defendants with a reasonable opportunity to obtain counsel by informing them of their right to have their own counsel. Rule 3.8(b). If the accused elects to proceed *pro se*, a prosecutor must negotiate directly with her, but she cannot urge an unrepresented person to waive important pretrial rights such as the right to a preliminary hearing. Rule 3.8(c).

Another ethical duty for a prosecutor is the obligation to make a "timely disclosure" to the defendant of exculpatory evidence, i.e., evidence that "tends to negate the guilt of the accused or mitigate the punishment." Rule 3.8(d). Such evidence includes information which is related to guilt or innocence, as well as impeachment evidence. This ethical duty is similar to the prosecutor's constitutional duty to disclose exculpatory evidence established in *Brady v. Maryland*, 373 U.S. 83 (1963), which requires disclosure of evidence that is favorable to the accused and material to either guilt or punishment.

In the post-conviction context, a prosecutor must promptly disclose to the court and the convicted defendant "new, credible and material evidence creating a reasonable likelihood" that she did not commit a crime for which she was convicted. The prosecutor also must investigate the matter further. Rule 3.8(g). If a prosecutor knows about "clear and convincing evidence" that a convicted defendant did not commit a crime for which she was convicted, the prosecutor must "seek to remedy the conviction," e.g., disclosing facts to the defendant, informing the court. Rule 3.8(h); Rule 3.8, Comment 8. Rules 3.8(g)–(h) are subject to a good faith safe harbor protecting the prosecutor from discipline if her good faith interpretation of the facts turns out to be incorrect. Rule 3.8, Comment 9.

A prosecutor is limited in the circumstances in which you as a lawyer can be subpoenaed. If the prosecutor "reasonably believes" that no privilege applies, the evidence you have is "essential" to the success of her investigation or prosecution, and she has no "feasible alternative" of obtaining the evidence she seeks from you, you can be subpoenaed. Rule 3.8(e).

F. LAWYER APPEARING IN NONADJUDICA-TIVE PROCEEDING

If you appear before a policy-making entity like a legislative committee or government agency to testify, you must disclose whether you are there in a representative capacity. Rule 3.9. (Your other duties in appearing before such nonadjudicative proceedings are found in Rule 3.3(a)–(c), Rule 3.4(a)–(c), and Rule 3.5.) Of course, you must obey the rules of the entity before which you are appearing. Rule 3.9, Comment 1.

When you know that the interests of your client may be significantly benefitted by a law reform decision in which you participate, such as testifying, you must disclose that fact to the committee or agency, even though you do not have to identify your client. Rule 6.4, Comment 1. The purpose of the disclosure is to preclude any suspicion that you are using improper influence to promote your client's interests. Thus, if you represent a private client and at the same time you are lobbying for a legal reform group by testifying before a legislative committee in support of the same issue as your private representation, you must disclose the fact of your representation to the legislative committee.

G. LAWYER REPRESENTING AN ENTITY OR OTHER ORGANIZATION

1. The Scope of Rule 1.13

When you are employed or retained by an entity as in-house counsel or outside counsel, you represent that entity acting through its agents. Rule 1.13(a). An entity includes corporations, unions, trade associations, general and limited partnerships, and government agencies. If someone associated with the entity misunderstands your role in representing the entity, it is your duty to clarify that misunderstanding. Rule 1.13(f). Toward that goal, you should not give legal advice to one of the entity's employees or agents. The result of giving such advice may be that you appear to the employee to be representing conflicting interests. No Rule prohibits such dual representation, but you must be sure to obtain informed consent from both "clients."

If you are in-house counsel, you have only one client. That fact reduces conflicts of interest because in-house lawyers usually do not encounter potential conflicts with other current and future clients. Because you have only one client, it is economically more difficult to terminate the relationship because you receive all of your compensation from the entity. As in-house counsel, you typically have a lot more information about your client than outside counsel as a result of your access to business and legal information, as well as informal sources of information. When you deal with officers or employees of the entity, you must explain to them that you represent the entity rather than any of them. Rule 1.13(g).

Outside lawyers have many clients, which creates the potential for conflicts of interest among those multiple clients. Although outside counsel has the same ethical obligations as you in the role of in-house counsel, you should probably seek the advice of the outside counsel when you are uncertain about some issue.

2. Protecting the Entity Client Under the Rules

Part of your responsibility in representing an entity is to act in its best interests. Rule 1.13(b) describes how you determine what the entity wants to do, how high up the corporate ladder you are required to go, and what happens when you reach the top of the ladder and you are still unsatisfied.

You have a special duty to protect the entity when you know that someone affiliated with your entity client is acting in a manner that is likely to directly or indirectly cause substantial harm to the client. This duty exists because organizational clients can act only through their duly authorized (but non-client) representatives such as managers. You must monitor those decisions when they threaten substantial injury to an entity client.

If a lawyer for an organization knows that an officer, employee or other person associated with the organization is engaged in action, intends to act or refuses to act in a matter related to the representation that is a violation of a legal obligation to the organization, or a violation of law which reasonably might be imputed to the organization, and that is likely to result in substantial injury to the organization, then the lawyer shall proceed as is reasonably necessary in the best interest of the organization.

Rule 1.13(b). Examples of a "legal obligation" to the entity include the failure to follow entity procedures, theft of entity property or opportunities, and damage to entity interests. Examples of a "violation of law" that others may reasonably impute to the entity include many the federal and state disclosure laws that permit government agencies to regulate corporate behavior.

The major source of injury for an entity is its financial interests. Because the focus of the ethical standard is on conduct likely to result in substantial injury to the entity, you are not required to be a whistle-blower for minor irregularities. You must act in a manner that is reasonably necessary in the entity's best interests. Rule 1.13(b).

Rule 1.13(b) refers to your duty to act when the misconduct is related "to a matter related to the representation." Your duty is a function of the breadth of the representation. If you represent the entity in a narrow context, your duty arises for what officers or others do that is related to that context and not to more general contexts. When you are general counsel or you do all of an entity's legal work, you always have a duty to prevent harm to the entity. You may conclude that it is necessary only to speak to a person and inform her about your position regarding the person's wrongful conduct. If the person refuses to follow your advice, you must refer the issue to a higher authority in the entity, including the highest authority like a Board of Directors that legally can act on behalf of the entity.

Your first duty is to exhaust the entity's internal remedies and seek assistance of those in the chain of authority who can influence the decision of the person who is acting contrary to the best interests of the entity. How best to proceed up the chain of command depends on the motives of the people involved, the seriousness of the violation, and the manner in which the entity has treated such issues in the past. Rule 1.13, Comments 4 & 5.

If your efforts to go up the chain of authority fail, you can reveal information to persons outside the entity if you still "reasonably believe that the violation is reasonably certain to result in substantial injury to the organization." Rule 1.13(c)(2). The Rule does not specify to whom you should reveal that information. Your disclosure must be confined to information necessary to prevent substantial injury to the entity, and disclosure may be made regardless of whether the Rule 1.6 confidentiality standard permits disclosure to protect the entity. Because of corporate frauds like Enron, your entity client receive less protection from disclosure of confidential information than non-entity clients receive. The entity's confidentiality was discussed in Chapter 3 on confidentiality.

Your obligation to exhaust the aforementioned internal remedies and to make permissive disclosures do not apply when the entity hires you specifically to investigate or defend it against legal wrongdoing. Rule 1.13(d). If you are fired or have withdrawn from representing the entity while performing your duties under Rule 1.13, you must attempt to contact the entity's highest authority who can act on behalf of the entity to assure that it knows that you were fired or forced to withdraw. Rule 1.13(e).

Rule 1.13 is not the only ethical or legal standard addressing crimes and frauds. Under the MRPC, you may be permitted or required to disclose fraud in litigation before a tribunal. Rule 3.3. Besides litigation, you may disclose when your client uses your services to perpetuate a fraud or crime likely to result in substantial financial harm to another person, Rule 1.6(b)(2), or to rectify or mitigate a past crime. Rule 1.6(b)(3). Disclosure is mandatory when you are directly involved in a client fraud against a third person. Rule 4.1. Finally, federal and state laws, such as the Sarbanes–Oxley Act, may apply in addition to Rule 1.13.

3. Model Rules v. SEC Regulations

In the wake of the Enron scandals during which thousands of people saw the value of their pensions disappear, the Sarbanes–Oxley Act required the Securities and Exchange Commission [SEC] to create regulations governing the professional responsibility of lawyers who represent corporations which issue publicly-traded securities. Those regulations are found in 17 CFR Part 205, which addresses a lawyer's duty to act in matters before the SEC.

Most of the Regulations impose broader duties on the lawyer involved in an SEC matter than Rule 1.13 requires of the lawyer for the entity. Unlike Rule 1.13(b), which applies to all lawyers representing an entity, the SEC Regulations apply only to people "appearing and practicing" before it and includes people who give securities advice. The lawyer's duties under Rule 1.13 must relate to the representation of the entity. Under the SEC Regulations, after a lawyer appears and practices before the SEC, she must follow the Sarbanes–Oxley Act procedures regardless of whether what she knows relates to the representation of her client.

While Rule 1.13 requires reporting of a violation that is likely to cause substantial injury to the entity, the broader SEC Regulations require the lawyer to report any "material violation" of federal or state (securities) law regardless of potential harm to the entity. Rule 1.13(b) requires the lawyer to "know" someone is engaged in wrongdoing before being required to report that person, but the SEC Regulation is triggered when the lawyer merely "becomes aware" of evidence of a material violation of law, even though it will be difficult for the lawyer to evaluate the risk to the entity.

The lawyer's reporting duties under the SEC Regulations are more specific than the Rule 1.13 standards. The lawyer must report a problem to the entity's chief legal officer who then must investigate the problem. Next, unless the reporting lawyer is told that there is no problem or that steps are being taken to prevent its recurrence, that lawyer must report the problem to the entity's audit committee or a different regulatory compliance committee set up by the entity. If the reporting lawyer receives inappropriate responses, she must explain that to the chief legal officer. If she is fired for reporting the problem, she may notify the entity's Board or the compliance committee about her termination and its reason. Thereafter, she may disclose the entity's conduct to the SEC to prevent or rectify conduct "likely to cause substantial injury to the financial interest of property of the issuer or investors." If the lawyer who learns the information works under the supervision of another lawyer, she may report the problem to her supervisor, who then must proceed through the aforementioned steps. None of the reporting requirements applies to a lawyer who has been retained by the entity to investigate wrongdoing that is reported by someone else.

4.   Representing Other Entities

Representing the entity and one or more constituents. When you represent an entity and you have a relationship with the entity's employees, you should explain and clarify the identity of your client if it appears that the entity's interests are adverse to those employees. Rule 1.13(f). If there is informed consent, you may represent both the entity and one or more of its officers or employees as long as someone "other than the individual who is to be represented" provides the entity's consent. Rule 1.13(g).

Representing partnerships and trade associations. Rule 1.13 applies to unincorporated associations, including partnerships. Rule 1.13, Comment 2. When you represent a partnership, generally you represent the entity rather than the individual partners. ABA Formal Opinion 91–361. In deciding whether you represent individual partners, relevant factors include whether you led the partner into believing that you represented her as an individual partner, whether she was individually represented when the partnership was formed, and whether evidence shows that the partner relied on you as her private counsel. The same rules do not apply to limited partnerships.

Rule 1.13 treats a trade association as an entity, meaning that you represent the trade association and not its members. However, a court may treat you as if you represent both the association and the individual member. *Westinghouse Electric Corp. v. Kerr–McGee Corp.*, 580 F.2d 1311 (7th Cir. 1978).

Representing related corporations. Suppose that your law firm represents Entity A, which asks you to file suit against Entity Z. Entity Z is not your client, but Entity Y is and Entity Z is a wholly owned subsidiary of Entity Y. May your law firm sue Entity Z at the same time it represents its wholly owned parent entity on an unrelated matter? ABA Formal Opinion 95–390 concluded that the MRPC do not prohibit a law firm from representing a party adverse to an entity merely because the law firm represents an affiliated entity in an unrelated matter. A "lawyer who has no reason to know that his potential adversary is an affiliate of his client will not necessarily violate Rule 1.7 by accepting the new representation without his client's consent." Relevant considerations are whether the subsidiary and parent are in effect operated as one entity, whether there is a prior agreement about treating the corporate family as the client, and whether your obligations to the parent will materially limit pursuit of a claim against the subsidiary corporation.

Representing government entities at the same time as private clients. Rule 1.13 treats the government as an organization, and the duties defined in Rule 1.13 apply to governmental organizations. Rule 1.13, Comment 9. Representing a governmental entity while representing an adverse private client in another case is analogous to the situation where you represent a subsidiary of a corporate entity. Under Rule 1.7(a)(1), for example, if you currently represent the school board, you cannot represent a private client against the school board even in an unrelated matter. If you represent the school board, you also may not be able to represent that private client against a different governmental entity in that jurisdiction. ABA Formal Opinion 97–405.

 ## DIFFERENT ROLES OF THE LAWYER CHECKLIST

A. **Lawyer as Advisor**

    1. You must give your client your realistic opinion about what a court is likely to do in her case, as well as the practical effects of the court's ruling.

    2. You are an evaluator if your opinion is given to the buyer or is made public but you are an advisor if your opinion is offered exclusively for the use of your client.

B. **Lawyer as Evaluator**

    1. You may exercise the role of an evaluator, even though it creates duties to non-clients.

    2. Disclosure of the evaluation to a third party necessarily removes client confidentiality for information found in the evaluation.

C. **Lawyer as Negotiator**

    1. The MRPC prohibit you from making false statements of material fact but you do not have a duty to do any research for the other side of the litigation or transaction or to volunteer factual information that could weaken your client's position.

    2. During a negotiation, you may exaggerate about facts and values.

D. **Lawyer as Arbitrator, Mediator, or Other Third–Party Neutral**

   1. A third-party neutral is an independent person who does not represent either party to a dispute, but who is seeking to promote the resolution of that dispute through the use of alternative dispute resolution (ADR) proceedings. Arbitrators and mediators are examples of third-party neutrals under the MRPC.

   2. A third-party neutral must inform unrepresented parties that he is not representing them.

E. **Special Prosecutorial Responsibilities**

   1. Prosecutors must provide a defendant with a reasonable opportunity to obtain counsel by informing her of their right to have her own counsel.

   2. A prosecutor cannot urge an unrepresented person to waive important pretrial rights.

   3. A prosecutor has an obligation to disclose to the defendant exculpatory evidence, i.e., evidence that "tends to negate the guilt of the accused or mitigate the punishment."

F. **Advocate in Nonadjudicative Proceedings.** If you appear before a policy-making entity like a legislative committee to testify, you must disclose whether you are there in a representative capacity.

G. **Lawyer Representing an Entity or Other Organization**

   1. When you are employed or retained by an entity as in-house counsel or outside counsel, you represent that entity acting thru its agents.

   2. Protecting the Entity Client under the Rules

      a. Potentially Substantial Harm to Entity

         1. You have a special duty to protect the entity when you know that someone affiliated with your entity client is acting in a manner that is likely to directly or indirectly cause substantial harm to the client.

         2. Your first duty is to exhaust the entity's internal remedies and seek assis-

tance of those in the chain of authority who can influence the decision of the person who is acting contrary to the best interests of the entity.

b. Scope of Disclosure

   1. If your efforts to go up the chain of authority fail, you can reveal information to persons outside the entity if you still "reasonably believe that the violation is reasonably certain to result in substantial injury to the organization."

   2. Your obligation to exhaust the aforementioned internal remedies and to make permissive disclosures do not apply when the entity hires you specifically to investigate or defend it against legal wrongdoing.

3. **Model Rules v. SEC Regulations**.

   a. SEC regulatory duties are broader than under the MRPC. Unlike the MRPC, the SEC Regulations apply only to people "appearing and practicing" before it and includes people who give securities advice.

      1. While the MRPC requires reporting of a violation that is likely to cause substantial injury to the entity, the SEC Regulations require the lawyer to report any "material violation" of federal or state law regardless of potential harm to the entity.

      2. The MRPC requires the lawyer to "know" someone is engaged in wrongdoing before being required to report that person, but the SEC Regulation is triggered when the

lawyer merely "becomes aware" of evidence of a material violation of law.

b. Lawyers' reporting duties under SEC regulations are more specific

    1. The lawyer must report a problem to the entity's chief legal officer who then must investigate the problem, and the lawyer must report the problem to the entity's audit committee.

    2. If the reporting lawyer is fired for reporting the problem, she may notify the entity's Board or the compliance committee about her termination and its reason.

4. Representing Other Entities

a. Representing Entities in Different Contexts

    1. When you represent a partnership, generally you represent the entity rather than the individual partners.

    2. The MRPC treats a trade association as an entity, meaning that you represent the trade association and not its members.

b. Concurrent Representation with Private Clients.

    1. If there is informed consent, you may represent both the entity and one or more of its officers or employees as long as someone "other than the individual who is to be represented, or the shareholders" provides the entity's consent.

    2. Where you represent a governmental entity while representing an adverse private client in another case is

analogous to the situation where you represent a subsidiary of a corporate entity.

1. Under Rule 1.7(a)(1), if you currently represent a governmental entity, you cannot represent a private client against the entity, even in an unrelated matter.

2. If you represent the entity, you may not be able to represent that private client against a different part of the governmental entity in that jurisdiction.

ILLUSTRATIVE PROBLEM

Continental Towing Company is the nation's largest operator of towboats. It also has a small manufacturing plant. A large Spanish corporation has been trying to acquire Continental. Very few people at Continental know about the acquisition possibility and the corporate CEO has instructed those few (including Maris, the General Counsel) not to tell anyone about it. The takeover almost certainly would result in the Spanish company selling off most of Continental's operations business with nothing remaining of the current Continental business but the small manufacturing entity. Jordan is the Associate General Counsel for Continental and seeks your advice. Last week, Continental's outside counsel told her that Maris and he were promoting the takeover by the Spanish corporation so that they could begin their own towing operation. Does Jordan have an ethical obligation to disclose her knowledge about the General Counsel's conduct and intent, and, if so, to whom?

Analysis

A lawyer for an entity represents the entity, and has an ethical obligation to act on her knowledge about an entity's agent's activities which are likely to result in substantial injury to the entity.

Rule 1.13(a) requires an lawyer representing an entity to under-stand that the entity, acting through its officers and others, is the client. When the lawyer knows that an agent of the entity has acted or intends to act in a manner which is likely to result in substantial injury to the entity, Rule 1.13 states that the lawyer shall proceed to act in a way which appears reasonably necessary to be in the best interest of the entity. Here, Jordan represents Continental Towing as the Associate General Counsel. She has knowledge about the General Counsel's intentions relating to the acquisition. Her aware-ness suggests that it is reasonably necessary to act in the best interest of the entity and speak to the CEO.

According to Rule 1.13(b), once Jordan knows about the likelihood of substantial injury to the entity by its agent, her possible actions include: 1) talking to the person whose conduct has produced the ethical dilemma, and urging him to reconsider its likely consequences for the entity; or 2) referring the matter to a higher authority in the organization, including referral to the highest internal authority such as a Chief Executive Officer. To speak directly to the General Counsel here appears futile, given her awareness of his previous conduct in trying to promote his own interest at the risk of harming the entity. The General Counsel may discharge Jordan immediately for her knowledge about his activi-ties and/or her questioning of his authority. Speaking first to the CEO may yield the same result in getting Jordan fired. If the CEO does not address Jordan's concerns, she may address the entity's highest authority, probably the Board of Directors, in an effort to protect the interests of the entity.

If despite her best efforts to comply with Rule 1.13(b), Jordan believes that the CEO and the Board are not addressing her concerns about the entity, Rule 1.13(c) permits her as lawyer for the entity to reveal information relating to the acquisition concerns if she reasonably believes that disclosure is necessary to prevent substantial injury to the entity.

POINTS TO REMEMBER
- You may exercise the role of an evaluator, even though it creates duties to non-clients. Disclosure of the evaluation to a

third party necessarily removes client confidentiality for information found in the evaluation.

- During negotiations, you cannot make false statements of material fact but you do not have a duty to do any research for the other side of the litigation or transaction or to volunteer factual information that could weaken your client's position. You may exaggerate about facts and values.

- A third-party neutral like an arbitrator must inform unrepresented parties that she does not represent them.

- A prosecutor must disclose to the defendant exculpatory evidence, i.e., evidence that "tends to negate the guilt of the accused or mitigate the punishment." Rule 3.8(d).

- If you appear before a policy-making entity like a legislative committee to testify, you must disclose whether you are there in a representative capacity. Rule 3.9.

- When you are employed or retained by an entity as in-house counsel or outside counsel, you represent that entity acting through its agents.

- You have a special duty to protect the entity when you know that someone affiliated with your entity client is acting in a manner that is likely to directly or indirectly cause substantial harm to the client.

- Your first duty is to exhaust the entity's internal remedies and seek assistance of those in the chain of authority who can influence the decision of the person who is acting contrary to the best interests of the entity.

- If your efforts to go up the chain of authority fail, you can reveal information to persons outside the entity if you still "reasonably believe that the violation is reasonably certain to result in substantial injury to the organization."

- While Rule 1.13 requires reporting of a violation that is likely to cause substantial injury to the entity, SEC Regulations require the lawyer to report any "material violation" of federal or state law regardless of potential harm to the entity.

- The lawyer must report a problem to the entity's chief legal officer who then must investigate the problem. The lawyer must report the problem to the entity's audit committee.

- If the reporting lawyer is fired for reporting the problem, she may notify the entity's Board or the compliance committee about her termination and its reason.

- When you represent a partnership, generally you represent the entity rather than the individual partners.

- If there is informed consent, you may represent both the entity and one or more of its officers or employees as long as someone "other than the individual who is to be represented, or the shareholders" provides the entity's consent. Rule 1.13(g).

- If you currently represent a governmental entity, you cannot represent a private client against the entity, even in an unrelated matter.

*

CHAPTER 9

Safekeeping Property

A. SAFEKEEPING PROPERTY

Keep client property separate. There are various reasons for you to possess your client's property, e.g., an advance fee, a settlement check, personal property which she owes to a third party. The MRPC seek to protect the property of others in your possession and to maintain both the fact and appearance of your honesty. You must keep separate identifiable trust fund accounts of clients' funds and they must not be commingled with your money. Rule 1.15(a). Your duty includes safeguarding legal fees and expenses which have been paid in advance until they have been earned or incurred. Rule 1.15(c). You must take reasonable steps to safeguard your clients' documents as well. Restatement, § 44, Comment b.

In the course of representing a client, you also may receive property such as a deed to property belonging to non-clients. You have a comparable duty to protect their property by placing it into a separate trust account or by keeping it in a safe deposit box and marked with identifying information about the owner. Rule 1.15(a).

Lawyers are disbarred for paying their debts out of client trust fund accounts. The proper procedure is to withdraw funds from the client's account when you are entitled to do so, place it in your account, and then write a check on your account for that amount.

The only time that you can deposit your own money in a client trust fund would be to cover the administrative costs of the account. After you receive funds belonging in a trust fund account, you must promptly notify the client or non-client third party. You also must promptly pay or deliver to the client any trust funds or property to which she is entitled.

With a contingent fee, you must make a written accounting to the client, stating "the outcome of the matter, and if there is a recovery, showing the payment to the client and the method of its determination." Rule 1.5(c). For other fee arrangements, you must provide an accounting upon request by your client. Rule 1.15(d).

You must maintain careful and current records of all client property for a period of years (even after the representation has ended) and provide her with an appropriate accounting. Rule 1.15(a). Only a lawyer admitted to practice law in the jurisdiction has the authority to be a signatory on trust accounts. In addition, withdrawals may be made only by either bank transfers or a check payable to a named payee (not "cash"). ABA Model Rule on Financial Recordkeeping, at B(1), (3).

B. DISPUTES ABOUT TRUST FUND PROPERTY

If you and your client have a dispute about trust fund property, you cannot withdraw the disputed portion of the fee until the dispute is resolved. Rule 1.15(e). For the undisputed portion, you must distribute it promptly. You must not coerce your client to give up her claim by refusing to deliver money that belongs to her. When your client and a third person have a dispute about the ownership of property, you must keep the disputed funds in a separate account.

Protection of client funds and trust fund accounts. The ABA has been active in protecting clients from lawyers' occasional abuse of client trust accounts. The ABA adopted a Model Rule for Payee Notification which requires an insurer, when paying out more than a certain amount of case proceeds to settle a third-party liability claim, to send written notice to the insured that the amount has been delivered to her lawyer or other representative. ABA Model Rule for Payee Notification, § A. Many lawyers include in their fee agreements with clients a provision for all settlement or verdict payments to be made jointly with the proceeds going into a trust account before disbursement. This practice preserves the lawyer's charging lien on the funds, as discussed in Chapter 2.

The ABA recommends that bar discipline counsel have access to all lawyers' trust fund accounts. Bar counsel may verify the accounts' accuracy with "probable cause" that they have not been maintained properly. The ABA also proposes random audits of lawyer trust fund accounts to deter the misuse of money and property. ABA Model Rule for Random Audit of Lawyer Trust Accounts, at § I. The ABA Model Rules for Trust Account Overdraft Notification protect clients from dishonest lawyers by requiring financial institutions maintaining lawyer trust fund accounts to notify lawyer disciplinary agencies of overdrafts.

C.   IOLTA PROGRAMS

Interest earned on client trust accounts does not belong to you; it is the client's private property. *Phillips v. Washington Legal Foundation*, 524 U.S. 156 (1998). Since the 1980s, states have used Interest on Lawyer Trust Accounts [IOLTA] to collect interest from pools of trust fund accounts and fund service projects like indigent legal services. In *Brown v. Legal Foundation*, 538 U.S. 216 (2003), the U.S. Supreme Court held that although the IOLTA program in the state of Washington was a physical taking of client property for a public purpose, the clients suffered no net loss and the program therefore owed no compensation to the clients under the Takings Clause of the Constitution's Fifth Amendment.

SAFEKEEPING PROPERTY CHECKLIST

A.   **Safekeeping Client Property**

   1.   You owe immediate fiduciary duties to a client or a third party who gives property to you as their agent.

       a.   You must keep client funds in a trust account and never commingle them with your personal or business accounts.

       b.   You also must safeguard property other than money. For all client property, you must promptly notify them when you receive it and promptly deliver it, unless you have made other arrangements.

2.   You must maintain "complete records" of all client property for a period of years (even after the representation has ended) and provide your client with an appropriate accounting.

3.   With a contingent fee, there must be a written accounting to the client, stating "the outcome of the matter, and if there is a recovery, showing the remittance to the client and the method of its determination." For other fee arrangements, you must provide an accounting upon request by your client.

B. Disputes About Trust Fund Property

1.   If you and your client have a dispute about trust fund property, you cannot withdraw the disputed portion of the fee until the dispute is resolved.

C. IOLTA Programs

1.   Interest earned on client trust accounts [IOLTA] is the client's private property. *Phillips v. Washington Legal Foundation*, 524 U.S. 156 (1998). Although IOLTA programs are a physical taking of client property for a public purpose, the program owes no compensation to the clients under the Takings Clause of the Fifth Amendment. *Brown v. Legal Foundation*, 538 U.S. 216 (2003).

ILLUSTRATIVE PROBLEM

Connie Jones recently represented a client in a lawsuit to recover a valuable necklace that had been wrongfully converted. The jury awarded Jones's client the necklace as well as $250,000 punitive damages. When Jones and the client earlier signed a fee contract, they agreed that Jones would receive 40% of all punitive damages. The client has told Jones that on a big recovery 40% is unfair. The client has offered to pay Jones 25%. The defendant in the case satisfied the judgment by giving Jones the necklace and a check for $250,000 payable to Jones. She immediately deposited the check in her client trust account and put the necklace around her neck until the fee dispute was resolved. Was it proper for Jones to put the $250,000 check into her trust account? Was it proper for Jones to wear the necklace?

Analysis

Under Rule 1.15, a lawyer can put the cash proceeds belonging to the client in her trust account only for a brief period until payment to the client can be made. The rule requires a lawyer to hold the property of a client that is in her possession in connection with a representation separate from her own property in a separate account. Complete records of those funds must be kept by the attorney. Rule 1.15(c) states that when, as a result of representing a client, a lawyer possesses property in which she and the client both claim interests, the property is to be kept separate by the attorney until there is an accounting and severance of their interests. When a dispute arises about the respective interests of the attorney and the client, the amount in dispute must be kept separate by the attorney until the dispute is resolved.

It was proper for Jones to put the $250,000 check in her trust account but only for a brief period. That account exists for (1) any sum belonging to the client until payment to the client can be made, and (2) any sum that is disputed. The initial deposit in the account was permissible, but the $150,000 (60% of the $250,00 corpus) to which the client was clearly entitled should have been paid the client promptly, and the attorney should have withdrawn her $62,500 which the client conceded was due. $37,500 is in dispute here, and the remainder cannot be held hostage in the dispute. Jones may not withdraw the $37,500, regardless of whether she thinks the client is wrong on the contract.

Under Rules 1.15(a) and (c), Jones must deposit the $250,000 check in her trust account, but must immediately pay the client the undisputed part of the fee. She also must promptly withdrawn her undisputed part of the fee. She cannot withdraw the disputed part of the fee.

Under Rule 1.15, a lawyer who is in possession of property in which a client has an interest must promptly notify the client and deliver the property to the client. Rule 1.15(a) requires a lawyer to hold the property of a client that is in her possession in connection with a representation separate from her own property. Under Rule 1.15(b), when a lawyer receives property in which her client has an interest, she must promptly notify her client. Unless otherwise agreed with the client, the lawyer must promptly deliver the property which the client is entitled to receive to the client.

In this case, non-cash property like the necklace must be safeguarded in a safe deposit box or other secure location. When Jones wore the necklace, she was neither safeguarding it nor returning it to the rightful owner—her client. She was treating the client's property as her own, in effect commingling the client's property with her own. Under Rules 1.15(a) and (b), upon receiving the necklace to which her client is entitled, Jones must immediately notify her client about the necklace and deliver it to the client. She is commingling her client's property with her own if she wears the necklace.

POINTS TO REMEMBER

- You owe immediate fiduciary duties to a client or a third party who gives property to you as their agent.

- You must keep client funds in a trust account and never commingle them with your personal or business accounts. Rule 1.15(a).

- You must safeguard property other than money, by notifying your client when you receive it, by promptly delivering it, and by promptly setting up proper accounting procedures and maintaining them for a period of years.

- With a contingent fee, there must be a written accounting to the client, stating "the outcome of the matter, and if there is a recovery, showing the remittance to the client and the method of its determination." Rule 1.5(c).

- If you and your client have a dispute about trust fund property, you cannot withdraw the disputed portion of the fee until the dispute is resolved. Rule 1.15(e).

- Interest earned on client trust accounts is the client's private property.

*

CHAPTER 10

Advertising and Solicitation

A. ADVERTISING AND OTHER PUBLIC COMMUNICATIONS ABOUT LEGAL SERVICES

1. Supreme Court Decisions About Advertising

In *Bates v. State Bar*, 433 U.S. 350 (1977), the Supreme Court invalidated state limitations on lawyer advertising. Free speech protects truthful newspaper advertising about lawyer availability and fees for "routine" legal services. But states may impose reasonable restrictions on the time, place and manner of lawyer advertising, as well as prohibited false or misleading ads.

Zauderer v. Office of Disciplinary Counsel, 471 U.S. 626 (1985) held that the state cannot discipline a lawyer who solicits business in a newspaper ad that contain nondeceptive illustrations and legal advice. State rules may regulate lawyer disclosures in ads that are reasonably related to the state's interest in preventing consumers from being deceived, not vague, and not unjustified or unduly burdensome. While upholding the state's right to publish nondeceptive ads, a state can discipline a lawyer who fails to include information necessary to make the ad not misleading. The ad stated that no legal fees would be owed "if there is no recovery," but it did not include information that the client might be liable for the costs of an unsuccessful litigation. Such disclosure was reasonably related to the state interest in preventing deceptive ads.

2. The Rules About Advertising

The MRPC have followed a course consistent with *Bates* and *Zauderer*. You cannot make affirmative statements in your ads that misrepresent the law or facts or omissions of fact that result in the statement as a whole being materially misleading. Rule 7.1. For example, you can state or imply that you practice in a law partnership or other organization only if that is true. Rule 7.5(d).

Statements in ads may violate the Rule either because they are false and misleading *or* because though truthful they are not accurate when considered as a whole. A third category of statements may violate Rule 7.1 as misleading "if there is a substantial likelihood that it will lead a reasonable person to formulate a specific conclusion about the lawyer or the lawyer's services for which there is no reasonable foundation." Rule 7.1, Comment 2.

If you advertise your past legal achievements, you may violate the prohibition on misleading statements if the statement leads "a reasonable person to form an unjustified expectation that the same results could be obtained for other clients in similar matters" regardless of the factual and legal circumstances of the case. Rule 7.1, Comment 3. You may include a disclaimer or qualifying language with your ad to eliminate or reduce unjustified expectations by the reader. Although client endorsements may also create such expectations, the Rule allows them as long as they are not false or misleading. If your ad provides an unsubstantiated comparison of your legal services to others, your ad may be misleading if it is "presented with such specificity as would lead a reasonable person to conclude that the comparison can be substantiated." Rule 7.1, Comment 3. Your ad cannot state or imply that you can achieve results for a client by means that violate the MRPC. Rule 8.4(e).

In the context of misleading statements, even in stationery or office nameplates, a former judge may continue to use his judicial title if she no longer practices law. ABA Formal Opinion 95–391. After she no longer practices, there is nothing that creates an unjustified expectation that the judge has special influence. You can refer to yourself as "of counsel" for a law firm on stationery and other communications, as long as there is an ongoing general relationship between you and the firm. If you work on only one case for a firm, your designation as "of counsel" on anything other than the court filings is misleading. ABA Formal Opinion 90–357.

The MRPC permit truthful advertising/communication through any ("written, recorded, or electronic") medium except "in-person solicitation," without regard to the ad's geographic reach. Rule 7.2(a). You must include the name and office address of at least one lawyer or your law firm responsible for the content of any such communication. Rule 7.2(c).

3. Firm Names and Letterheads

Peel v. Attorney Registration and Disciplinary Commission of Illinois, 496 U.S. 91 (1990) reversed the public censure of a lawyer whose letterhead truthfully stated that he was a civil trial specialist certified by a national private group of lawyers. The Court found that the facts on his letterhead were verifiable and truthful; therefore they were constitutionally protected. The Court noted that the state's interest in preventing consumers from being misled may justify having standards for asserting areas of specialty and for screening certifying organizations.

Under the MRPC, you cannot use a firm name, letterhead or other professional designation that is false or misleading. You may use a trade name, e.g., "Fourth Street Clinic," as long as it is not false or misleading, and does not suggest a connection with either a governmental agency or a legal services organization. Rule 7.5(a). When your firm has offices in more than one state, it may use the same firm name in all its offices. If you are admitted to practice in fewer than all of the states where the law firm has its offices, your jurisdictional limits must appear on the law firm letterhead and law firm publicity. Rule 7.5(b).

If you hold a public office, you cannot use your position to obtain a proper an improper advantage for your client. Your firm may continue to use your name in the firm name only if you have an active, regular practice with the your firm. Rule 7.5(c). Otherwise, it is misleading for the firm to use your name in its communications.

You may use the name of a deceased or retired member of your law firm in the firm name in a line of succession. Rule 7.5, Comment 1. Otherwise, the names that can appear in the law firm name are lawyers who currently practice actively and regularly with the firm. These standards also apply to professional designations in electronic media like websites and emails.

B. SOLICITATION—DIRECT CONTACT WITH PROSPECTIVE CLIENTS

1. Supreme Court Decisions

A state can regulate lawyer in-person solicitation to protect the public from false or deceptive commercial practices, as long as the regulations are reasonable and present no danger to the public. The state has an interest in protecting the "unsophisticated, injured, or distressed lay person" from "those aspects of solicitation that involve fraud, undue influence, intimidation, overreaching, and other forms of 'vexatious conduct.' " *Ohralik v. Ohio State Bar*, 436 U.S. 447 (1978). In that case, the lawyer solicited an accident victim who was in traction in a hospital and who was "especially incapable of making informed judgments or of assessing and protecting their own interests." The solicitation for private gain was prohibited without a showing of harm to the solicited person, due to the misleading, deceptive and overbearing conduct.

A solicitation on behalf of a nonprofit organization that litigates as a form of political expression may be regulated only when there is a showing of misleading conduct. *In re Primus*, 436 U.S. 412 (1978). The Court emphasized two factors distinguishing the *Ohralik* result from *Primus*: the presence of pressure tactics and a major pecuniary award.

Shapero v. Kentucky Bar Association, 486 U.S. 466 (1988) struck down state prohibitions against lawyers sending any targeted direct mail advertising. The mailed letters sent to people facing specific legal problems were truthful and not misleading. Because of the nature of the solicitation, there was no pressure on the recipient for an immediate response. The mere potential for abuse does not justify a blanket prohibition. The Court later prohibited such correspondence sent too soon after the event which raised the need for legal representation. In *Florida Bar v. Went for It, Inc.*, 515 U.S. 618 (1995), the Court held that a state may ban targeted mailings for thirty days after the event. The Court, however, did uphold the lawyer's right to send untargeted letters to the general public.

2. The Rules

All in-person, live telephone, and real-time electronic (as with chat rooms or instant messaging) solicitations of a prospective client are prohibited when your significant motive is your own compensation. Defining prohibited solicitations requires enumeration of permitted solicitations. You can solicit another lawyer for business. Rule 7.3(a)(1). You also can contact your family members who are in need of legal services, as well as people with whom you have a close personal relationship. Both of these groups know about your competence and that you are not going to take advantage of them. Rule 7.3(a)(2).

Finally, you can always contact former clients, who know whether they were satisfied with your previous work. Rule 7.3(a)(2). When you leave a law firm, can you contact a client whom you served while practicing at your old firm? You may contact persons with whom you had direct contact. The notice should relate to pending matters, and convey sufficient information to enable the client to decide whether her legal work will remain with your old firm or will be transferred to you in your new professional association. ABA Formal Opinion 99–414.

The MRPC address permissible targeted mailing in a broader manner. You cannot solicit professional employment from a prospective client in person or through any form of communication, either when that person has made known to you her desire not to be solicited by you or when your solicitation involves coercion, duress, or harassment. Rule 7.3. That Rule applies to plaintiffs' lawyers who are looking for class members after the filing but before the certification of a class action. ABA Formal Opinion 07–445. Notice that the Rule does not include the thirty-day restriction allowed by the Supreme Court in *Florida Bar v. Went for It, Inc.*

You must include the words "Advertising Material" in any written, recorded or electronic communication that you send to solicit employment from a prospective client who is known to be in need of legal services, unless the recipient is another lawyer or has a family, close personal, or prior professional relationship with you. Rule 7.3(c).

C.   GROUP LEGAL SERVICES

The general prohibition on solicitation of new clients does not apply to your participation in a prepaid or group legal services plan that you do not own or direct, when your in-person or telephonic solicitation is for membership in the plan for people not known by you to need legal services in a particular matter. Rule 7.3(d).

D.   REFERRALS

You cannot give anything of value in exchange for a recommendation of your services, but you may pay reasonable costs for media advertising. Rule 7.2(b)(1). You cannot pay anyone to promote your services or to distribute your business cards. You also cannot pay a nonlawyer an amount connected to the amount of business she sends to you. You must supervise any nonlawyer employed by you so that she does not violate the MRPC. Rule 7.2, Comment 5.

You may pay the "usual charges" of a lawyer referral service conducted by a legal services plan, a not-for-profit, or a qualified lawyer referral service. Rule 7.2(b)(2). Unless the referral plan is a not-for-profit or a qualified plan, you cannot become involved in paying an entity for referring cases to you. ABA Formal Opinion 87–355 permits your participation in a for-profit prepaid legal services plan. You also may agree with a referring, not-for-profit *pro bono* organization to turn over all or some of any court-awarded legal fees. ABA Formal Opinion 93–374.

You may enter into reciprocal referral agreements with another lawyer or nonlawyer professional, if that agreement is not exclusive and your client is told about the existence and nature of the agreement. Rule 7.2(b)(4). Otherwise, you cannot pay anyone for sending professional work your way. Rule 7.2, Comment 6. The purpose of these Rules is that you must be independent of other persons.

E. COMMUNICATIONS REGARDING FIELDS OF PRACTICE AND SPECIALIZATION

In re R.M.J., 455 U.S. 191 (1982) invalidated restrictions on lawyer advertising that the state bar had claimed were misleading. The case specifically concerned advertising about fields of practice. R.M.J.'s ads had gone beyond the prescribed language for listing fields of practice, e.g., he listed "real estate" as a field of practice instead of the approved word "property". While ads listing areas of practice potentially were misleading, they could not be prohibited if the information could be presented in a non-deceptive manner.

Generally, under the MRPC you may call yourself a specialist in a particular field or fields of law under limited circumstances. Rule 7.4(a). Such claims must be truthful and not false or misleading. Rule 7.1. The MRPC recognize historic specialties in admiralty law and patent law, clearly prescribing the method of communicating those areas of specialization. Rule 7.4(b), (c). If a state has a system for certifying specialists in specific areas of the law, you can publicize your certification as a specialist from a state-approved or ABA-accredited group. The name of the certifying organization must appear clearly in the communication. Rule 7.4(d)(1)–(2).

INFORMATION ABOUT LEGAL
SERVICES CHECKLIST

A. **Advertising**

    1. ***Bates v. State Bar***, 433 U.S. 350 (1977). Free speech protects truthful newspaper advertising about lawyer

availability and fees for "routine" legal services. States may impose reasonable restrictions on the time, place and manner of lawyer advertising, as well as prohibited false or misleading ads.

2. ***Zauderer v. Office of Disciplinary Counsel***, 471 U.S. 626 (1985). The state cannot discipline a lawyer who solicits business in a newspaper ad that contain nondeceptive illustrations and legal advice.

   a. State rules may regulate lawyer disclosures that are reasonably related to the state's interest in preventing consumers from being deceived, not vague, and justified or not burdensome.

   b. The state can discipline a lawyer who fails to include information necessary to make the ad not misleading.

3. Under the MRPC, you cannot make affirmative statements in your ads that misrepresent the law or facts or omissions of fact that make a statement as a whole materially misleading.

   a. Statements in ads may violate the Rule either because they are false and misleading or because though truthful they are not accurate when considered as a whole.

   b. You may include a disclaimer or qualifying language with your ad to eliminate or reduce unjustified expectations by the reader, as long as they are not false or misleading.

   c. If your ad provides an unsubstantiated comparison of your legal services to others, your ad may be misleading if it is "presented with such specificity as would lead a reasonable person to conclude that the comparison can be substantiated."

4. The MRPC permit truthful advertising/communication through any ("written, recorded, or electronic") medium except "in-person solicitation," without regard to the ad's geographic reach.

5. Firm Names and Letterheads

    a. You cannot use a firm name, letterhead, or other professional designation that is false or misleading. You may use a trade name, e.g., "Fourth Street Clinic," as long as it is not false or misleading, and does not suggest a connection with either a governmental agency or a legal services organization.

        1. When your firm has offices in more than one state, it may use the same firm name in all its offices.

        2. If you are admitted to practice in fewer than all of the states where the law firm has its offices, your jurisdictional limits must appear on the law firm letterhead and law firm publicity.

    b. You may use the name of a deceased or retired member of your law firm in the firm name in a line of succession. Otherwise, the names that can appear in the law firm name are lawyers who currently practice actively and regularly with the firm.

B. Solicitation

1. ***Ohralik v. Ohio State Bar***, 436 U.S. 447 (1978). A state can regulate lawyer in-person solicitation to protect the public from false or deceptive commercial practices, as long as the regulations are reasonable and present no danger to the public.

2. ***In re Primus***, 436 U.S. 412 (1978). A solicitation on behalf of a nonprofit organization that litigates as a form of political expression may be regulated only when there is a showing of misleading conduct. The Court distin-

guished *Ohralik* from *Primus* on two grounds: the presence of pressure tactics and a major pecuniary award.

3. ***Shapero v. Kentucky Bar Association***, 486 U.S. 466 (1988). The Court struck down state prohibitions against lawyers who send targeted direct mail advertising. The mailed letters to people facing specific legal problems were truthful and not misleading.

4. ***Florida Bar v. Went for It, Inc.***, 515 U.S. 618 (1995). The Court prohibited targeted mailings sent thirty days after an event calling for legal representation. The Court, however, did uphold the lawyer's right to send untargeted letters to the general public.

5. Under the MRPC, all in-person, live telephone, and real-time electronic (e.g., chat room, instant messaging) solicitations of a prospective client are prohibited when your significant motive is your own pecuniary gain. Exceptions are:

    a. You can solicit another lawyer for business.

    b. You also can contact your family members who are in need of legal services, as well as people with whom you have a close personal relationship.

    c. You can always contact former clients, who know whether they were satisfied with your previous work.

6. When you leave a law firm, you may contact a client whom you served while practicing at your old firm.

7. As for targeted solicitations, you cannot solicit professional employment from a prospective client in any form, either:

    a. When that person has made known to you her desire not to be solicited by you, or

    b. When your solicitation involves coercion, duress, or harassment.

    c. There is no thirty-day restriction in the MRPC.

8. You must include the words "Advertising Material" in most targeted mailings.

C. **Group Legal Services.** The general prohibition on solicitation is inapplicable when you participate in a prepaid or group legal services plan that you do not own or direct and when your membership in the plan is for people who do not need legal services in a particular matter.

D. **Referrals**

1. You cannot give anything of value in exchange for a recommendation of your services, e.g., to promote your services or to distribute your business cards, unless you are paying for reasonable costs for media advertising.

2. You may pay the "usual charges" of a lawyer referral service conducted by a legal services plan or a not-for-profit or qualified lawyer referral service.

3. You may enter into reciprocal referral agreements with another lawyer or nonlawyer professional, if that agreement is not exclusive and your client is told about the existence and nature of the agreement.

E. **Communicating Fields of Practice and Specialization**

1. *In re R.M.J.*, 455 U.S. 191 (1982). R.M.J.'s ads had gone beyond the prescribed language for listing fields of practice. He listed "real estate" as a field of practice instead of the approved word "property". While ads listing areas of practice potentially were misleading, they could not be prohibited if the information could be presented in a non-deceptive manner.

2. You may call yourself a specialist in a particular field or fields of law if it is truthful and not false or misleading.

3. The MRPC recognize historic specialties in admiralty law and patent law.

4. If a state has a system for certifying specialists in specific areas of the law, you can publicize your certification as a specialist from a state-approved or ABA-accredited

group. The name of the certifying organization must appear clearly in the communication.

ILLUSTRATIVE PROBLEM

Michael Weinstein is a famous estate planner throughout the western United States. He is renowned for knowing the probate laws of every western state, as well as memorizing the regulations of the Internal Revenue Service regarding all types of trust instruments. Because of his expertise, he has spoken about estate planning to more than twenty state bar conventions and has appeared on national estate planning talk shows. His skill and knowledge have produced a large client base which he attempts to serve as efficiently and effectively s possible. Is it ethically proper for Michael to send the persons for whom he has drafted wills and trust instruments an annual notice, suggesting that they contact him in order to review their will and trusts for any necessary updating?

Analysis

What Weinstein intends to do is ethically proper, and does not constitute an improper solicitation. He wants to send a bulk mailing to people for whom he has already done legal work. The contact is not prompted by a particular event affecting all of Weinstein's clients, unless in a given year the laws pertaining to all wills dramatically change. While the mailing recommends Weinstein's services, it advises contacting him because of the prior lawyer-client relationship. Weinstein would contend that his communication is to ensure that the services he has performed for them continue to be regarded by the government as legal and proper.

The general proscriptions against solicitation apply to prospective clients. For example, Rule 7.3(a) prohibits a lawyer from soliciting "professional employment from a prospective client when a significant motive for the lawyer's doing so is the lawyer's pecuniary gain." The targets of all Weinstein mailings are to former clients. An exception to the general rule permits a contact with persons who have a "a family, close personal, or prior professional relationship with the lawyer." Rule 7.3(a)(2).

POINTS TO REMEMBER

- States may impose reasonable restrictions on the time, place and manner of lawyer advertising.

- You cannot make affirmative statements in your ads that misrepresent the law or facts or omissions of fact that make a statement as a whole materially misleading. Rule 7.1.

- Statements in ads may violate the Rule either because they are false and misleading *or* because though truthful they are not accurate when considered as a whole.

- If your ad provides an unsubstantiated comparison of your legal services to others, your ad may be misleading if it is "presented with such specificity as would lead a reasonable person to conclude that the comparison can be substantiated." Rule 7.1, Comment 3.

- You may use a trade name such as "Fourth Street Clinic," as long as it is not false or misleading, and does not suggest a connection with either a governmental agency or a legal services organization. Rule 7.5(a).

- You may use the name of a deceased or retired member of your law firm in the firm name in a line of succession. Rule 7.5, Comment 1. The other names that can appear in the law firm name are lawyers who currently practice actively and regularly with the firm.

- A state can regulate lawyer in-person solicitation to protect the public from false or deceptive commercial practices, as long as the regulations are reasonable and present no danger to the public.

- A solicitation on behalf of a nonprofit organization that litigates as a form of political expression may be regulated only when there is a showing of misleading conduct.

- Generally, in-person, live telephone, and real-time electronic solicitations of a prospective client are prohibited when your significant motive is your own pecuniary gain.

- As for targeted solicitation, you cannot solicit professional employment from a prospective client in any form, either when that person has made known to you her desire not to be solicited by you, or when your solicitation involves coercion, duress, or harassment. Rule 7.3(b).

- You may solicit new clients when you participate in a prepaid or group legal services plan that you do not own or direct and when your contact is for membership in the plan for people not known to need legal services in a particular matter. Rule 7.3(d).

- You cannot give anything of value in exchange for a recommendation of your services, unless you are paying for reasonable costs for media advertising. Rule 7.2(b)(1).

- You may call yourself a specialist in a particular field or fields of law if it is truthful and not false or misleading. Rule 7.4(a).

CHAPTER 11

Duties to the Public and the Legal System

A. VOLUNTARY *PRO BONO* SERVICE

Pro bono work by lawyers refers to legal services provided without a fee being charged or the expectation of a normal fee. The MRPC encourage lawyers to engage in *pro bono* activities. Rule 6.1. *Pro bono* services may be provided for causes as well as for clients, and may include testifying on behalf of law reform, lobbying for law reform, and participating in bar association activities. When a non-profit *pro bono* organization asks you to accept *pro bono* litigation, you can agree in advance or later to give all or part of your court-awarded fee to that organization. If you enter into such an agreement, you should disclose it to your client, because of concern about improper interference with your exercise of independent judgment. ABA Formal Opinion 93–374.

The MRPC urge you "to render at least (50) hours of *pro bono publico* legal services per year." Each state is free to specify a different number of hours, but no state has adopted a mandatory *pro bono* requirement. If the hours are unmet through legal representation, lobbying, or mentoring people of limited means, you can do *pro bono* work for groups or individuals seeking to protect their civil or public rights or you can perform *pro bono* work for charitable, religious, or bar organizations. Rule 6.1(b), Comments 5–8. In addition to delivering *pro bono* services, the MRPC encourage you to "support all proper efforts" of legal services programs by providing financial support. Rule 6.1, Comment 3. You should "voluntarily contribute financial support to organizations that provide legal services to persons of limited means." Rule 6.1.

B.   ACCEPTING COURT APPOINTMENTS

There are types of cases which you *must* decline, such as when you're too busy, Rule 1.1, or the case is frivolous or is brought to harass another, Rule 3.1. You should *not* decline just because the client or her cause is unpopular. Rule 6.2, Comment 1. You should not refuse a court appointment in a *pro bono* case except for "compelling reasons" or for "good cause." One example of good cause occurs if the representation "is likely to result in a violation of the Rules . . . or other law," such as a conflict of interest with another client.

A second type of good cause occurs when accepting the appointment would result in "an unreasonable financial burden." Rule 6.2(b). For example, if you have recently accepted several court appointments, you may decline the current appointment because of the need to earn money from paying clients in order to pay your bills and to support your dependents. The third category of good cause justifying turning down a court appointment is when "the cause is so repugnant to the lawyer" so as to impair the lawyer-client relationship or the quality of your representation. Rule 6.2(c). You may decline the representation if your feelings are so strong that you could not do a competent job.

C.   SERVING IN LEGAL SERVICES ORGANIZA-TIONS

If you are a lawyer in a law firm, you also may serve as an officer or director of a legal services organization, even if the organization's clients have interests adverse to your client. Rule 6.3. However, you cannot knowingly participate in a decision or action of the organization if your participation would be inconsistent with the obligations you owe to your current client or could have a "material adverse effect" on the organization's client. Rule 6.3(a)–(b).

D. LAW REFORM ACTIVITIES AFFECTING CLIENT INTERESTS

You may serve as an officer, director, or member of a law reform organization, even though the law reform may affect your client's interests. When you know that your client's interests may be materially benefitted by a decision in which you participate in that law reform organization, you must disclose that fact but you do not have to identify your client. Rule 6.4.

E. CRITICISM OF JUDGES AND ADJUDICATING OFFICIALS

If you make a false statement about the qualifications or integrity of a judge, judicial candidate, or public legal officer, you are subject to discipline if you made that statement knowingly or with reckless disregard for the truth. Rule 8.2(a). The Comments note the importance of improving the administration of justice by encouraging you to express "honest and candid opinions." Rule 8.2, Comment 1. The Comments support "efforts to defend judges and courts unjustly criticized." Rule 8.2, Comment 3. If what you say is understood as an opinion rather than as a statement, discipline is inappropriate. There is no violation if you (1) tell the truth about the judge, even if you do so out of a sinister motive, or (2) spoke falsely but you did not know of the falsity of the statement. If you decide to seek a judicial position, either by election or appointment, you must comply with the Code of Judicial Conduct applicable in your state. Rule 8.2(b).

F. POLITICAL CONTRIBUTIONS

The MRPC prohibit you or your law firm (which includes a "political action committee owned or controlled by" you) from accepting a governmental "legal engagement" or a judicial appointment if you made or solicited political campaign contributions for the purpose of obtaining or being considered for that type of engagement or appointment. Rule 7.6. It is said that the Rule prohibits "pay-to-play contributions." The MRPC does not address the issue of a lawyer receiving the contribution; only the payment is important to lawyer discipline. The scope of discipline applies both to you and your law firm, which is unique among the MRPC. The Rule applies only when you accept the appointment you sought.

G. IMPROPER CONTACT WITH GOVERN-MENT OR JUDICIAL OFFICIALS

You can never state or even imply that you are able to influence improperly a government agency or official, or to achieve results by means that violate the law or the MRPC, *even if* you actually lack the ability to exercise influence. Rule 8.4(e). You also cannot knowingly assist a judge to violate the Code of Judicial Conduct, such as accepting a bribe. Rule 8.4(f).

DUTIES TO THE PUBLIC AND THE LEGAL SYSTEM CHECKLIST

A. **Voluntary *Pro Bono* Service**

    1. *Pro bono* work

        a. Legal services provided without either a fee being charged or the expectation of a normal fee.

        b. The MRPC encourage lawyers to engage in *pro bono* activities.

        c. *Pro bono* services may include testifying or lobbying for law reform, and participating in bar association activities.

    2. The Rules urges you "to render at least (50) hours of *pro bono publico* legal services per year," but no state has adopted a mandatory *pro bono* requirement.

3. When a non-profit *pro bono* organization asks you to accept *pro bono* litigation, you should disclose to your client any agreement you have made to give all or part of your court-awarded fee to that organization.

B. Accepting Court Appointments

1. You should not refuse a court appointment in a *pro bono* case except for "compelling reasons" or for "good cause." There are three categories of good cause:

   a. If the representation "is likely to result in a violation of the Rules . . . or other law," as when you would have a conflict of interest with another client.

   b. When accepting the appointment would result in "an unreasonable financial burden," as when you have recently accepted several court appointments.

   c. When the client's "cause is so repugnant to the lawyer" so as to impair the lawyer-client relationship or the quality of your representation.

C. Serving in Legal Services Organizations

1. You may serve as an officer or director of a legal services organization, even if the organization's clients have interests adverse to your client.

2. You cannot knowingly participate in a decision of action of the organization if it would result in a conflict of interest with the obligations you owe to your current client or could have a "material adverse effect" on the organization's client.

D. Law reform activities affecting client interests

1. You may serve as an officer, director, or member of a law reform organization, even though the law reform may affect your client's interests.

2. When you know that your client's interests may be materially benefitted by a decision in which you partici-

pate in that law reform organization, you must disclose that fact but you do not have to identify your client.

E. **Criticism of Judges and Adjudicating Officials**

    1. If you make a false statement about the qualifications or integrity of a judge, judicial candidate, or public legal officer, you are subject to discipline if you made that statement knowingly or with reckless disregard for the truth.

    2. If what you say is understood as an opinion rather than as a statement, discipline is inappropriate.

F. **Political Contributions**. The Rule prohibits you or your law firm from accepting a governmental "legal engagement" or a judicial appointment if you made or solicited political campaign contributions for the purpose of obtaining or being considered for that type of engagement or appointment.

G. **Improper Contact with Government or Judicial Officials**. You cannot state or imply an ability to influence improperly a government agency or official, or to achieve results by any means that violate the Rules.

ILLUSTRATIVE PROBLEM

Eugene King is a lawyer who is deeply involved in local political matters, including judicial politics. When the election campaigns begin for the judges who are elected every four years, Eugene is one of the first lawyers to contribute to both candidates so that he can say that he backed the election winner. The size of his contribution is usually the equivalent of the average political contribution. When Eugene's caseload began to decrease, he decided that perhaps he could realize a benefit from all his campaign donations. Last year, after Judge Pfeiffer was reelected, Eugene successfully requested to be put at the top of the judge's list for court appointments for exclusive positions such as guardians *ad litem*. Has Eugene acted improperly?

Analysis

Rule 7.6 prohibits a lawyer from accepting a political or judicial appointment if that lawyer makes or solicits political contributions in order to obtain that appointment. The prohibition applies only to contributions that would not have been made but for the lawyer's desire to the political or judicial appointment. If the motive for Eugene's contributions simply was to be on the winning side, his acceptance of the guardian appointments would not support an inference of impropriety, especially when the amount of his contribution was average compared to the contributions from others. Similarly, judicial appointments made on a rotating basis from a list compiled without regard to the fact or amount of a campaign contribution are excluded from the Rule's application. On the other hand, if only Eugene's latest contribution was motivated by his need to become the only guardian in Judge Pfeiffer's court, Eugene has violated Rule 7.6.

POINTS TO REMEMBER

- *Pro bono* work involves legal services provided without either a fee being charged or the expectation of a (normal) fee. The Rules encourage lawyers to engage in *pro bono* activities. Rule 6.1.

- The MRPC urge you "to render at least (50) hours of *pro bono publico* legal services per year," but no state has adopted a mandatory *pro bono* requirement.

- You should not refuse a court appointment in a *pro bono* case except for "compelling reasons" or for "good cause." Rule 6.2(a).

- A lawyer in a law firm may serve as an officer or director of a legal services organization, even if the organization's clients have interests adverse to your client. Rule 6.3.

- When you know that your client's interests may be materially benefitted by a decision in which you participate in that law reform organization, you must disclose that fact but you do not have to identify your client. Rule 6.4.

- If you make a false statement about the qualifications or integrity of a judge, judicial candidate, or public legal officer, you are subject to discipline if you made that statement knowingly or with reckless disregard the truth. Rule 8.2(a).

- The MRPC prohibit you or your law firm from accepting a governmental "legal engagement" or a judicial appointment if you made or solicited political campaign contributions for the purpose of obtaining or being considered for that type of engagement or appointment. Rule 7.6.

- You can never state or imply an ability to influence improperly a government agency or official, or to achieve results by any means that violate the Rules.

CHAPTER 12

Judicial Ethics

A. MAINTAINING THE INDEPENDENCE AND IMPARTIALITY OF THE JUDICIARY

This section discusses the obvious ethical obligations for judges found in Canon 1 of the CJC. First, a judge must comply with the law, including the CJC. CJC Rule 1.1. At all times, she must act so as to promote "public confidence in the independence, integrity, and impartiality of the judiciary." A judge also must "avoid impropriety and the appearance of impropriety." CJC Rule 1.2. A judge must not abuse the prestige of judicial office to promote either the personal interests or the economic interests of the judge or others, or allow others to do so. CJC Rule 1.3.

B. PERFORMING JUDICIAL DUTIES IMPARTIALLY, COMPETENTLY AND DILIGENTLY

When deciding cases, a judge must interpret and apply the law as she understands it, performing all her judicial duties fairly and impartially. CJC Rule 2.2. Applying the law objectively means that she makes decisions regardless of whether she "approves or disapproves of the law in question."

She must perform all of her duties without her "words or conduct" showing bias or prejudice. CJC Rule 2.3(A). A judge also must not engage in harassment "based upon race, sex, gender, religion, national origin, ethnicity, disability, age, sexual orientation, marital status, socioeconomic status, or political affiliation." She must not allow anyone subject to her direction to engage in such bias, prejudice, or harassment. CJC Rule 2.3(B)–(C). A judge must not be influenced "by public clamor or fear of criticism," and she must not allow "family, social, political, financial, or other interests or relationships to influence" her judicial conduct or judgment. She must not suggest or permit others to suggest an "impression that any person or organization is in a position to influence" her. CJC Rule 2.4(A)–(C). A judge may encourage the parties and their lawyers to settle matters but she must never coerce anyone into settling their case. CJC Rule 2.6(B).

While a judge must maintain order and decorum in proceedings before the court, she also must be "patient, dignified, and courteous to litigants, jurors, witnesses, lawyers, court staff, court officials, and others with whom" she deals in an official capacity. She must "not commend or criticize jurors for their verdict other than in a court order or opinion in a proceeding." CJC Rule 2.8(C).

Judges must not make "any public statement that might reasonably be expected to affect the outcome or impair the fairness of a matter pending or impending in any court, or make any nonpublic statement that might substantially interfere with a fair trial or hearing." CJC Rule 2.10(A). Subject to that requirement, she "may respond directly or through a third party to allegations in the media or elsewhere" about her conduct in a matter. CJC Rule 2.10(E). However, she can make public statements while she is performing her judicial duties, explain court procedures, and comment on any proceeding in which she is a litigant in a private capacity. CJC Rule 2.10(D).

In connection with cases, controversies, or issues that are likely to come before her, a judge must not "make pledges, promises, or commitments that are inconsistent with the impartial performance of the adjudicative duties of judicial office." CJC Rule 2.10(B). She must require that anyone subject to her direction and control refrain from doing what she herself is prohibited from doing. CJC Rule 2.10(C).

When a judge makes administrative appointments, she must do so "impartially and on the basis of merit," avoiding nepotism, favoritism and unnecessary appointments. CJC Rule 2.13(A). She also must not approve compensation for any appointee that is "beyond the fair value of services rendered." CJC Rule 2.13(C). She must not "appoint a lawyer to a position if the judge either knows that the lawyer, or the lawyer's spouse or domestic partner, has contributed more than" a particular dollar amount to her election campaign. CJC Rule 2.13(B).

If a judge reasonably believes that a lawyer or another judge "is impaired by drugs or alcohol, or by a mental, emotional, or physical condition," she must "take appropriate action, which may include a confidential referral to a lawyer or judicial assistance program." CJC Rule 2.14. If a judge knows either that another judge has violated the CJC or that a lawyer has violated the Rules of Professional Conduct, raising a substantial question about his honesty, trustworthiness or general fitness to serve, she must inform the appropriate authority. CJC Rule 2.15(A)–(B). These Rules parallel the lawyer reporting requirement in MPRC 8.3. If a judge "receives information indicating a substantial likelihood that another judge" or a lawyer has violated those ethical standards, she must take appropriate action. CJC Rule 2.15(C)–(D).

A judge must "cooperate and be candid and honest with judicial and lawyer disciplinary agencies." CJC Rule 2.16(A). A judge must "not retaliate, directly or indirectly, against a person known or suspected to have assisted or cooperated with an investigation of a judge or a lawyer." CJC Rule 2.16(B).

C. *EX PARTE* COMMUNICATIONS

Subject to several exceptions, the general ethical standard bans a judge from two types of communications: (1) initiation, permission or consideration of *ex parte* communications; or (2) consideration of other communications made to the judge outside the presence of the parties or their lawyers, concerning a pending or impending case. CJC Rule 2.9(A). If a judge inadvertently receives an unauthorized *ex parte* communication about the substance of a matter, she must provide for prompt notice to all other parties about the substance of the communication and give them an opportunity to respond. CJC Rule 2.9(B).

D.   DISQUALIFICATION

Although most disqualification issues are decided under the CJC, under the Due Process Clause disqualification may be constitutionally required when the judge (1) has a financial interest in the outcome of the case, (2) is trying a defendant for certain cases of contempt, or (3) receives a large campaign contribution from a person with a stake in a pending or imminent case. *Caperton v. A.T. Massey Coal Co., Inc.*, 129 S.Ct. 2252 (2009). Disqualification standards under the CJC are listed in the following paragraphs.

A judge must disqualify or recuse herself "in a proceeding in which the judge's impartiality might reasonably be questioned." CJC Rule 2.11(A). This general standard of "whether the judge's impartiality might reasonably be questioned" is applicable when the Code does not specifically describe a situation where the judge's partiality is presumed. CJC Rule 2.11(A)(1)–(6) lists specific situations in which he judge's partiality is presumed, i.e., when the judge:

- has a personal bias or prejudice about a party or the party's lawyer;
- has personal knowledge about the disputed facts in the proceeding;
- knows that she, her spouse or her domestic partner, or a person within the third degree of relationship to either of them, or the spouse or domestic partner of such a person is:
    - a party in the proceeding, or an officer, director, general partner, managing member, or trustee of a party;
    - a lawyer in the proceeding;
    - a person with more than a *de minimis* interest that could be substantially affected by the proceeding; or
    - likely to be a material witness in the case;
- knows that she, individually or as a fiduciary, or her spouse, domestic partner, parent, or child, or any other member of the her family residing in the judge's household, has an

economic interest in the subject matter in controversy or is a party in the case;

- knows or learns through a timely motion that a party, a party's lawyer, or the law firm of a party's lawyer has within the previous [insert number] year[s] made aggregate contributions to her campaign in an amount that [is greater than $[insert amount] for an individual or $[insert amount] for an entity] [is reasonable and appropriate for an individual or an entity];
- while a judge or a judicial candidate, has made a public statement, other than in a court proceeding, judicial decision, or opinion, that commits or appears to commit her to reach a particular result or rule in a particular direction in the proceeding;
- served as a lawyer in the matter, or was associated with a lawyer who participated substantially as a lawyer in the matter during such association;
- participated in governmental employment personally and substantially as a lawyer or public official concerning the case, or publicly expressed in that capacity an opinion about the merits of the case;
- was a material witness concerning the matter; or
- previously presided as a judge over the case in another court.

For example, when a lawyer concurrently represents a judge on a personal matter and also represents a client whose unrelated case is before the judge, the judge must recuse herself and may not seek a waiver (see the next paragraph) if she believes that she has a personal bias for her lawyer or the lawyer's firm as a result of the representation. ABA Formal Opinion 07–449.

A judge must keep informed about her personal and fiduciary economic interests. In addition, she must make a reasonable effort to keep informed about the personal economic interests of her spouse or domestic partner and minor children residing in her household. CJC Rule 2.11(B).

A judge disqualified under CJC Rule 2.11 may disclose on the record the basis for her disqualification and may ask the parties and their lawyers to *waive* any disqualifying grounds, except for personal bias or prejudice. CJC Rule 2.11(C).

E. EXTRAJUDICIAL ACTIVITIES

A judge may engage in extrajudicial activities, except those prohibited by law or by CJC Rule 3.1. The Rule then offers a general list of restrictions on a judge's participation in such activities. Per CJC Rule 3.1(A)–(E), she cannot participate in activities or engage in conduct that:

> (1) will interfere with the proper performance of her judicial duties, (2) will lead to her frequent disqualification, (3) would appear to a reasonable person to undermine her independence, integrity, or impartiality, (4) would appear to a reasonable person to be coercive, or (5) make use of court premises, staff, stationery, equipment, or other resources, except for incidental use for activities that concern the law, the legal system, or the administration of justice, or unless such additional use is permitted by law.

Generally, a judge must not make a voluntary appearance at a public hearing or consult with an executive or legislative branch official. However, per CJC Rule 3.2(A)–(C), she may appear in connection with: (1) matters concerning the law, the legal system, or the administration of justice, (2) matters about which the judge acquired knowledge or expertise in the course of the judge's judicial duties, or (3) the judge acting *pro se* in a matter involving the judge's legal or economic interests, e.g., a zoning proposal affecting her own property, or when the judge is acting in a fiduciary capacity.

Unless she is properly summoned, a judge cannot be a character witness in any adjudicatory proceeding, or otherwise vouch for the character of a person in a legal proceeding. CJC Rule 3.3.

A judge must not accept an appointment to a public committee, board, commission, or other position, unless it concerns the law, the legal system, or the administration of justice. CJC Rule 3.4. She also must not intentionally disclose or use nonpublic information acquired in a judicial capacity for any purpose unrelated to her judicial duties. CJC Rule 3.5.

A judge cannot be a member of any organization that practices invidious discrimination on the basis of race, sex, gender, religion, national origin, ethnicity, or sexual orientation. CJC Rule 3.6(A). A judge also must not use the benefits or facilities of such an organization if she knows or should know that it practices invidious discrimination on one or more of the above grounds. However, she does not violate the Rule by attending an event in a facility of an organization when her attendance is "an isolated event that could not reasonably be perceived as an endorsement of the organization's practices." CJC Rule 3.6(B).

Subject to the requirements of CJC Rule 3.1, a judge may participate in privately or publicly sponsored activities that are "concerned with the law, the legal system, or the administration of justice, and those sponsored by or on behalf of educational, religious, charitable, fraternal, or civic organizations not conducted for profit." CJC Rule 3.7(A). Such activities include those listed in CJC Rule 3.7(B). Merely attending an event, whether or not it has a fund-raising purpose, is not a violation.

A judge cannot accept an appointment to a fiduciary position such as an executor, except for the estate, trust, or person of a member of the judge's family, as long as such service will not interfere with the proper performance of her judicial duties. CJC 3.8(A). She also cannot serve if she as a fiduciary will likely be engaged in proceedings that would ordinarily come before her, or if the "estate, trust, or ward becomes involved in adversary proceedings in the court on which the judge serves, or one under its appellate jurisdiction." CJC Rule 3.8(B). If a person serving as a fiduciary becomes a judge, she must comply with this CJC Rule as soon as reasonably practicable, but in no event later than [one year] after becoming a judge. CJC Rule 3.8(D). A judge acting in any fiduciary capacity is subject to the same restrictions on engaging in financial activities that apply to a judge personally, per CJC 3.11. CJC Rule 3.8(C).

A judge cannot be an arbitrator or a mediator, or perform other judicial functions apart from her official duties, unless expressly authorized by law. CJC Rule 3.9. A judge also cannot practice law, but she may act *pro se* and can without compensation give legal advice to and/or draft or review documents for a member of her family. However, she is prohibited from serving as the family member's lawyer in any forum. CJC Rule 3.10.

A judge may hold and manage investments of the judge and members of her family, but she cannot serve as an officer, director, manager, general partner, advisor, or employee of any business entity. CJC Rule 3.11(A). But she must not engage of any of the above financial activities that will interfere with the proper performance of her judicial duties, or lead to her frequent disqualification. CJC Rule 3.11(C).

A judge may accept reasonable compensation for extrajudicial activities permitted by the CJC or other law, unless accepting it would create an appearance of impropriety. CJC Rule 3.12. She also cannot accept any things of value, if acceptance is prohibited by law or would create the appearance of impropriety. CJC Rule 3.13(A). However, she may accept things of value such as ordinary social hospitality, gifts from friends or relatives, publications sent to her for her official use, or commercial opportunities as long as all person have the same opportunities.

Unless otherwise prohibited by CJC Rules 3.1 and 3.13(A) or other law, a judge can accept reimbursement of necessary and reasonable expenses for travel, food, lodging, or other incidental expenses, or a waiver or partial waiver of fees or charges for registration, tuition, and similar items, from sources other than her employing entity, if the expenses or charges are associated with her participation in extrajudicial activities permitted by the CJC. CJC Rule 3.14(A). Reimbursement of expenses for necessary travel, food, lodging, or other incidental expenses must be limited to the actual costs reasonably incurred by the judge. CJC Rule 3.14(B).

 JUDICIAL ETHICS CHECKLIST

A. **Maintaining the Independence and Impartiality of the Judiciary**

    1. A judge must comply with the law, including the Code of Judicial Conduct.

    2. A judge must "avoid impropriety and the appearance of impropriety."

3. A judge must not abuse the prestige of judicial office to promote either the personal interests or the economic interests of the judge or others, or allow others to do so.

B. **Performing the Duties of Judicial Office Impartially, Competently and Diligently**

1. When deciding cases, a judge must interpret and apply the law as she understands it, performing all her judicial duties fairly and impartially.

2. A judge must perform all of her duties without her "words or conduct" showing bias or prejudice.

3. A judge cannot be influenced "by public clamor or fear of criticism," and cannot allow "family, social, political, financial, or other interests or relationships to influence" her judicial conduct or judgment.

4. Every person who has a legal interest in a proceeding, or that person's lawyer, must be accorded the "right to be heard according to law."

5. While a judge must maintain order and decorum in proceedings before the court, she also must be "patient, dignified, and courteous to litigants, jurors, witnesses, lawyers, court staff, court officials, and others with whom" she deals in an official capacity.

6. Judges must not make "any public statement that might reasonably be expected to affect the outcome or impair the fairness of a matter pending or impending in any court, or make any nonpublic statement that might substantially interfere with a fair trial or hearing."

7. If a judge reasonably believes that a lawyer or another judge "is impaired by drugs or alcohol, or by a mental, emotional, or physical condition," she must "take appropriate action, which may include a confidential referral to a lawyer or judicial assistance program."

8. Responding to judicial and lawyer misconduct

   a. If a judge knows either that another judge has violated the CJC or that a lawyer has violated the Rules of Professional Conduct, raising a substantial question about his honesty, trustworthiness or general fitness to serve, she must inform the appropriate authority.

      b.   If a judge "receives information indicating a substantial likelihood that another judge" or a lawyer has violated those ethical standards, she must take appropriate action.

C. *Ex parte* communications

1. Subject to several exceptions, the general ethical standard bans a judge from two types of communications: (1) initiation, permission or consideration of *ex parte* communications; or (2) consideration of other communications made to the judge outside the presence of the parties or their lawyers, concerning a pending or impending case.

2. A judge is prohibited from investigating "facts in a matter independently, and shall consider only the evidence presented and any facts that may properly be judicially noticed."

D. Disqualification

1. A judge must disqualify or recuse herself "in a proceeding in which the judge's impartiality might reasonably be questioned."

2. Specific situations in which he judge's partiality is presumed, i.e., when the judge:

      a.   Has a personal bias or prejudice about a party or her lawyer;

      b.   Has personal knowledge about the disputed facts in the proceeding;

      c.   Knows that she, her spouse or her domestic partner, or a person within the third degree of relationship to either of them, or the spouse or domestic partner of such a person is:

           1.   A party in the proceeding, or an officer, director, general partner, managing member, or trustee of a party,

2. A lawyer in the proceeding,

3. A person with more than a *de minimis* interest that could be substantially affected by the proceeding, or

4. Likely to be a material witness in the case,

d. Knows that she, individually or as a fiduciary, or her spouse, domestic partner, parent, or child, or any other member of the her family residing in the judge's household, has an economic interest in the subject matter in controversy or is a party in the case,

e. Knows or learns through a timely motion that a party, a party's lawyer, or the law firm of a party's lawyer has within the previous time period made aggregate contributions to her campaign in an amount exceeding a certain amount,

f. While a judge or a judicial candidate, has made a public statement, other than in a court proceeding, judicial decision, or opinion, that commits or appears to commit her to reach a particular result or rule in a particular direction in the proceeding,

g. Served as a lawyer in the matter, or was associated with a lawyer who participated substantially as a lawyer in the matter during such association,

h. Participated in governmental employment personally and substantially as a lawyer or public official concerning the case, or publicly expressed in that capacity an opinion about the merits of the case,

i. Was a material witness concerning the matter, or

j. Previously presided as a judge over the case in another court.

3. A judge must keep informed about her personal and fiduciary economic interests, and must make a reasonable effort to keep informed about the personal economic interests of her spouse or domestic partner and minor children residing in her household.

4. A judge disqualified under the foregoing provisions may disclose on the record the basis for her disqualification and may ask the parties and their lawyers to waive any disqualifying grounds, except for personal bias or prejudice.

E. **Extrajudicial activities**

1. A judge may engage in extrajudicial activities, except those prohibited by law or by the CJC.

2. Prohibited activities are those that

    a. Will interfere with the proper performance of her judicial duties,

    b. Will lead to her frequent disqualification,

    c. Would appear to a reasonable person to undermine her independence, integrity, or impartiality,

    d. Would appear to a reasonable person to be coercive, or

    e. Make use of court premises, staff, stationery, equipment, or other resources, except for incidental use for activities that concern the law, the legal system, or the administration of justice, or unless such additional use is permitted by law.

3. Generally, a judge must not make a voluntary appearance at a public hearing or consult with an executive or legislative branch official. However, she may appear in connection with matters concerning the law, the legal system, or the administration of justice

4. A judge cannot be a member of any organization that practices invidious discrimination on the basis of race, sex, gender, religion, national origin, ethnicity, or sexual orientation.

5. Appointments to Fiduciary Positions

    a. A judge cannot accept an appointment to a fiduciary position such as an executor, except for the estate, trust, or person of a member of the judge's family, as long as such service will not interfere with the proper performance of her judicial duties.

    b. A judge shall not serve in a fiduciary position if the judge as fiduciary will likely be engaged in proceedings that would ordinarily come before her, or if the "estate, trust, or ward becomes involved in adversary proceedings in the court on which the judge serves, or one under its appellate jurisdiction."

    c. If a person serving as a fiduciary becomes a judge, she must comply with this CJC Rule as soon as reasonably practicable, but in no event later than [one year] after becoming a judge.

6. A judge cannot practice law, but she may act *pro se* and can without compensation give legal advice to and/or draft or review documents for a member of her family.

7. A judge may hold and manage investments of the judge and members of her family, but she cannot serve as an officer, director, manager, general partner, advisor, or employee of any business entity.

8. A judge may accept reasonable compensation for extra-judicial activities permitted by the CJC or other law, unless accepting it would create an appearance of impropriety.

9. She may accept things of value, such as ordinary social hospitality, gifts from friends or relatives, publications sent to her for her official use, or commercial opportunities as long as all person have the same opportunities.

10. Reimbursement of expenses for necessary travel, food, lodging, or other incidental expenses must be limited to the actual costs reasonably incurred by the judge.

ILLUSTRATIVE PROBLEM

Frank Benjamin graduated from law school three years ago and works as an associate in a Kansas City law firm, Johnson, Jones and Smith PLLC, which has 27 law partners and 37 salaried associates. His mother, Lisa Benjamin, is a trial judge in downtown Kansas City. During his first two years of practice, no lawyers appearing before Judge Benjamin moved to disqualify her in cases where Johnson, Jones and Smith was their adversary firm. Recently, though, motions to disqualify Frank's mother from sitting in Johnson, Jones and Smith cases have begun to proliferate, regardless of whether Frank is counsel of record or even working on the case. Assuming that the 2007 version of the Model Code of Judicial Conduct [CJC] applies to Judge Benjamin, what is her ethical obligation to recuse herself in cases where Johnson, Jones and Smith is counsel of record?

Analysis

Section 2.11 of the CJC requires a judge to recuse herself in cases where any relative within the third degree of relationship is counsel of record in the proceeding. She also is disqualified from sitting in a case when her son is known to have more than a *de minimis* interest that could be substantially affected by the proceeding. The scope of Judge Benjamin's duty to recuse herself under this provision depends upon whether her son is a person who will realize a direct financial benefit as a Johnson, Jones and Smith law partner from the law firm's success in the case. If her son is neither counsel of record nor will realize a direct financial benefit as a law partner from a successful outcome in the case, Judge Benjamin's duty to recuse depends on whether her "impartiality might reasonably be questioned" under the CJC. She has to decide whether his status as a salaried associate in the firm of record creates an appearance of partiality, requiring her recusal. In any of the preceding three factual contexts, she may disclose on the record her relationship with Frank, and his role in the case and in the law firm, and thereafter seek a waiver of the disqualifying conflict from all the parties and lawyers.

POINTS TO REMEMBER

- A judge must comply with the law, including the Code of Judicial Conduct and "avoid impropriety and the appearance of impropriety." CJC Rule 1.2.

- A judge must perform all of her duties without her "words or conduct" showing bias or prejudice. CJC Rule 2.3(A).

- A judge cannot not be influenced "by public clamor or fear of criticism."

- Judges must not make "any public statement that might reasonably be expected to affect the outcome or impair the fairness of a matter pending in any court."

- When a judge makes administrative appointments, she must do so "impartially and on the basis of merit." CJC Rule 2.13(A).

- If a judge reasonably believes that a lawyer or another judge "is impaired by drugs or alcohol, or by a mental, emotional, or physical condition," she must "take appropriate action." CJC Rule 2.14.

- If a judge knows either that another judge has violated the CJC or that a lawyer has violated the Rules of Professional Conduct, she must inform the appropriate authority. CJC Rule 2.15(A)–(B).

- A judge cannot generally initiate, permit, or consider *ex parte* communications concerning a pending or impending case.

- A judge is prohibited from investigating "facts in a matter independently, and shall consider only the evidence presented and any facts that may properly be judicially noticed." CJC Rule 2.9(C).

- A judge must disqualify or recuse herself "in a proceeding in which the judge's impartiality might reasonably be questioned." CJC Rule 2.11(A).

- A judge is disqualified if she

  - Has a personal bias or prejudice about a party or her lawyer;

- Has personal knowledge about the disputed facts in the proceeding;

- Knows that she, her spouse or her domestic partner, or a person within the third degree of relationship to either of them, or the spouse or domestic partner of such a person is:

- A party in the proceeding, or an officer, director, general partner, managing member, or trustee of a party;

- A lawyer in the proceeding;

- A person with more than a *de minimis* interest that could be substantially affected by the proceeding; or

- Likely to be a material witness in the case;

- Knows that she, individually or as a fiduciary, or her spouse, domestic partner, parent, or child, or any other member of the her family residing in the judge's household, has an economic interest in the subject matter in controversy or is a party in the case;

- While a judge or a judicial candidate, has made a public statement, other than in a court proceeding, judicial decision, or opinion, that commits or appears to commit her to reach a particular result or rule in a particular direction in the proceeding;

- Served as a lawyer in the matter, or was associated with a lawyer who participated substantially as a lawyer in the matter during such association;

- Participated in governmental employment personally and substantially as a lawyer or public official concerning the case, or publicly expressed in that capacity an opinion about the merits of the case;

- Was a material witness concerning the matter; or

- Previously presided as a judge over the case in another court.

- A judge disqualified under CJC Rule 2.11 may disclose on the record the basis for her disqualification and may ask the parties and their lawyers to waive any disqualifying grounds, except for personal bias or prejudice. CJC Rule 2.11(C).

- Generally, a judge must not make a voluntary appearance at a public hearing or consult with an executive or legislative branch official.

- A judge cannot be a member of any organization that practices invidious discrimination. CJC Rule 3.6(A).

- A judge cannot accept an appointment to a fiduciary position such as an executor, except for the estate, trust, or person of a member of the judge's family. CJC 3.8(A).

- A judge cannot practice law, but she can give legal advice to and/or draft or review documents for a member of her family. CJC Rule 3.10

- A judge may accept things of value, such as ordinary social hospitality, gifts from friends or relatives, publications sent to her for her official use, or commercial opportunities as long as all person have the same opportunities.

- Reimbursement of expenses for necessary travel, food, lodging, or other incidental expenses must be limited to the actual costs reasonably incurred by the judge.

*

Conclusion:
General Examination Tips

Now that you have the full set of checklists for each of the topics that you will be covering on your examination, there are some bits of advice to help you ace your Professional Responsibility examination or the Multistate Professional Responsibility Examination (MPRE):

Before the Examination

- Prepare early for examinations by reviewing information learned as you go along rather than waiting until the end of the semester.

- Review the material by working on hypothetical problems. It is important to gain experience answering and writing out answers to problems before the examination.

- Meet with your professor regularly to gain useful insight into what he or she feels is important about particular topics and to develop a deeper understanding of the material. This time can also be used to obtain information regarding what type of analysis the professor expects on an examination.

- Synthesize the material by recognizing the connections between different topics covered within the course to develop a more comprehensive view of the material.

- Do not neglect information regarding the policy underpinnings or implications of various legal principles learned in the course. These policy issues become important in giving you the ability to resolve tough questions and to provide rationales for particular legal outcomes.

- Do not rely on a mere mastery of the substantive material to prepare for the exam. What is equally important is a deep understanding of the material which will enable you to engage in high level analysis of the problems that you will face on the exam.

During the Examination

- Before writing an essay to a question, be sure you understand precisely what the professor is asking you to do, e.g., giving the arguments on both sides of an issue or on behalf of only one party, assuming the role of the judge writing an opinion in the case. Outline the answer to facilitate your ability to provide a clear, organized response and to structure your thinking about the question to ensure that your answer covers all of the issues that need to be addressed.

- On the exam, professors are not simply looking for students to apply the law they have been taught to a given set of facts to achieve a result. In addition, superior exam takers demonstrate a depth of understanding beyond the black-letter law. The recognition of difficult questions and reference to underlying policies is the mark of a good answer.

- Always identify your assumptions. If you are assuming certain facts as the basis for your answer, make those assumptions explicit.

- Unless the question asks for a very brief answer, never give a simple conclusion regarding the proper result as your answer on an exam. Provide a full explanation showing your analysis. How you reach your conclusion is much more important than the conclusion.

- Rather than simply reaching a particular result because a certain case calls for that result, reason toward a conclusion by identifying key facts in the question, similar facts in other relevant cases, and any policy issues that support the outcome you intend to reach.

- Regardless of how difficult the question may seem, an answer to an examination question must reach a result. Do not equivocate, unless a factual ambiguity invites you to explore alternative analytical paths. Use legal judgment, reasoning, and analysis to identify a superior position and provide arguments for your choice.

- Generally, consider the arguments on both sides of an issue and state them. Then take the opportunity to apply your understanding of the principles and policies involved as well as any relevant precedent to side with a particular result.

- When deciding between two competing approaches to resolving an issue, clearly state which approach you intend to apply and articulate the arguments for why that is the better approach.

- Distinguish yourself by engaging in an analysis that demonstrates depth of knowledge and true understanding rather than rote memorization or dexterity with available source material (for open-book exams).

- In addition to the quality of one's answer, make sure to provide an answer that identifies all of the issues raised in the question. Working on practice questions is a good way to develop the ability to spot issues, making it critical that you work with practice questions prior to the exam.

After the Examination

Don't waste time talking with other classmates about the exam. You'll just create more anxiety for yourself. Focus on the next exam; or, if Professional Responsibility is your last exam, celebrate being done!

*

APPENDIX:

Mini-Checklists

In this Appendix, you will find brief versions of the checklists for each topic, for quick reference and use when it is necessary to find something quickly under a time crunch during an exam. These reduced versions cover the key points that need to be checked in your analysis. Proper use and understanding of these "mini-checklists" requires a complete understanding of the full checklists presented in the main text of this book.

Regulation of the Legal Profession

A. **Powers of Courts and Other Bodies to Regulate Lawyers**. The courts of each state have the inherent power to regulate members of the legal profession for their conduct, both in-court and elsewhere.

B. **Admission to the Profession**. A bar applicant cannot "knowingly make a false statement of material fact."

C. **Regulation after Admission—Lawyer Discipline**

   1. Misconduct

      a. You are subject to discipline for wrongful conduct committed while you are acting in your capacity as a lawyer or for illegal conduct or conduct "involving dishonesty, fraud, deceit, or misrepresentation."

      b. Discipline may be imposed for crimes that reflect "adversely on the lawyer's honesty, trustworthiness or fitness as a lawyer."

      c. You are subject to discipline for "conduct that is prejudicial to the administration of justice," as when you make remarks that were racist, sexist, or politically incorrect.

   2. Disciplinary Authority. If you admitted in State A, you are subject to discipline there, even if your misconduct occurs outside State A.

   3. Choice of Law. If you are admitted to practice in State A but you are temporarily admitted in a court in State B and your alleged misconduct occurred there, discipline by State A would be governed by the Rules of State B.

D. **Mandatory and Permissive Reporting of Professional Misconduct**

   1. You have a general obligation to report information about another lawyer's conduct that raises a "substantial question" about the other lawyer's "honesty, trustworthiness or fitness as a lawyer."

2. Your duty when your client tells you that another lawyer has engaged in serious misconduct, or you represent a lawyer who has herself committed serious misconduct.

E. **Unauthorized Practice of Law**. You violate the unauthorized practice rules, by practicing in a state where you are not admitted or by helping a lay person in her unauthorized practice of law.

F. **Multijurisdictional Practice**

1. You cannot open a law office in a state where you are not admitted, but you may open an office with a lawyer admitted there.

2. You may be admitted by a court to practice one case in another state *pro hac vice*.

3. If you are an employee-lawyer for an entity like a corporation, you may represent it anywhere you are not admitted to practice. If that representation results in litigation, you must seek *pro hac vice* admission to the court where the lawsuit is pending. Rule 5.5(d)(1).

G. **Fee Division with a Nonlawyer**. Subject to exceptions in Rule 5.4(a), you or your firm cannot share legal fees with a nonlawyer, to control nonlawyer involvement in the delivery of legal services. You cannot be in a partnership with a nonlawyer if practicing law is any part of the partnership's business.

H. **Law Firm and Other Forms of Practice**

1. Law–Related Services. Before you contract for such law-related services such as title insurance, you must disclose to your client that those law-related services do not constitute law practice.

2. Short-term Legal Services. You may participate in a short-term legal services program sponsored by a nonprofit organization or a court. Under that circumstance, the current or former client conflict Rules (1.7 and 1.9) do not apply.

3. Subject to collateral restrictions in Rule 1.17(c), you may sell either your entire practice or an entire area of practice to one or more lawyers or law firms. Rule 1.17.

I. **Responsibilities of Partners, Supervisory, and Subordinate Lawyers**

1. Supervisory Responsibilities of Lawyers. The partners in a law firm and those with supervisory authority over other lawyers must make reasonable efforts to assure that lawyers and nonlawyer assistants they supervise comply with the MRPC.

2. Subordinate Lawyers' Responsibilities. You cannot escape your responsibility for ethical misconduct by claiming that you were just following orders, but if an ethical violation is not clear, you can defer to the judgment of your supervising lawyer.

J. **Restrictions of Right to Practice**. Except for agreements for retirement benefits, the MRPC prohibit agreements that restrict your right to practice after you leave your law firm.

The Lawyer–Client Relationship

A. **Formation of a lawyer-client relationship** is governed by both general contract principles and the specific agreement with the client.

B. **Scope, Objective, and Means of Representation**

  1. You may limit the scope of your representation if the limitation is reasonable and your client gives you her informed consent. You cannot assist a client in criminal or fraudulent conduct.

  2. If a client lacks the capacity to make considered decisions, you must explain things to her in words that she can understand and that allow her to make decisions. If your client has a diminished capacity, you may take action when she "is at risk of substantial physical, financial, or other harm unless action is taken."

C. **Decision–Making Authority**. As the agent for your client, you must follow her "decisions concerning the objectives of representation," but you also can act on your client's behalf in a manner which is "impliedly authorized to carry out the representation."

  1. Your authority extends to decisions about which witnesses to call, methods of cross-examination, jury selection, motions and objections to make, and other strategic or tactical decisions.

  2. Decisions about settlement, testifying and pleading guilty are for the client.

D. **Termination of the Lawyer–Client Relationship**

  1. If a court refuses to grant its permission to withdraw, you have to continue representing your client even though the MRPC may provide a duty or right to withdraw.

  2. Regardless of the reason for the withdrawal, you must make reasonable efforts to protect your client's interests, e.g., turning over her papers and property.

3. You must withdraw if your continued employment would result in violating the ethical rules or other law, your physical or mental condition has a materially adverse effect on your client, or she fires you.

4. You may withdraw if there is good cause.

E. **Communication**. You must keep your clients informed about what is going throughout the representation and to promptly answer their reasonable requests. You must explain to your client the possible consequences of any proposed action you intend to take.

F. **Fees**. You may not negotiate for, charge, or collect an unreasonable fee or an unreasonable amount for expenses. Rule 1.5(a) lists eight factors as examples of relevant concerns in determining the fair market value of your services.

1. A contingent fee arrangement provides that you will receive a fee if you are successful in obtaining recovery for your client. You cannot ethically use a contingent fee in a criminal case or a domestic relations matter.

2. Lawyers in different firms may divide fees in proportion to the services performed by each lawyer or if each of them assumes joint responsibility for the case, and the client agrees in writing to the division.

Confidentiality

A. **Lawyer–Client Privilege**.

1. Communication. The privilege applies to communications from the client to her lawyer, and to communications from the lawyer to her client.

2. Made in confidence. The client must intend for the information to be treated as confidential.

3. To a lawyer. The lawyer must be acting as a legal advisor with respect to the particular client.

4. By a client. If a prospective client consults a lawyer, their preliminary communications are privileged even if the lawyer is not ultimately retained.

5. For the purpose of seeking or obtaining legal advice. Communications while using a lawyer as a scrivener is not covered by the privilege, because these activities could be performed by persons with other occupations.

B. **Work Product Doctrine**. Work product consists of tangible material or its intangible equivalent in oral or unwritten form, other than underlying facts, prepared by a lawyer either for current litigation or in anticipation of future litigation. Opinion work product are the opinions and mental impressions of a lawyer. Other work product is known as ordinary work product. Subject to exceptions, work product is not discoverable.

C. **Professional Obligation of Confidentiality** has two facets—the ethical duty of confidentiality and the evidentiary principle known as the lawyer-client privilege.

1. The ethical duty of confidentiality is based upon the MRPC. Generally you are not to talk about a client's case to anyone in the course of the representation, except as the client permits.

2. You cannot use your current client's confidential information to her disadvantage. As to a former client, you cannot use confidential information that has not become generally known.

3. For the privilege to apply, the client must intend that the communication to be in confidence. The ethical duty applies to you whether or not your client has told others the same information that she had told to you.

4. Only information obtained from the client or her agent is privileged. By contrast, any information relating to the representation of your client is protected by the ethical duty.

5. No privileged information can be disclosed, even involuntarily, unless your client consents or if the information is within your discretion to disclose. For the ethical duty, you cannot *voluntarily* disclose. Only by court order, consent, or by a discretionary exception can you disclose information about the representation.

6. Your obligation to preserve your client's confidential information generally survives the end of your lawyer-client relationship with her and continues after the death of your client.

7. Although the elements of the lawyer-client privilege exist, the privilege may be waived explicitly or implicitly.

8. Your client may inadvertently lose protection of the lawyer-client privilege, if she reveals a privileged communication to someone other than her lawyer.

D. **Disclosures Expressly Authorized by Rules**

1. You "may reveal information relating to the representation of a client to the extent the lawyer reasonably believes necessary" to "prevent reasonably certain death or substantial bodily harm."

2. You may disclose confidential information if you reasonably believe that disclosure is necessary, for example, to sue your client for an unpaid fee, or to defend a malpractice, disciplinary, or criminal charge.

3. You may disclose confidential information in order "to comply with other law or a court order" such as revealing client perjury.

4. You may disclose information about past, present, or future client fraud or client crime that has caused or reasonably certain to cause financial harm to another person. Your right to disclose is based on your client's breach of her duty not to use your services in this manner.

E. **Disclosures Implicitly Authorized to Carry Out the Representation**. Lawyers in the same firm frequently discuss their clients' cases, even if the client hired only one of the lawyers. When you represent more than one client in the same matter, you must tell them about the joint client exception to the lawyer-client privilege.

Conflicts of Interest

A. **Current Client Conflicts**

1. Rule 1.7(a)(1) prohibits you from representing a client if that representation "will be directly adverse to another client," as when you represent plaintiff and defendant in the same lawsuit.

2. Rule 1.7(a)(2) prohibits representation if there is a significant risk that the representation will be "materially limited" by your responsibilities to another, whether that client is a current client, a former client, a third person, or even yourself.

3. General rule: you cannot sue a Client B on behalf of Client A, while you represent Client B on an unrelated matter. If you represent two directly adverse clients in different lawsuits, if they do not consent to the conflict, you usually must withdraw from representing both parties in the two cases.

4. Rule 1.7 permits a written client waiver, if you make a full disclosure to your clients, by explaining to them the relevant circumstances that created the conflict and the risks and benefits of one lawyer representing all of them as opposed to each of them having separate lawyers.

B. **Current Client Conflicts—Lawyer's Personal Interest or Duties**

1. You cannot have a sexual relationship with a client, unless that consensual relationship already existed prior to the beginning of the lawyer-client relationship.

2. No matter how large the gift, the Rules do not prohibit gifts from your client to you, if the gifting does not require you to draft a legal instrument. Exceptions: If you cannot accept a gift, neither can anyone related to you unless you or the other gift recipient is related to the client.

C. **Former Client Conflicts**

1. If you formerly represented a client in a matter, you cannot represent a new client in the same or substantially related matter if your new client has interests that are "materially adverse" to your old client. A "matter" is not limited to lawsuits.

2. Waiver of former client conflict. The otherwise disqualified lawyer may represent a new client against the prior client who gives informed consent in writing.

D. **Prospective Client Conflicts**. A "prospective client" is a "person who discusses with a lawyer the possibility of forming a client-lawyer relationship with respect to a matter."

1. You have a duty of confidentiality to the prospective client, no matter how brief your initial conference was.

2. If the prospective client never becomes a client, generally you cannot represent another client who has interests "materially adverse to those of a prospective client in the same or substantially related matter if the lawyer received information from the prospective client that could be significantly harmful to that person in the matter." Rule 1.18(c).

E. **Imputed Conflicts**

1. When you are disqualified from representing a client, generally none of the lawyers with whom you are affiliated can represent that client. Rule 1.10.

2. A client affected by imputed disqualification principles may waive its protections if each client gives informed consent in writing, and each lawyer reasonably believes that she will be able to provide competent and diligent representation.

3. Rule 1.10(a) provides for screening as a method of curing the disqualification when you leave one firm and go to another firm, in order to avoid the firm's imputed disqualification based on your individual conflict of interest.

4. Except for sexual relations (a personal, not professional, conflict with a client), all Rule 1.8 conflicts between you and your client are imputed to other lawyers in your firm. Rule 1.8(k). '

F. **Acquiring an Interest in Litigation**.

1. You generally cannot acquire a financial interest in your client's litigation because of the risk that your independent professional judgment will be affected.

2. You cannot negotiate with your client for literary or media rights to a particular matter while you are still working for her on that case.

3. You cannot support your client financially by giving her money for her living expenses or medical bills, but you can advance or even guarantee litigation expenses and court costs without your client being ultimately responsible for paying them.

G. **Business Transactions with Clients**. You can conduct a business transaction with your current client if it is fair and reasonable to your client, its terms are given to her in writing in clear language so that she can understand the terms, she is advised in writing that she can consult another lawyer, and she consents in writing.

H. **Third Party Compensation and Influence**.

1. Because your obligations are to your client, you cannot allow the third party payer to interfere with your exercise of professional judgment. You must obtain her consent to that fee arrangement.

2. In representing multiple clients, you may negotiate an aggregate settlement of their civil claims or plea bargains of their criminal charges. Each client must consent in writing after consultation.

I. **Lawyers Currently or Formerly in Government Service**

1. After you leave government employment, you can never represent a client in connection with a matter in which you

participated personally and substantially as a government employee, unless the appropriate government agency consents in writing.

2. While working for the government, you cannot negotiate for private work with a party who is involved in a matter in which you are then participating personally and substantially.

3. If you personally and substantially worked on a matter while in nongovernmental employment and then began working for the government, you are disqualified from working on that same matter unless the government agency consents in writing.

J. **Former Judges Moving to the Private Sector**

1. Any lawyer who participated personally and substantially on the merits as a judge or other adjudicative officer cannot accept or negotiate for private employment in a matter in which she acted in a judicial capacity. An exception permits representation if all parties to the former proceeding consent in writing.

2. As long as she first notifies the judge for whom she works, while working for the government, a law clerk may negotiate for private work with a party who is involved in a matter in which the clerk participated personally and substantially.

Lawyer–Client Relationship Basics

A. You are a competent lawyer if you have "the legal knowledge, skill, thoroughness and preparation reasonably necessary for the representation."

B. You must maintain competence through complying with CLE requirements and controlling workload.

C. Reasonable diligence requires that you assess the work that needs to be done on your client's behalf and to exercise reasonable promptness in completing that work.

D. You may be subject to discipline for having performed your legal work incompetently or negligently. In a claim based on negligence, your former client must prove that you owed her a duty of care and breached that duty, the breach caused injury to your client in the form of damages, and that without your negligence your client would have been more successful in the underlying matter.

E. You can make an agreement with your client that prospectively limits your liability to her for malpractice if she is independently represented by counsel.

Litigation and Other Forms of Advocacy

A. **Meritorious Claims**. When a client consults you to be her advocate, you may present any nonfrivolous interpretation of the law that favors her. You cannot present frivolous claims, defenses, or motions, but a good faith argument for extending, modifying, or reversing existing law is permitted.

1. A court's inherent powers and its procedural rules (FRCP 11) also provide methods to deal with frivolous advocacy.

2. In criminal cases, the prosecutor's obligation is not to bring charges if she knows that they are not supported by probable cause, and defense counsel's duty is to put the prosecution to its burden of proof.

B. **Expediting Litigation**. You must make "reasonable efforts to expedite litigation" that are "consistent with the interests of the client."

C. **Candor to the Tribunal**

1. You have a duty to voluntarily disclose to the tribunal any legal authority in the controlling jurisdiction that you know is directly adverse to your client's position and which your adversary has not disclosed.

2. As with statements of law, you cannot make false statements of fact to a tribunal, and you must correct any statement of fact that you learn was both false and material to the proceeding.

3. There is no constitutional right for a party to lie or for you to assist in that perjury. *Nix v. Whiteside*, 475 U.S. 157 (1986).

4. You must not offer evidence that you know is false, Rule 3.3(a)(3), even when your client insists.

5. If you learn before the conclusion of the proceedings that a piece of evidence you offered was false when admitted, you must take reasonable remedial measures, first to convince

your client or the witness to correct the false evidence, and then to consider withdrawing from the representation. If withdrawal is not possible, you must disclose the information to the tribunal which then must decide how to proceed.

6. If you learn that your client intends to engage or has engaged in fraud or bribery, you must take reasonable remedial measures, including disclosure to the court.

D. **Fairness to Opposing Party and Counsel**

1. You cannot unlawfully obstruct access to, alter, or conceal evidence or witnesses, and you cannot encourage a witness to testify falsely.

2. You cannot disobey the rules of a tribunal, which include the court's local rules.

3. During trial, you may allude only to matters that you reasonably believe are relevant or admissible, and in closing argument you cannot assert your personal opinion or knowledge about the facts.

E. **Improper Contact with Judge, Jurors and Other Officials**. You cannot attempt to influence a judge, juror, prospective juror, or other official by illegal means such as bribery, and you cannot engage in improper *ex parte* communications with jurors or prospective jurors during the proceedings.

F. **Trial Publicity**. The general standard is to restrict speech that "will have a substantial likelihood of materially prejudicing an adjudicative proceeding in the matter," from the view of the reasonable lawyer making the statement. Rules 3.6(b)–(c) describe categories of permissible out-of-court statements

G. **Lawyer as Witness**. Subject to exceptions, if you will be testifying in a case where you are counsel of record, you must withdraw as counsel. No imputed disqualification applies to the disqualified lawyer's law firm.

Communications With Non–Clients

A. **Truthfulness in Statements to Others**

1. While you represent a client in a litigation or a nonlitigation setting, you cannot knowingly "make a false statement of material law or fact to a third person." The Rules applies to statements of material fact, not to opinions.

2. If you realize that your client is committing a crime or fraud against another person, you must inform her that you cannot participate further. If the fraud or crime is ongoing and you have provided legal services connected with the crime of fraud, you must withdraw if your client refuses to change her conduct, informing the opposing party of your withdrawal as well as disaffirming any false documents.

B. **Communications with Represented Persons**. If you represent a client and you know that another person is represented by her own lawyer, you cannot communicate with that person about that matter, unless the other lawyer consents or the contact is authorized by law or court order.

C. **Communications with Unrepresented Persons**. If a person has no lawyer, on behalf of your client you cannot state or imply that you are disinterested and you should not provide legal advice to her.

D. **Respect for Rights of Third Persons**

1. In representing a client, you must not use means that serve no substantial purpose other than to "embarrass, delay, or burden a third person. . . . "

2. If you receive a document relating to a representation and you know or reasonably should know that the document was delivered to you inadvertently, you must inform the sender promptly.

Different Roles of the Lawyer

A. **Lawyer as Advisor**. You must give your client your realistic opinion about what a court is likely to do in her case, as well as the practical effects of the court's ruling.

B. **Lawyer as Evaluator**. You may exercise the role of an evaluator, even though it creates duties to non-clients.

C. **Lawyer as Negotiator**. The MRPC prohibit you from making false statements of material fact, but you do not have a duty to do any research for the other side of the litigation or transaction or to volunteer factual information that could weaken your client's position. During a negotiation, you may exaggerate about facts and values.

D. **Lawyer as Arbitrator, Mediator, or Other Third–Party Neutral**. A third-party neutral must inform unrepresented parties that he is not representing them.

E. **Special Prosecutorial Responsibilities**. Prosecutors must disclose to the defendant exculpatory evidence, i.e., evidence that "tends to negate the guilt of the accused or mitigate the punishment."

F. **Advocate in Nonadjudicative Proceedings.** If you appear before a policy-making entity like a legislative committee to testify, you must disclose whether you are there in a representative capacity.

G. **Lawyer Representing an Entity or Other Organization**. When you are employed or retained by an entity as in-house counsel or outside counsel, you represent that entity acting thru its agents.

   1. You have a special duty to protect the entity when you know that someone affiliated with your entity client is acting in a manner that is likely to directly or indirectly cause substantial harm to the client. Your first duty is to exhaust the entity's internal remedies and seek assistance of those in the chain of authority who can influence the decision of the person who is acting contrary to the best interests of the entity.

2. If your efforts to go up the chain of authority fail, you can reveal information to persons outside the entity if you still "reasonably believe that the violation is reasonably certain to result in substantial injury to the organization."

3. SEC regulatory duties are broader than under Rule 1.13. SEC Regulations require the lawyer to report any "material violation" of federal or state law regardless of potential harm to the entity. The lawyer must report a problem to the entity's chief legal officer who then must investigate the problem. The lawyer must report the problem to the entity's audit committee. If the reporting lawyer is fired for reporting the problem, she may disclose the entity's conduct to the SEC to prevent or rectify conduct "likely to cause substantial injury to the financial interest of property of the issuer or investors."

Safekeeping Property

A. **Safekeeping Client Property**

1. You must keep client funds in a trust account and never commingle them with your personal or business accounts. You also must safeguard property other than money.

2. With a contingent fee, there must be a written accounting to the client, stating "the outcome of the matter, and if there is a recovery, showing the remittance to the client and the method of its determination." For other fee arrangements, you must provide an accounting upon request by your client.

3. If you and your client have a dispute about trust fund property, you cannot withdraw the disputed portion of the fee until the dispute is resolved. Rule 1.15(e).

Communication About Legal Services

A. **Advertising**. You cannot make affirmative statements in your ads that misrepresent the law or facts or omissions of fact that make a statement as a whole materially misleading.

    1. The MRPC permit truthful advertising/communication through any ("written, recorded, or electronic") medium except "in-person solicitation," without regard to the ad's geographic reach.

    2. You cannot use a firm name, letterhead, or other professional designation that is false or misleading. You may use a trade name, e.g., "Fourth Street Clinic," as long as it is not false or misleading, and does not suggest a connection with either a governmental agency or a legal services organization.

    3. If you are admitted to practice in fewer than all of the states where the law firm has its offices, your jurisdictional limits must appear on the law firm letterhead and law firm publicity.

B. **Solicitation**. All in-person, live telephone, and real-time electronic (e.g., chat room, instant messaging) solicitations of a prospective client are prohibited when your significant motive is your own pecuniary gain.

    1. Exceptions are when you solicit another lawyer for business, your family members in need of legal services, people with whom you have a close personal relationship, and former clients.

    2. As for targeted solicitation, you cannot solicit professional employment from a prospective client in any form, either when that person has made known to you her desire not to be solicited by you, or when your solicitation involves coercion, duress, or harassment.

C. **Group Legal Services**. The general prohibition on solicitation is inapplicable when you participate in a prepaid or group legal services plan that you do not own or direct and when your contact is for membership in the plan for people not known to need legal services in a particular matter.

D. **Referrals**

1. You cannot give anything of value in exchange for a recommendation of your services, unless you are paying for reasonable costs for media advertising.

2. You may pay the "usual charges" of a lawyer referral service conducted by a legal services plan or a not-for-profit or qualified lawyer referral service.

E. **Communicating Fields of Practice and Specialization**

1. You may call yourself a specialist in a particular field or fields of law if it is truthful and not false or misleading.

2. The MRPC recognize historic specialties in admiralty law and patent law, clearly prescribing the method of communicating those areas of specialization.

3. If a state has a system for certifying specialists in specific areas of the law, you can publicize your certification as a specialist from a state-approved or ABA-accredited group. The name of the certifying organization must appear clearly in the communication.

Duties to the Public and the Legal System

A. **Voluntary *Pro Bono* Service**. *Pro bono* work is a legal service provided without either a fee being charged or the expectation of a normal fee. The MRPC encourage lawyers to engage in *pro bono* activities.

B. **Accepting Court Appointments**. You should not refuse a court appointment in a *pro bono* case except for "compelling reasons" or for "good cause."

C. **Serving in Legal Services Organizations**

   1. A lawyer in a law firm also may serve as an officer or director of a legal services organization, even if the organization's clients have interests adverse to your client.

   2. You cannot knowingly participate in a decision of action of the organization if it would result in a conflict of interest with the obligations you owe to your current client or could have a "material adverse effect" on the organization's client.

D. **Law reform Activities Affecting Client Interests**. You may serve as an officer, director, or member of a law reform organization, even though the law reform may affect your client's interests.

E. **Criticism of Judges and Adjudicating Officials**. If you make a false statement (not an opinion) about a judge, judicial candidate, or public legal officer, you are subject to discipline if you made that statement knowingly or with reckless disregard for the truth.

F. **Political Contributions**. Neither you nor your law firm can accept a governmental "legal engagement" or a judicial appointment if you made or solicited such political campaign contributions for the purpose of obtaining or being considered for that type of engagement or appointment.

G. **Improper Contact with Government or Judicial Officials**. You cannot state or imply an ability to influence improperly a government agency or official, or to achieve results by any means that violate the MRPC.

Judicial Ethics

A. **Maintaining the Independence and Impartiality of the Judiciary**

    1. A judge must comply with the law, and "avoid impropriety and the appearance of impropriety."

    2. A judge must not abuse the prestige of judicial office to promote either the personal interests or the economic interests of the judge or others, or allow others to do so.

B. **Performing the Duties of Judicial Office Impartially, Competently and Diligently**

    1. When deciding cases, a judge must interpret and apply the law as she understands it, performing all her judicial duties fairly and impartially, without regard to "public clamor or fear of criticism."

    2. A judge must be "patient, dignified, and courteous to litigants, jurors, witnesses, lawyers, court staff, court officials, and others with whom" she deals in an official capacity.

    3. Judges must not make "any public statement that might reasonably be expected to affect the outcome or impair the fairness of a matter pending or impending in any court, or make any nonpublic statement that might substantially interfere with a fair trial or hearing."

    4. If a judge knows either that another judge has violated the CJC or that a lawyer has violated the Rules of Professional Conduct, raising a substantial question about his honesty, trustworthiness or general fitness to serve, she must inform the appropriate authority.

    5. If a judge "receives information indicating a substantial likelihood that another judge" or a lawyer has violated those ethical standards, she must take appropriate action.

C. *Ex parte* **Communications**. Subject to several exceptions, the general ethical standard bans a judge from two types of communications: (1) initiation, permission or consideration of *ex parte* communications; or (2) consideration of other communications made to the judge outside the presence of the parties or their lawyers, concerning a pending or impending case.

D. **Disqualification**

1. A judge must disqualify or recuse herself "in a proceeding in which the judge's impartiality might reasonably be questioned." CJC Rule 2.11(A).

2. Specific situations in which he judge's partiality is presumed, i.e., when the judge

   a. Has a personal bias or prejudice about a party or her lawyer,

   b. Has personal knowledge about the disputed facts in the proceeding,

   c. Knows that she, her spouse or her domestic partner, or a person within the third degree of relationship to either of them, or the spouse or domestic partner of such a person is a party in the proceeding, an officer, director, general partner, managing member, or trustee of a party, a lawyer in the proceeding, a person with more than a *de minimis* interest that could be substantially affected by the proceeding, or likely to be a material witness in the case,

   d. Knows that she, individually or as a fiduciary, or her spouse, domestic partner, parent, or child, or any other member of the her family residing in the judge's household, has an economic interest in the subject matter in controversy or is a party in the case,

   e. Knows or learns through a timely motion that a party, a party's lawyer, or the law firm of a party's lawyer has within the previous time period made aggregate contributions to her campaign in an amount exceeding a certain amount,

f.   While a judge or a judicial candidate, has made a public statement, other than in a court proceeding, judicial decision, or opinion, that commits or appears to commit her to reach a particular result or rule in a particular direction in the proceeding,

g.   Served as a lawyer in the matter, or was associated with a lawyer who participated substantially as a lawyer in the matter during such association,

h.   Participated in governmental employment personally and substantially as a lawyer or public official concerning the case, or publicly expressed in that capacity an opinion about the merits of the case,

i.   Was a material witness concerning the matter, or

j.   Previously presided as a judge over the case in another court.

3.   A judge must keep informed about her personal and fiduciary economic interests, and must make a reasonable effort to keep informed about the personal economic interests of her spouse or domestic partner and minor children residing in her household.

4.   A judge disqualified under CJC Rule 2.11 may disclose on the record the basis for her disqualification and may ask the parties and their lawyers to waive any disqualifying grounds, except for personal bias or prejudice.

E.   **Extrajudicial Activities**. A judge may engage in extrajudicial activities, except those prohibited by law or by the CJC.

1.   A judge cannot be a member of any organization that practices invidious discrimination on the basis of race, sex, gender, religion, national origin, ethnicity, or sexual orientation.

2.   A judge cannot accept an appointment to a fiduciary position such as an executor, except for the estate, trust, or person of a member of the judge's family, as long as such service will not interfere with the proper performance of her judicial duties.

3. A judge also cannot practice law, but she may act *pro se* and can without compensation give legal advice to and/or draft or review documents for a member of her family.

4. A judge may hold and manage investments of the judge and members of her family, but she cannot serve as an officer, director, manager, general partner, advisor, or employee of any business entity.

5. She may accept things of value, such as ordinary social hospitality, gifts from friends or relatives, publications sent to her for her official use, or commercial opportunities as long as all person have the same opportunities.

†